WRITING FROM THESE ROOTS

WRITING FROM THESE ROOTS

Literacy in a Hmong-American Community

John M. Duffy

UNIVERSITY OF HAWAI'I PRESS

HONOLULU

This publication is made possible in part by support
from the Institute for Scholarship in the Liberal Arts,
College of Arts and Letters, University of Notre Dame.

Library of Congress Cataloging-in-Publication Data
Duffy, John.
  Writing from these roots : literacy in a Hmong-American community / John
Duffy.
      p.   cm.
  Includes bibliographical references and index.
  ISBN 978-0-8248-3095-3 (hardcover : alk. paper)
  1. Hmong Americans—Education.   2. Literacy—Social aspects—United
States.   3. Hmong language—Writing—History.   4. Hmong (Asian people)—
China.   5. Hmong (Asian people)—Laos.   I. Title.
  LC3501.H56D83 2007
  371.829'95942—dc22
                                                          2007002858

Designed by Paul Herr
Printed by The Maple-Vail Book Manufacturing Group

To San,
For love and sustaining faith

Why ever did those horses have to eat the books of our forefathers, many, many years ago? Those Meo kings were the first there were in the whole great northern kingdom. Indeed in those days we had a land of our own. A Meo king ruled over us. We were the most powerful nation on earth. But the wicked Chinese were more cunning than we. They fell upon us in great hordes. They had better weapons than we had. We fought bitterly and courageously, but it was in vain. The Chinese knew no mercy. They murdered, enslaved, and pillaged. We had to surrender. But not quite everyone gave in; whoever could escape did so. When the exhausted fugitives came to a wide river they rested, leaving their packs among the bushes. They were all overcome with sleep. When at last they woke up— O horror—the horses had eaten up all the Meo books! Not a single one remained. Since then we have possessed neither books nor a script.

—Quoted in N. Tapp, *Sovereignty and Rebellion*

In 1960, five Americans came from the CIA and had us sign documents. We couldn't write, so we put our handprints on it instead. It said: "You help us, you hide us. We will fight the communists and if we lose and you don't have anywhere to go, we will give you a radio, a saw, an axe so you can cut trees and live in the forest. If you go into the jungle, we'll drop rice." I was involved with this for ten years.

—S. Reder, *The Hmong Resettlement Study*

My teacher in the writing class, he taught me one thing. He said, "Lue, you must start thinking like an American before you understand my class." And then he asked, "Have you ever dreamed an American dream?" And I said, "No, I still dream in Hmong. I still keep dreaming Hmong dreams." So he said, "You must change that. If you don't change that, you're going to have a difficult time learning the English language. Think American," he said.

—Thao Lue, in an interview recalling his high school English class
  in Wausau, Wisconsin

Contents

Acknowledgments

The acknowledgments section of a book is often the place where the author uses too many words to say not enough. Many people contributed to the completion of this project, offering knowledge, critique, and inspiration. My debts are numerous.

First, I must express my profound gratitude to the Hmong people who consented to speak with me and share something of their lives with me. Listening to their stories, I learned about Hmong culture, about literacy, and about grace of spirit. I am forever indebted to those who welcomed me into their homes, workplaces, and churches. *Ua tsaug ntau.*

The project was supported, over the years, by the Wisconsin Center for Education Research of the University of Wisconsin-Madison, by an anonymous foundation in Wausau, Wisconsin, and by the National Endowment for the Humanities. I must also thank Masako Ikeda at the University of Hawai`i Press, whose enthusiasm has been a blessing, and Susan Biggs Corrado, who clarified numerous ambiguities in the text. A special sort of gratitude is owed to Michael K. Lecky, who performed exhaustive line-by-line editing of the entire manuscript, and whose fierce attentions repeatedly rescued me from my many offenses against clear thinking and writing. *Il miglior fabbro* indeed.

In Wausau, John Staples and Susan Warden were friends to this book from the start, sharing their ideas and passions as we drank countless cups of tea in their kitchen overlooking the Wisconsin River. Phyllis Bermingham offered encouragement, good questions, and a model for how to balance intellectual commitments and community activism. Peter Yang and Houa Lee answered more questions than anyone ever deserves to be asked, and Chang Yang offered a place to live while I conducted the research. Taosia Lo in Wausau and Lee Yang in Madison were able and thoughtful Hmong language interpreters.

At the University of Wisconsin-Madison, I was fortunate to work with colleagues who care deeply about issues of language, literacy, and rhetoric. Karen Redfield, Rebecca Nowacek, Nelson Graff, Carl Battaglia, and Jeff Weimelt read early versions of the work and offered direction. Kim Marie

Cole patiently allowed me to talk through ideas, even the most inchoate, and Andrew Hansen introduced me to the study of rhetoric. Jane Collins, Ceci Ford, and Cathy Prendergast challenged me to think more deeply about research methods, language, and literacy.

Others deserve thanks. William A. Smalley welcomed me into his home and shared his vast knowledge of literacy and the Hmong. He was a learned and compassionate man, and I am one of the many whose lives have been touched by his work. Nicholas Tapp provided important clarifications, and Paoze Thao corrected several of my many misunderstandings about Hmong culture and history. Brad Hughes was a steadfast supporter, and Martin Nystrand was an encouraging reader, teacher, and friend. An unpayable debt is owed to Bryan Trabold, who read my early chapters as though they were his own and whose passions stoked mine. Peter Mortensen read the manuscript carefully and critically, offering insights I would never have arrived at on my own.

Harvey Graff was a mentor and inspiration. His work remains the benchmark for anyone who cares seriously about the historical study of literacy, and his personal generosity is an example for all to emulate. Stuart Greene offered me a home at Notre Dame and steadied me when I felt myself faltering. I continue to be enriched by his friendship. Deborah Brandt has been, from start to finish, the guiding spirit of this book. Deborah read early drafts, provided tough, necessary criticism, and quietly inspired me to continue. Her scholarship remains the model not only for my work, but for countless others in our field.

Finally, I must express my everlasting gratitude to the person who most helped me and who more than anyone made this book possible: Kathy Opel. Her faith has sustained me, her guidance improved me, and her love made me whole. This work belongs to her.

Notes on Language, Orthography, and Transcription

Language and Spelling

The Hmong language has at least two forms, White Hmong, *Hmoob Dawb* (mong daw), and Blue/Green Hmong, alternatively known as Blue Hmong, *Hmoob Njua* (mong njua), or Green Hmong, *Hmoob Leeg* (mong leng). While many linguists regard these as dialects of the same language, some Hmong reject that designation and see *Hmoob Leej* as a separate language, which they call Mong *(Moob Lub Neej)*. There is considerable controversy in the Hmong community over these claims (for a scholarly discussion, see Thao 1999). In its written form, White Hmong is commonly represented by the Romanized Popular Alphabet (RPA), while Blue/Green Hmong is often represented by a variant of the RPA.

In this book, I use either the RPA or commonly accepted English equivalents to represent Hmong place names and selected vocabulary items. The criteria for choosing between the RPA and its English equivalent is intuitive and based on how widely known the term is to English-language speakers. So, for example, I use the English spelling of the word "Hmong," which is commonly used by English and Hmong speakers, rather than the RPA spelling of *Hmoob*. In the same way, I represent Hmong names in their English-language spellings rather than in Hmong RPA spellings: "Lee" rather than *Lis,* "Thao" rather than *Thoj,* "Xiong" rather than *Xyooj,* and so on. Alternatively, I use RPA spellings for terms less widely known to English speakers or for which there may be no English equivalent. Thus, I represent the Hmong term for a traditional love song in its RPA spelling, *kwv txhiaj* (kuh tziah). As is apparent from the previous examples, words represented in the RPA appear in *italics,* while English spellings appear in conventional font. For Hmong words that may represent a particular pronunciation challenge to non-Hmong speakers, such as *kwv txhiaj,* I provide a suggested pronunciation following the RPA spelling. The pronunciation suggestions appear in parentheses following the RPA spellings, as above, and are intended as informal guides rather than phonetically accurate representations of the language. For a technical introduction to Hmong language and pronunciation, including Hmong tones, see Thao 1999; also Heimbach 1969.

Transcriptions

Much of the data for this book comes from oral testimonies collected from Hmong adult men and women, none of whom spoke English as their first language. In some cases, I have edited the transcripts for clarity and to reflect standard English usage. While practitioners of the "new ethnography" call attention to the unequal power relations among informants and scholars and insist that scholars not tamper with informants' narratives, I side with Sucheng Chan (1994), who argued that to represent Hmong speakers in nonstandard English is to expose adult men and women to the patronizing attitudes and overt racism directed at refugees and immigrants who are not fluent in English. I have edited the transcripts used in this project to both avoid such characterizations and to clarify what I believe to be the speakers' meanings.

Introduction

In the offices of the Wausau Area Hmong Mutual Association in Wausau, Wisconsin, a picturesque city surrounded by dairy farms and forests, is a collection of dog-eared scrapbooks. An employee of the association maintains these scrapbooks, which serve as an informal archive of the Hmong experience in Wausau and which contain virtually every newspaper article, editorial, and letter to the editor written about the Hmong and published in the local newspaper since the Hmong and other Southeast Asian refugees began arriving in the city at the end of the Vietnam War.

Collected in the scrapbooks are newspaper stories explaining how Laotian Hmong farmers were recruited by the U.S. Central Intelligence Agency (CIA) to serve as a covert army in support of U.S. military objectives in Southeast Asia in the 1960s; how Hmong gueril;las rescued U.S. pilots shot down over Laos; and how the Hmong suffered casualties so devastating that twelve-year-old boys were eventually pressed into battle. Other stories describe the defeat of L'Armée Clandestine in 1975 and the exodus of thousands of Hmong to the United States, where they arrived as economically impoverished refugees. Still other accounts focus on the perceived "otherness" of Hmong cultural practices, such as the early marriage age of women or the role of shamans in Hmong cosmology.

Also pasted into the scrapbooks are the numerous editorials and letters to the editor about the Hmong that have been published in the local paper, *The Wausau Daily Herald,* over the years. Many of these pieces are harshly critical, variously accusing the Hmong of abusing the welfare system, having too many children, refusing to learn English, and eating local dogs.[1] There are letters published under such captions as "Send refugees back to Asia," "No friend of Wausau Hmong," and "New Citizens—adopt our values to be Americans." The following excerpt provides a sampling of the criticism.

> EDITOR: I too am becoming increasingly angry at the "so called" plight
> of the Hmong in the Wausau area. Where else would they be able to live
> as they do? Certainly not in their homeland. Perhaps they were hard

working farmers in years gone by but I certainly don't perceive them as hard workers at all in the United States, but I guess they don't have to be. They know where their next meal is coming from. ("Hmong 'plight' doesn't make sense," *The Wausau Daily Herald*, June 1993)

Such letters reflected the uncertainties felt by many Wausau residents about the changing demographics of the city. Prior to the arrival of the Hmong and other Southeast Asian refugees, Wausau was populated primarily by the descendants of German, Polish, and Scandinavian immigrants (Kronenwetter 1985).[2] The arrival of the Hmong began to change the city's demographics, however, as the refugee population increased from a few isolated families in 1976 to 3,128 individuals in 1990, to 4,403 in 1995, or approximately 10 percent of the total city population (Wausau Area Hmong Mutual Association, 2000).[3] Hmong people were drawn to Wausau by the possibilities for employment, by the rural environment—which, if very different from Laos was less alien than the urban centers where many Hmong were originally resettled—and by Wisconsin's comparatively generous public assistance programs. As the refugee community began to establish itself, more Hmong came to join family members already settled in the city, further increasing the size of the Southeast Asian population. The letters collected in the Hmong Association scrapbooks document the social tensions that accompanied Wausau's demographic shift—tensions that became so pronounced as to draw national attention, including an article in *The Atlantic Monthly* (Beck 1994) and a segment on the television program *60 Minutes*.

Initially, few Hmong wrote to respond to criticisms made of them in *The Wausau Daily Herald*. Indeed, it is impossible to know precisely how many Hmong were reading the newspaper or were aware of its contents. Most Hmong refugees in the United States in the 1980s did not speak English, and many were not literate in any language, including their native Hmong. A people who trace their origins to China, the Hmong have long been known in the West as a "preliterate" or "oral" culture—terms that obscure more than they reveal but are meant to indicate a situation in which most members of a culture do not read or write. While the existence of so-called "preliterate" cultures may be a historical fiction (Besnier 1995), and while Hmong culture has long reflected a mixture of oral and literate influences, it is nevertheless accurate to state that the majority of Hmong who arrived in the United States in the 1970s and early 1980s had received limited education and did not read or write in the Laotian, Hmong, or English languages (Green and Reder 1986; Reder 1985a, 1985b; Strand and Jones 1985).

By the early 1990s, however, letters and op-ed essays written by Hmong people began appearing in *The Wausau Daily Herald* with increasing frequency. In these writings, Hmong residents of the city replied to criticisms of Southeast Asians and sought to explain something of Hmong culture, values, and history to the majority community. The following editorial by a Hmong man, for example, addresses an accusation, widely circulated in the city and published in a previous letter to the editor, that Hmong people receiving public assistance were buying new cars and "$80,000 houses."

> What about the Hmong man who buys an $80,000 house when he has been here only a couple of years, when there are so many people who were born in this country who cannot afford a $30,000 home? Before getting mad at this person, maybe we can all learn something from him and try to live our lives as he did. Obviously, if he bought an $80,000 house, he is not on welfare....I can almost guarantee that he neither smokes, nor drinks, nor goes out to eat regularly, nor drives a $20,000 car, and a portion of [his down payment] came from his family. ("Expand the clan; we're all one Wausau family," *The Wausau Daily Herald,* n.d.)

Similarly, a letter written by a Hmong woman responds to criticism of the Hmong people for speaking their native language in public.

> EDITOR: I also would like to respond to the article called "Asians shouldn't speak native tongue but adapt!" There are many like myself who have been here in the U.S. for about 14 years and still want to, and can, speak Hmong. I am glad to be a bilingual. ("Don't blame Hmong, but work to solve problems," *The Wausau Daily Herald,* September 11, 1993)

And an op-ed essay authored by a Hmong military veteran reminds Wausau readers of the Hmong alliance with the United States during the Vietnam War and the drastic consequences of this for the Hmong people.

> When the United States withdrew its troops from Southeast Asia, you let your enemies take revenge on us because of what you did to the Vietnamese and the communist Laotians. We were killed and gassed with chemical weapons—bleeding agents that tore our skin and made it impossible for us to breathe and eat. We died because we fought with you. ("U.S. turns deaf ear to killing fields of Laos and Hmong allies," *The Wausau Daily Herald,* May 19, 1993)

This book tells the story of how these letters came to be written.

More precisely, the book tells a story of literacy development in a midwestern community of Laotian Hmong, a people whose language had no widely accepted written form until the late twentieth century. Consequently, the Hmong have often been described in scholarly and popular literature as "preliterates," "non-literates," or members of an "oral culture." While such terms are fraught with empirical and conceptual problems, it is true, as previously noted, that the majority of Hmong did not read or write in any language when they arrived in the United States. For this reason, the Hmong provide a unique opportunity to study the forces that influence the development of reading and writing abilities in cultures in which writing is not widespread, and to do so within the context of the sociopolitical developments that have defined our own historical moment.

Unlike studies of literacy development set in the distant past—in ancient Athens (Havelock 1982), the Middle Ages (Clanchy 1979), or colonial New England (Lockridge 1974)—the Hmong literacy narrative is located in the context of twentieth-century life and can be told, to a great extent, in the words of those who lived the experience. And unlike modern anthropological studies that examine the literacy development of so-called "non-literate" cultures in fixed geographical locations, such as the Pacific Islands (Clammer 1976; Topping 1992; Besnier 1995), the Hmong literacy story is situated in the welter of political, economic, religious, military, and migratory upheavals that we classify as "globalization." One of the reasons the Hmong story is so compelling, then, is for its temporal proximity, for the unique vantage point it offers on questions of literacy both past and present, in both stable and shifting cultural settings.

In relating the particulars of the Hmong story, we seek insights into broader questions, still urgent and unresolved, about the nature of literacy development generally.

- How do people learn to read and write? What are the processes through which people come to make sense of graphical marks upon a page and then reproduce these? How do cultures become literate, shifting from conditions in which literacy is absent or limited to conditions in which it is widely practiced?
- How does literacy develop in minority cultures, including refugee and immigrant cultures, in which literacy has not historically had a deep purchase? What are the forces that direct the literacy experiences of such cultures in the twentieth century?
- What are the effects of literacy? How does it serve those who disseminate it, and what does it offer those who learn to practice it? Literacy is

a notoriously malleable property: "an instrument for the enslavement of mankind," in Levi-Strauss' (1964) dark phrase, but equally a means for liberation and "reading the world" in the more hopeful language of Paulo Freire (1970). But whose understandings of literacy prevail as people learn to read and write, and why? How are the contradictions of literacy negotiated? And how is literacy implicated in our constructions of identity, perceptions of reality, and exertions of power over one another?

- Finally, what do these questions and their possible answers mean for literacy education and scholarship? What does the Hmong narrative add to our understandings of these activities? Of what reading and writing ultimately mean?

In addition to addressing these questions, the book will seek to provide another perspective on the Asian-American experience, which has been historically constructed through two distinct narratives, both pernicious. In the first of these narratives, Asian immigrants to the nineteenth-century United States were inscribed by white Americans as "strangers" and "heathens," barbaric and essentially unassimilable (Takaki 1993, 7). Chinese, Japanese, Filipino, and other Asian immigrants to America's Western shore were thought to constitute a threat to Anglo-American sovereignty and white racial purity. Such racist attitudes were not mere abstractions but were codified by law, including the Chinese Exclusion Act of 1882, which restricted the numbers of Chinese allowed to emigrate to the United States, and the National Origins Act of 1924, which prohibited Japanese immigration altogether (Takaki 1989, 14). An 1885 San Francisco board of supervisors report written in response to a Chinese-American effort to integrate the public schools of the city captured the prevailing attitudes.

> Meanwhile, guard well the doors of our public schools, that they [Chinese children] do not enter. For however hard and stern such a doctrine may sound, it is but the enforcement of the law of self preservation, the inculcation of the doctrine of true humanity, and an integral part of the enforcement of the iron rule of right by which we hope presently to prove that we can justly and practically defend ourselves from this invasion of Mongolian barbarism. (In Okihiro 1994, 159)

In this exclusionist narrative, the "racial uniform" of Asians (Takaki 1989, 13) obscured all else, including their diverse cultures and nationalities.

In the second and superficially opposite narrative, Asian Americans are viewed as the "model minority," immigrants whose educational and economic achievements speak to their successful assimilation in the United

States. While the "model minority" narrative ostensibly praises Asian Americans for their achievements, it too imposes a homogenous and essentialist identity, as Lisa Lowe (1996) has argued, subsuming the differences of class, gender, and nationality under the single all-encompassing category of "race" (68). As a result, Ronald Takaki (1989) writes, "Asian Americans find their diversity denied: many feel forced to conform to the 'model minority' mold and want more freedom to be their individual selves" (477). Gary K. Okihiro (1994) has argued that the racialized "stranger" and "model minority" narratives are not in fact separate stories but represent a "seamless continuum" (141). Both constructs, Okihiro contended, give credence to the problematic construct of a "White" identity, whether as a race of people threatened by hordes of "heathen" strangers or as the ideal for hard-working, obedient immigrants that have accepted the status quo of white domination (139–142). Both stories deny what Lowe called "Asian American heterogeneities"—the existing cultural, political, gender, and other differences among peoples of Asian origin that mark them as discrete, as diverse, and as human beings.

In relating the literacy development of the Hmong, this book contributes to the dialogue within Asian-American studies by recovering another episode of what Morris Young (2004) called the "hidden histories" of Asian Americans (9). The book offers an alternative to essentializing constructs—whether the "model minority" trope or the still virulent racism of the "Stranger" narrative (see Takaki 1989, 479–483)—by exploring the history of one group of Asian Americans, the Hmong of Laos, and demonstrating how the distinctiveness of that history influenced Hmong literacy development.

To tell this story, I examine the literacy histories of Hmong refugees— men and women, elders and young adults, college educated and those who have never learned to read or write—resettled in one American community. Interviewed at their homes, workplaces, and churches, these people recalled their memories of learning to read and write in Laos, in refugee camps in Thailand, and finally in the United States. In these interviews, Hmong people describe the circumstances under which they learned to read and write, the identities their literacy training offered them, and the various ways they appropriated their literacy skills for the purpose of advancing their own complex and divergent cultural, political, spiritual, and economic agendas.

From these narratives I have derived a theoretical account of literacy development, one that offers a critical vocabulary for talking about the ways in which people learn to read and write in diverse settings and across the boundaries of cultures, states, languages, economies, and writing systems. I call this theoretical framework, this way of thinking and talking about literacy, the "rhetorical conception of literacy development" and elaborate upon it below. In offering this conception, I seek to contribute to the interdisciplinary study of reading and writing that has become known as "New Literacy Studies" (Collins 1995; Street 1993).

Before going further, let me say what I mean by "literacy." In this book, "literacy" refers to the activities of reading and writing at a basic level: "the ability to decode and comprehend written language at a rudimentary level—that is the ability to say written words corresponding to ordinary oral discourse and to understand them" (Kaestle 1991, 3; see also Graff 1987, 5). However, since literacy can be understood as both an activity and a condition, let me specify further. "Literacy" in this work refers to the ability to read and write at the primary school level or above. "Literate" means possessing the skills to perform these acts. And "literacy development" refers to the gradual accumulation of these skills over a span of years, in the case of individuals, or decades or centuries, in the case of cultures.

In the remainder of this introduction I describe New Literacy Studies and what this book seeks to contribute to it, discuss the research methods used for collecting the ethnographic and historical data presented in this work, and elaborate upon the "rhetorical conception" on literacy development. The introduction concludes with a brief overview of the book's chapters.

New Literacy Studies at the Crossroads: Perspectives on Learning to Read and Write

Over the last few decades, ideas about the nature of literacy, and in particular about how people learn to read and write, have changed profoundly. Well into the 1980s, literacy was considered a product of individual cognition, an essentially solitary act of mind. In the United States, the understanding of reading and writing as individual activity has been most clearly articulated in psychology, particularly the branch of psychology associated with behaviorism. Mike Rose (1985) has written that when turn-of-the-century educational psychologists such as E. L. Thorndike began studying the teaching of writing, they discarded the study of classically influenced grammars in favor of more scientific conceptions of mind, language, and literacy. However, the model of language from which they proceeded, according to Rose, was narrowly reductive, "a mechanistic paradigm that studied language by reducing it to discrete behaviors and that defined language growth as the accretion of these particulars" (343). Literacy was seen as one of the "discrete behaviors," and its development was construed in terms of appropriate mental conditioning.

Pedagogy proceeding from this conception of literacy was similarly reductive. Teaching and learning were modeled on the principles of industrial scientific management and stressed the importance of drills and language exercises as the means to develop "habit formation," which Rose calls "the behaviorist equivalent to learning—the resilience of an acquired response being dependent upon the power and number of reinforcements" (344). In the "skill-based approach," as this perspective became known, everything could be broken into isolated parts, and all the parts could subsequently be taught, learned, and ultimately tested (Barton 1994, 162). Students were expected to learn to decode the preexisting meanings of texts, and reading programs were based upon the "gradual mastery of subskills such as letter recognition, sound blending, word recognition, and ultimately deciphering meaning" (Olson 1977, 262). Literacy in this conception becomes a kind of mechanical puzzle in which parts can be disassembled, spread over the pages of a primer or basal reader, and examined in analytical isolation from one another.

Significantly, skills-based approaches to literacy were conceived of as objective, disconnected from the social and moral content of everyday life, while learning was regarded as the responsibility of the individual learner. In the skills-based approach, each human being acts, as Ira Shor (1992, 92) has written, as a "lone entrepreneur" operating independently of social institutions and economic systems. This is the conception of literacy that has for years dominated in the schools, where reading and writing have been understood and assessed in terms of individual ability, motivation, and effort (Luke, Comber, and O'Brien 1996). In this sense, the individual conception of literacy has been more influential than any other and has directed the schooling and literacy experiences of students from the elementary to the college levels.

Dissatisfied with the limitations of the skills-based approach, scholars in the 1980s began to move away from thinking of literacy in terms of individual mentality, or as a private act of mind, to conceiving of it as fundamentally social, or as an expression of cultural practices, values, and beliefs. Such studies, which have become known collectively as the New Literacy Studies, have drawn upon interdisciplinary perspectives and methods of inquiry, including those of psychology (Hayes 1996; Scribner and Cole 1981), linguistics (Chafe 1985; Gee 1996), history (Brandt 2001; Gere 1997), and anthropology (Besnier 1995; Street 2001). This work, while diverse, is typically characterized by fine-grained observation of a culture, by description of the features and patterns of reading and writing within that culture, and by attention to the details of daily existence that make visible, as Brian Street (2001) has written, "the complexity of local, everyday community literacy practices" (7). Moreover, unlike the putatively "value-neutral" position of the skills-based approach, New Literacy Studies acknowledges "the ideological character of the processes of acquisition and of the meanings and uses of different literacies" (Street 1993, 7).

The contributions of New Literacy Studies have been profoundly important, shifting the focus away from the individual and psychological perspectives that have dominated education research over the last century to reveal the socially situated nature of written communication. Among other things, New Literacy Studies scholars have complicated our understandings of oral and literate communication (Heath 1983), explored the relationships of literacy and ethnicity (Ferdman 1990), legitimized the nonstandard literacy practices of minority populations (Moss 1994), and examined the intersections of home and school literacies (Rose 1989).

In recent years, however, there has been an increasing sense that New Literacy Studies may have arrived at a crossroads of sorts; may have reached the limits of its explanatory powers. The problem is that while culturally based approaches have provided insights into the socially situated nature of reading and writing, these same approaches too often fail to delineate the historical relationships that have shaped the very practices being described. Consequently, literacy practices may end up being represented as though they were self-generating, a product of unique cultural characteristics rather than an outcome of historical and often violent contacts between peoples of unequal power. The result can be models of the world that become, as anthropologist Eric Wolf (1982) wrote of ethnography in his discipline, "a global pool hall in which [self-contained] entities spin off each other like so many hard and round billiard balls" (6).

Failing to make such connections in literacy research, Street (2001) has warned, leaves us with "the old reifications" in which "a particular group of people become associated with a particular literacy; another group of people become associated with another literacy" (9). Literacy scholars have yet, Cushman et al. (2001) argue, "to compile these specific studies into a larger theoretical understanding of literacy" (11), one that can connect the local, historical, and hierarchical relationships that govern literacy development. Street (2003) has gone so far as to suggest that New Literacy Studies may be at an "impasse," having produced many necessary studies of literacy in cultural context yet still not having fully engaged the structural forces that shape the meanings of literacy and the implications of those forces for learners, especially minority learners.

What is needed, then, it seems, is literacy research that transcends what Brandt and Clinton (2002) call "the limits of the local" in such a way as to connect the diamond-sharp observations of ethnographic studies to the larger structural, systemic, and global forces that shape local contexts. That is the undertaking of this book, which attempts to contribute to the interdisciplinary project of New Literacy Studies by examining the literacy development of one people, the Hmong of Laos, in a way that connects ethnographic, historical, and theoretical perspectives. The book is *ethnographic* in that it is located in a single community and attempts to represent literacy development from the perspective of community members, communicating their diverging values, beliefs, and attitudes about reading and writing. It is *historical* in that it considers how literacy in the "ethnographic present" may be seen as a product of a culture's encounters with other cultures, states, institutions, and other powers in the past. Finally, the book offers a *theoretical* framework, an interpretive lens and language through which to understand the "general tendencies that hold across diverse case studies." *Writing from These Roots* thus attempts to offer a path beyond the current impasse by presenting a model for tracing the ethnographic, historical, and theoretical dimensions of literacy development.

Stories as History: Notes on Research Methods

To understand the Hmong experience of literacy, contemporary and historical, I went to what seemed to me the most direct source: Hmong people who had lived the experience. In living rooms and kitchens, workplaces and churches, over cups of tea, rich Hmong meals, and the occasional bottle of beer, I asked people how, when, where, and why they had learned to read and write. In the course of these conversations, often conducted while children were clambering about the room or a television set was blaring in the background, I listened to stories of rural life, civil war, exile, and, interwoven and entangled among all these, literacy development.

In the social sciences, the term for this kind of storytelling and listening is the *life history interview,* or the qualitative data-gathering method in which the researcher seeks to understand the relationships between patterns of daily life as described in the stories of ordinary people and the larger patterns of social relations that govern cultures, states, and societies (Bertaux 1982, 1981). In life history research, patterns of historical experience and change are interpreted from the vantage of the individual, whose story represents a perspective often missing from historical and ethnographic writings (Marshall and Rossman 1995, 88). Life history research looks to individual narratives for what Bertaux (1981) called "a progressive elucidation of the historical movement of social relations" (41). From the mosaics of the particular, in other words, may come some apprehension of the whole.

This was my approach in interviewing the Hmong. In the interviews, I wanted to learn how individual experiences of learning to read and write might be representative of larger patterns of literacy development. Though each of the testimonies I collected was in its own way compelling, I read them for a larger story, looking for the ways in which individual testimonies might reveal a broader narrative. In this sense, I offer in this book an example of what the historian Paul Thompson (1978) called "cross-hatching" in oral history, or the mining of a diverse collection of oral narratives to construct a larger argument.

While qualitative research offers an array of methodological options for collecting data (Marshall and Rossman 1995, 78–107), the life history approach seemed the best possible method for conducting this project, given my aims. First, the approach is fundamentally historical. Recalling Bertaux's (1981) admonition that "the only knowledge we may hope to reach is of a *historical* character: our present is our past" (35), I wanted to go beyond the "ethnographic present" and locate much of my study in the past. The life history approach promised a means to that end.

Also, the life history approach was a methodology of necessity. As the Hmong do not have long-established traditions of reading and writing, there was no body of Hmong documentation to call upon in researching my study, no Hmong archives to which I might turn. To be sure, there are Hmong academics today writing scholarly accounts of their culture and history, and there are numerous studies of Hmong culture and history written by Western authors. (For recent and excellent examples of both, see Tapp et al. 2004.) In addition, there are other sources on the Hmong from which to draw, such as newspaper accounts, public documents, and government records. None of these published sources, however, offered the insights into Hmong literacy development provided by the oral testimonies of people who had experienced it.

The final reason for choosing the life history method was my desire to collaborate with Hmong people in writing a small piece of their history. One of the characteristics of life histories and oral histories is the way in which they seek to "repair the historical record," as Shulamit Reinharz (1992) puts it, by co-constructing history with those who have traditionally been excluded from historical writings. In the life history interview, the act of knowledge making is not reserved for the researcher but is shared by storyteller and listener (Bertaux 1981; Thompson 1978). Indeed, one of the strengths of life history research is the place it reserves for people—women, working people, minorities—who have been marginalized in standard histories of an era or event (see Reinharz 1992, 126–144). In this way can oral history, as Thompson has written, "give back to the people who made and experienced history, a central place" in the way it is written (1978, 2). In writing this book, I sought to create a narrative in which participants might speak for themselves, recalling and interpreting their own histories of life and literacy development. Ultimately, I did not fully realize this goal, for reasons I shall explain presently.

Interviews and Analysis

Who was interviewed, and how were they selected? In this project, I relied upon a network of personal contacts to suggest people whom I might interview and to facilitate the meetings. As a former employee of the local Hmong Association in the city where the research was conducted, I had excellent contacts with the educated class of Hmong professionals, including teachers, social workers, business people, and community leaders. However, I did not have the same access to other segments of the Hmong population, including elders, women, and non-English speakers, who had less education but whose insights promised a richer understanding of the Hmong literacy experience. My procedure for reaching these individuals was to go to my contacts, explain what I was interested in, and ask them to recommend people I might interview. These contacts would then typically schedule the interviews by telephone and in some cases accompany me to the home of the person to be interviewed. In the language of social science, this is the form of nonprobability sampling known as "purposive" or "snowball" sampling (Bernard 1988, 97–98), in which the researcher selects a topic of interest, locates people qualified to talk about it, interviews them, and then asks them to recommend additional interviewees. This is essentially the procedure followed in this book.

Over a two-year period, I interviewed forty-one people, conducting fifty interviews in all. Counted in this number were interviews with several non-Hmong, including the late William A. Smalley, one of the creators of the Romanized Popular Alphabet (RPA), the script that has become widely used by many Hmong in the United States and throughout the world. The number of interviews was not preordained but was arrived at when I came to feel that I understood the historical relationships that had most influenced Hmong literacy development. This is the point in life history research that Bertaux (1981) calls the "saturation of knowledge," or when the life history interviews have revealed the underlying social relations that are the object of the study. Shortly after arriving at this point, I concluded the interviews.[4]

Interviews were open-ended and generally informal. Though I brought a question script to each interview, I never asked all the questions I had prepared; rather, the script was used as a compass, to point in directions I might wish to go.[5] Interviews were two to six hours long, were taped on audiocassettes, and were subsequently transcribed.[6] The transcripts were then organized into categories to create what Anne Haas Dyson (1993) called "a vocabulary of sorts" (28) for interpreting the material. The purpose of the categories was to help me understand, as Anselm L. Strauss (1987) puts it, "What's the main story here, and why?" (31).[7]

Interviews were conducted in either the Hmong or English languages, and sometimes in both. While many of the people interviewed for this project were fluent English speakers, others were not comfortable speaking English or did not speak it at all. Although I have studied *Hmoob Dawb* (mong daw), the White Hmong dialect of the language, I do not speak it well enough to conduct Hmong-language interviews without assistance. When necessary, then, I worked with an interpreter, who translated my questions and the interviewees' responses through the course of the interview. The tapes of these discussions were then transcribed by another Hmong speaker who translated, for a second time, the Hmong-language portions of the interview tapes. In this project, eleven of the fifty interviews called for the use of an interpreter; of those eleven interviewees, seven spoke Hmong and some English, and four spoke only Hmong.[8]

Along with oral testimonies, I also collected a limited number of Hmong-authored writings in both the Hmong and English languages, including personal narratives, poetry, songbooks, historical documents, business plans, school essays, and a screenplay in the Hmong language on the subject of generational conflict. Along with these, I collected letters and editorials written by Hmong authors and published in *The Wausau Daily Herald* and in various Hmong newsletters. I discuss these texts in chapter 6.

"Passionate Attachments": Writing and Representation

To what extent did the Hmong people who consented to speak with me reclaim, as I had hoped, the "central place" in telling their history? To what extent did they "co-author" this narrative? Whose knowledge is, ultimately, represented in this work, and whose voices are privileged? Such questions reflect the increasing self-consciousness that qualitative researchers have come to feel about their methods and their acknowledgment that in seeking to give voice to others they are in fact writing from a specific cultural, political, and ethnographic position (Clifford 1988; Clifford and Marcus 1986; Rosaldo 1993; Tapp 2004). Researchers working with so-called "marginal" or "disenfranchised" populations must address the issue of who speaks in a research project, whose story gets told, and whose interests are represented. Moreover, the "subjects" of research have in some cases refused their traditional identities as the silent partner in ethnographic research and offered counter-narratives and identities to those created for them by the researcher.

I wrestled with these issues in writing about the Hmong. My vantage point was that of a white, middle-class male. I was introduced to the Hmong in the 1980s, when I worked in refugee camps in the Philippines and Thailand. I came to know the Hmong in Wausau through working in the early 1990s for the local Hmong Association, doing English-language development and community organizing. Through this work, I came to admire the Hmong people both generally and as individuals. In writing this book, I sought to acknowledge my respect for the Hmong by giving them a central place in telling the story of their literacy development. But this is not what finally happened. As the project went on, my own questions, motivations, interests, and limitations predominated. In the questions I asked, the categories I created, the testimonies I edited, the project became more my own and less the property of those who spoke with me. And while I have tried to represent faithfully and ethically what the interviewees told me, what I ultimately present here are my own interpretations, polemics, and conclusions about the Hmong experience of literacy. This statement in no way absolves this work of the questions of representation raised above, but it is my way of acknowledging my own "passionate attachments," as Jacqueline Jones Royster (2000, 280) termed the stance and commitments of the researcher. This story, then, is not "*the* Hmong story" or even "a Hmong story," even if we could sort out the definitions of such terms. Rather, it is a story told by a scholar about one aspect of the Hmong experience—their literacy development. So must this book be judged.

The "Rhetorical Conception": A Theoretical Framework for Literacy Development

The life history approach revealed the breadth of settings, purposes, and even writing systems implicated in the narrative of Hmong literacy development. Hmong people I met with variously recalled learning to read and write in rural villages, military bases, and church basements. They spoke of becoming literate so that they might write letters, read bibles, or compose autobiographies. They recounted studying scripts representing the Lao, Hmong, and English languages. Listening to these stories, I was struck by the extent to which Hmong people learning to read and write did so in contexts of distinctly different symbolic environments—environments that offered them unique ways of understanding themselves and their positions in the world.

Becoming literate, it seemed, meant learning to manipulate a graphical code not for its own sake, not simply to read and write for its own sake, but so that one might enter a particular symbolic universe and take up any one or many of the social identities—student, Christian, soldier, refugee— offered in that universe. Becoming literate also meant, the Hmong stories suggested, refusing or re-imagining these identities and using literacy to create alternative understandings of self and the world. Listening to the testimonies, I came to think that what mattered were not so much the actual practices of reading and writing, but rather the symbolic worlds in which these acts were given meaning. In this book, I call these symbolic worlds "rhetorics" and posit what I call the "rhetorical conception of literacy development."

Let me say what I mean by "rhetoric," which is a troublesome term, one laden throughout its history with cultural baggage, much of it pejorative. In this book, when I refer to "rhetoric" I do not mean the classical arts of persuasion or the ornamentation of elite discourse. Nor am I referring to the popular conceptions of rhetoric as a synonym for doubletalk, manipulation, or bombast. Rather, rhetoric as I mean it here refers to *the ways of using language and other symbols by institutions, groups, or individuals for the purpose of shaping conceptions of reality.* This means that we may think of "rhetorics" in the plural rather than imagining a single, coherent, and all-unifying "rhetoric." For example, the languages of governments, schools, and media I think of as "rhetorics," and the ways these operate within community life I consider "rhetorical." Rhetorics provide the frameworks in which individual acts of reading and writing take place.

I derived this view from Kenneth Burke (1969, 1966, 1945, 1937), the critic, philosopher, and boundary-breaking thinker whose vast landscape of work anticipated much of the contemporary conversation concerning discursive formations of identity.[9] Burke extended "the range of rhetoric" beyond the classical function of persuasion to what he called "identification," sometimes called "consubstantiality," by which Burke meant the use of symbols for the purpose of inducing identification and cooperation with others (1969, 20–23). Rather than simply persuading people, Burke suggested, rhetoric socializes them, inducing individuals to identify with one another and to assent to the communicative norms of their society. While rhetorical language is instrumental, a means for gaining advantage and deflecting "the... regions of malice and the lie," it is also the means by which listeners and speakers come to know themselves and their place within cultural and material hierarchies. Rhetoric in this sense offers, Burke suggested, "sheer 'identities' of the Symbolic... the identifications whereby a specialized activity makes one a participant in some social or economic class" (1969, 27–28).

This is the rhetoric of identity making, or the ways in which language has been used to invite human beings to understand themselves within the framework of tribe—a nation, culture, faith, institution, or family. "Our basic principle," Burke wrote, "is our contention that all symbolism can be treated as the ritualistic naming and changing of identity" (1937, quoted in Eddy 2003, 2). Burke's notion of "identity" does not refer to a single, solitary, and unified self, but rather, as Timothy W. Crusius (1999) puts it, to the particular "pattern of identifications" (40) or engagements with different forms and practices of symbolic activity that make up an individual's world. In this, Burke anticipated more recent understandings of identity not as an individuated and private essence, but rather as a gathering place of diverse symbols, commitments, and social practices (Ivanic 1998).

Symbolic identities are not merely individual, but also public. Paul Stob (2005) has argued that for Burke, language was fundamentally social and "transforms the individual into a specific type of social being" (236). "The mind, being formed by language," Burke wrote in *Attitudes Toward History*, "is formed by a *public grammar*" (1959, quoted in Stob 2005, 236). In this formulation, rhetoric's identity-making functions, the ways in which it constitutes the individual as an individual, as a citizen, soldier, family member, or other, are regarded as prior to the persuasive devices recognized by classical theorists. Before the citizens may be persuaded, they must first identify themselves as citizens. "If it is easier to praise Athens before Athenians than before Laecedemonians," Maurice Charland (1987) has written in a twist of Aristotle's famous observation, "we should ask how those in Athens come to experience themselves as Athenians" (134). Human beings define themselves, in other words, within the symbols and ideology of a given rhetoric. In doing so, they build for themselves and inhabit a social identity that is subject to persuasion. "We are invited by the rhetoric," in Edwin Black's (1993) words, "not simply to believe something but to *be* something. We are solicited by the discourse to fulfill its blandishments with our very selves" (172). In this way of understanding, rhetoric does not merely persuade but helps to create the ideological identifications that make persuasion possible.

I use the term "ideology" here not as a synonym for "false consciousness" or adherence to a particular doctrine, but rather, after James Berlin (1987), as "the pluralistic conceptions of social and political arrangements that are present in a society at any given time" (4). Rhetorics are the languages of ideologies and offer the symbolic means through which ideologies become known and are imposed, shared, understood, or overthrown. Rhetoric and ideology are in this sense enmeshed, impossible to separate. Rhetorics are ideological, and ideologies rhetorical.

In a rhetorical conception of literacy, individual acts of reading and writing, of decoding and encoding, have little meaning in themselves. They are largely technical operations that assume significance only in what Burke (1969) called the "wider context of motives" (31), or the shaping ideology of the rhetoric. This means that all elements of literacy instruction, including the selection of reading materials, the choice of teaching methodologies, the assignment of essay topics, and even the teacher's conception of the learner are ultimately rhetorical and ideological, ultimately intended to promote a vision of the world and the place of learners within it. To see literacy development as rhetorical is to consider the influence of rhetorics on what writers choose to say, the audience they imagine in saying it, the genres in which they elect to write, and the words and phrases they use to communicate their messages. It is also to acknowledge the influence of rhetorics on what people refrain from saying and the expressive possibilities that are foreclosed to them. Literacy in this sense is a product of powerfully shaping rhetorics that work to define, inscribe, and organize human activity.

What I am calling a rhetoric is closely related to the concept of "discourse," another term used across disciplines to suggest a range of theoretical and general meanings. Literacy scholars have called upon the term "discourse" in examining the material, social, and political dimensions of literacy and how these affect individual learners (e.g., Gee 1990; Street 1995; Yagelski 2000). James Gee (1990) defines discourse as the "socially accepted association among ways of using language, of thinking, feeling, believing, valuing, and of acting that can be used to identify oneself as a member of a socially meaningful group ... or to signal (that one is playing) a socially meaningful 'role' [within the group]" (143). In this view, literacy operates as a discursive practice that works to construct identity and one's position within a group or culture.

This work has been indispensable in explaining the role of symbolic activity in shaping human identities and positions, and the ideas presented in this book are indebted to such scholarship. However, I choose to use the terms "rhetoric" and "rhetorics of literacy" over "discourse" and "discourses of literacy" to emphasize the role of human agents, in this case readers and writers, to negotiate these shaping discourses, and to construct new identities and social positions. The term "rhetoric," for all its elitist history, its cyclic declines in reputation, and its popular connotations of bombast, misdirection, and deceit, yet retains its associations with agency, social action, and democratic practice. Rhetoric, Burke reminds us, is a kind of symbolic action, a means through which individuals may respond to and influence the institutional forces that work to define human possibilities. There is, therefore, a tension in the definition of rhetoric offered here. Rhetorics are the specialized collections of symbols and languages used by institutions to control human beings. Yet rhetorics may also be understood as the response, the opposing set of symbols and languages used by individuals and groups to negotiate or resist institutional pressures. So if institutions can "control people by controlling their literacy," in Beth Daniell's (1999) words, so it is also possible, again quoting Daniell, for "individuals and groups to use literacy to act either in concert with or in opposition to this power" (406). The terms "rhetoric" and "rhetorics of literacy" are meant to indicate these opposing possibilities—the ways in which reading and writing can be used to define, control, and circumscribe, but also the ways in which human beings can use written language to turn aside, re-create, and re-imagine.

Finally, the rhetorical conception stands in sharp contrast to standard treatments of literacy acquisition by immigrants, refugees, and adults generally, which are often framed in terms of life-skill competencies (Seufert 1999), vocational training (Grognet 1997), and citizenship (Nixon and Keenan 1997). Such treatments typically view literacy as instrumental, a means for assimilation into the dominant culture, political institutions, and economy of the United States. Students learn to read and write so that they may competently "function" within the new culture, or find a job, or become an American citizen. In the rhetorical conception of literacy, however, the emphasis is on symbolic activities that offer learners their "sheer identities of the symbolic," whether those of new resident, employee, or citizen, and what these may mean for readers and writers who may be new to the United States.

Overview of the Book

Chapters 1 and 2 provide the historical background necessary for understanding the Hmong literacy narrative. In chapter 1, I review Hmong history in China and Laos, concentrating on those events that led to the Hmong involvement in the Vietnam War. The chapter traces the beginning of Hmong history in China, follows the Hmong migration to Southeast Asia in the nineteenth century, and examines Hmong entanglements with the French, Laotian, and U.S. governments in the twentieth century. All of these historical episodes, I argue, played a part in the way Hmong people have come to use and value literacy. In chapter 2, I consider the history of the writing systems developed for the Hmong language and the role of these systems in the construction of individual and cultural identity. Reviewing the array of scripts invented for the Hmong language by assorted governments, missionary organizations, and messianic Hmong leaders, I look at how each of these scripts invented for the Hmong language offered readers and writers a place in a larger social, cultural, political, or religious hierarchy.

In chapter 3, I examine the concept of Hmong "preliteracy." Drawing upon testimonies I have collected, I critique the widely held notion of Hmong "preliteracy" by arguing that this term and its cognates—"nonliterate," "semi-literate," and so forth—are rhetorical constructions that devalue the cultures to which they are applied and obscure the historical processes through which literacy is promoted or suppressed. The chapter documents the ways in which Hmong preliteracy, far from being an expression of Hmong values, practices, or aspirations, should be seen as a result of the Hmong historical interactions with the Chinese, Laotian, French, and U.S. governments.

In chapter 4, I draw again upon the testimonies, as well as upon published ethnographies and histories of the Hmong, to argue that when the Hmong in Laos did encounter literacy, it came in the context of three powerfully shaping rhetorics: those of Laotian public schooling, Hmong military life, and missionary Christianity. I suggest that each of these rhetorics influenced the ways in which literacy was taught, learned, and practiced and that each also offered learners different conceptions of themselves and the world. The chapter also considers the ways in which Hmong people began appropriating their newfound literacy skills for their own purposes, such as writing personal letters, keeping journals, and organizing political resistance after the communist victory in Laos.

Chapters 5 and 6 move the story to the United States. In chapter 5, I consider the rhetorics that shaped reading and writing instruction in the United States and the implication of these for Hmong learners. Specifically, I examine the rhetorics of U.S. public schooling, Christian churches, and the workplace. As in chapter 4, I also recount the ways in which Hmong people came to use literacy learned in these settings for purposes of their own. In chapter 6, I examine literacy practiced outside of institutional contexts. I look at personal narratives authored by Hmong adult refugees, at the writings and literacy histories of Hmong women in the local community, and finally at the letters and essays published by Hmong writers in the public forum of the daily newspaper. I consider how all these literacy practices and texts offered alternatives to majority inscriptions of the Hmong and suggested new readings of the Hmong experience in the United States at the end of the twentieth century.

The book concludes by considering what implications the Hmong story and the rhetorical conception of literacy might have for other literacy learners, in other settings, inscribed in other rhetorics. I consider, too, some of the practical implications of this study, what it might mean to literacy teachers and learners in schools, community centers, prisons, colleges, and other institutional contexts. My intent in the final chapter is to demonstrate how the Hmong story offers a constructive way of thinking about the question of how people learn to read and write in the twenty-first century and what these practices may mean for individuals and society.

CHAPTER 1

Lost Books and Broken Promises
The Hmong People in China and Laos

Why ever did those horses have to eat the books of our forefathers, many, many years ago? Those Meo kings were the first there were in the whole great northern kingdom. Indeed in those days we had a land of our own. A Meo king ruled over us. We were the most powerful nation on earth. But the wicked Chinese were more cunning than we. They fell upon us in great hordes. They had better weapons than we had. We fought bitterly and courageously, but it was in vain. The Chinese knew no mercy. They murdered, enslaved, and pillaged. We had to surrender. But not quite everyone gave in; whoever could escape did so. When the exhausted fugitives came to a wide river they rested, leaving their packs among the bushes. They were all overcome with sleep. When at last they woke up—O horror—the horses had eaten up all the Meo books! Not a single one remained. Since then we have possessed neither books nor a script.

—Quoted in N. Tapp, *Sovereignty and Rebellion*

As we have seen, the Hmong of Laos have long been portrayed as an oral people, lacking an alphabet and knowledge of basic literacy processes. In this narrative, the Hmong were introduced to literacy only in the 1950s, and only through the efforts of missionary linguists from France and the United States. Prior to this, the Hmong supposedly lived in what Walter Ong (1982) might call a "primary oral culture," where knowledge of the very existence of literacy was so scant that most Hmong had never seen a book, much less held a pencil. This, at any rate, is the story of the Hmong that has so often been told in American schools with Hmong students, in government agencies serving Hmong refugees, and in popular media reports about Hmong refugees in the United States.

The Hmong have their own narratives, however, and in one of their oldest they once ruled a kingdom in China where they possessed their own lands, their own armies, and their own indigenous alphabet. In the continuous warfare against the expansionist Manchu dynasty, the Hmong king was eventually killed, his family butchered, and great numbers of Hmong people driven south. In the course of their escape the Hmong "book," the metonym for the Hmong alphabet and knowledge of writing, fell into the waters of the Yellow River and was lost. Or it was eaten by horses as the Hmong slept, exhausted from their flight. Or it was eaten by the Hmong themselves, who were starving. Such are the stories of the Hmong book (Enwall 1994, 45–58; Tapp 1989, 121–130).

The British historian Alun Munslow (1997) has argued that while the writing of history was formerly thought to be an objective act, a disinterested reconstruction of the past, contemporary historians have increasingly acknowledged the "story-shaped" character of their work, or the degree to which they are imposing their own narratives upon a series of disparate events. History, Munslow suggests, is not a collection of objective facts waiting to be discovered but is instead constituted in stories that reflect the worldview of the storyteller, the historian. Such narratives are not politically or socially innocent, moreover, but act as "a mechanism for the exercise of power in contemporary society" as some stories flourish and others are suppressed (13). In this view, the stories we tell about ourselves, and those that others tell about us, have material and political consequences.

Perhaps few groups have experienced the contingent nature of historical narrative more dramatically than the Hmong, a people whose history continues to be refracted through a prism of competing stories. Sally Peterson (1990) points out that written histories of the Hmong reflect the social and political interests of the people who have written them. In nineteenth-century China, for example, where the Hmong were despised and feared, accounts described a violent and subhuman race, the *yau-jin,* or wild people, who came down from the hills to trade and who were said to have short tails "like monkeys" (Geddes 1976, 14). On the other hand, the Hmong pacts with the CIA in the 1960s and 1970s and the role of the Hmong in fighting the communists in Vietnam have won the Hmong a privileged place in American historiography about the Vietnam War.[1] For stalwart supporters of U.S. policy in Vietnam, such as former CIA director William Colby (1991), the Hmong involvement in the war was "an inspiring story of courage and skill by a brave mountain people determined to fight for their freedom from an outside invader, who developed a unique relationship of trust and affection with faraway Americans" (34). To historians of the American Left, the Hmong were described, at least initially, as a mercenary army intent on "destroying and plundering" the local landscape under the direction of the CIA (Chomsky 1971; see also Yang 1993, 38–41). Hmong refugees in the United States, meanwhile, have been positioned in still other narratives, which have commonly described them as intellectual primitives and political victims (Koltyk 1995, 99). Since Hmong people are just beginning to write their own histories (Ng 1993), the imposed narratives of others have defined the Hmong for many people in the United States.

In what follows, I will attempt to provide some historical context for these competing narratives by presenting an introduction to the Hmong people and their history in China, Laos, and the United States. The premise of this chapter is that histories of literacy are also histories of peoples and that it is ill advised to discuss the literacy development of a culture without a corresponding discussion of the wider historical events that shaped that culture. The Hmong literacy story, in other words, is deeply enmeshed with other stories—of warfare, missionary work, migration, and exile—all of which have influenced the reading and writing skills that Hmong people learned, practiced, and valued. Hmong literacy development is so intimately tied to larger historical processes that discussions of learning to read and write have little meaning if they are not situated in their historical context.

This historical overview addresses two broad questions. First, who are the Hmong people and where did they come from? Second, why and how did they become involved in the Vietnam War? Limiting the discussion to these two topics, both of which are prerequisites to further considerations of Hmong literacy, means that much of the richness and complexity of the Hmong world are absent from this chapter. The chapter does not explore the strength of Hmong family structures, the elegance of Hmong music, the artistry of Hmong silversmithing, or the beauty of the Hmong language. Readers are encouraged to look elsewhere for treatments of these.[2] Similarly, my discussion of the events leading to the involvement of the Hmong in the Vietnam War can only begin to address the complexities of that fateful encounter. For readers interested in more comprehensive treatments, I suggest other sources.[3]

Finally, I feel obliged to say that my recounting of the Hmong experience with the West is not impartial. My selection of materials and sources reflects my biases about what has been most significant in shaping the course of Hmong history in the twentieth century—specifically, the recruitment of the Hmong by the CIA and their subsequent participation in the Vietnam War. These events would eventually lead to the devastation of Hmong ways of living in Laos and to the emigration of Hmong people throughout the world. Virtually every aspect of contemporary Hmong life, including Hmong reading and writing processes, has been changed by this experience. My retelling of the Hmong story reflects this point of view.

"Obstinate and Rebellious": Chinese Origins
of the Hmong

The origins of the Hmong are obscure and much debated.[4] Hmong culture has several tales of origin, the most widely known perhaps being the story of the great flood (Lee 1996). In this account, Hmong beginnings are traced to a disastrous flood that leaves only two people living on earth, a brother and sister. The brother wants to marry the sister, but she refuses him, thinking their union would displease the Lord of the Sky. The brother proposes several tests to prove that their marriage is the will of the God, and the couple is subsequently married. However, the infant born of their union is deformed, having neither head, nor hands, nor feet. Thinking the child is an egg, the parents proceed to cut it open. They find no other children within it, but each bit of flesh that touches the ground grows into a separate whole child. In this way is the world repopulated (Geddes 1976).

The earliest written mention of people who may have been the Hmong is found in Chinese annals dating to the third century BCE. In these annals, a people called the San-Miao, or "three Miao," were described as defiant and troublesome, an "obstinate and ungratefully rebellious [people], which would not submit" (in Geddes 1976, 5)—a representation that likely reflected Chinese fears of the rebellious Hmong. In a recent essay, Nicholas Tapp (2004) argues that there is much confusion and misrepresentation on the subject of early Hmong history and that many earlier accounts accepted as plausible by those interested in the Hmong are egregiously misinformed. What is not controversial, according to Louisa Schein (2004), is that virtually all Hmong who speak on the matter refer to China as the "homeland" and locate their origins somewhere in the Chinese state (274).

If the origins of the Hmong people are contested, so too are the names by which the Hmong have been known in China, Laos, and the United States. In China, the people who today call themselves the "Hmong" were known as "Miao," a term broadly applied by the Chinese to ethnic groups living mainly in southern China. While many scholars regard "Miao" as a neutral term, derived from the Chinese characters "plants" and "fields" and connoting "sons of the soil" (Geddes 1976, 13) or "seedlings" (Enwall 1992), Hmong in the United States have rejected the term and its Laotian derivative, "Meo," as pejorative, preferring to call themselves "Hmong." Yang Dao writes,

> The word "Miao," meaning barbarian, was used originally during the expansionist conquests of the Han dynasty to refer to all peoples of other than Chinese origin. Later, the epithet "Miao" was confined to

certain refractory ethnic groups, including the Hmong, who fought against Chinese domination. Introduced in the late nineteenth century to French Indochina, "Miao" degenerated into "Meo," a derogatory term categorically denounced by the Hmong. (1993, xvi)

Joakim Enwall (1992) disputes this view, arguing that "Miao" does not mean "barbarian" in any Chinese dialect and that Yang provides no etymological proof of his claim. Enwall faults Yang for "prejudice" and sees his use of "Hmong" as having political rather than linguistic significance. Schein (2004) contends that while many Hmong outside China oppose the term "Miao," it is in China a neutral term encompassing all the various minority subgroups.[5] The Hmong scholar Gary Yia Lee (1996) states that most Hmong people are hesitant about the meaning of "Hmong" and "simply do not know" the meanings of the word, even as they use it, while Paoze Thao (1999) argues that "the origin of the word 'Mong' or 'Hmong' is itself unknown" (3).

Hmong naming was further politicized in Laos when the Royal Laotian Government (RLG), before its downfall in 1975, sought to bring together all of its sixty-eight recognized minority peoples by classifying them as "Lao." The RLG further sorted the Lao into three general categories: "Lao Loum" for lowland ethnic Lao, "Lao Thueng" for "mountain slope" dwellers such as the Khmu people, and "Lao Soung" for "mountain summit dwellers," meaning the Hmong and Yao peoples (Stuart-Fox 1986, 44–48). The RLG's intention, in this nationalist taxonomy, was that these disparate groups would begin to think of themselves as Laotian citizens rather than as members of independent ethnic groups. The education and literacy development of many Hmong people, as we shall see in chapter 4, would be influenced by this policy. In this book, I use the term "Hmong" because it is the designation preferred by most Hmong people. "Miao" is used only when discussing the Hmong in China and only to reflect consistency with historical sources cited in this chapter.

By whatever name, the people now called the Hmong were in their earliest history engaged in warfare against the Chinese. Chinese annals chronicle wars in which the Miao were driven off the fertile Yellow River and Yangtze River basins and into the remote provinces of Szechwan, Yunnan, Hunan, and Kweichow sometime between 2700 and 2300 BCE (Geddes 1976, 5). Deprived of their fertile lands, the Miao began migrating south, toward what are now the Yunnan and Kweichow provinces of China (Mottin 1980, 7). From here there are gaps in the story, as the Miao disappear from written histories until the fifth century BCE, when they once again reemerge and take up a protracted armed rebellion against ruling Chinese dynasties. The historian Herold J. Weins (1954), for example, reports more than forty Miao uprisings between 403 and 561 ACE.

In the seventeenth century, the ruling Manchu dynasty (1644–1911) decided to take control of the lands occupied by the Miao and began to confront the Miao militarily. In a campaign that historian Alfred J. McCoy (1972, 65) called as brutal as that waged by the U.S. Seventh Cavalry against the Plains Indians fifty years later, the Manchus set out to destroy the Miao. Manchu military campaigns, conducted with what Lee (1982) called "truly barbaric cruelty," resulted in widespread destruction and death. In one campaign, Chinese troops reportedly burnt more than 12,000 villages, killed 17,000 Miao in battle, and took 27,000 prisoners in the space of three years (Mottin 1980, 35).

Unable to maintain their lands or ensure their own survival, thousands of Miao began to retreat southward between 1810 and 1820 (Geddes 1976). Initially, the Miao migrated into northern Vietnam, where they were met by Vietnamese elephant battalions and driven into the mountains (McCoy 1972, 80). Other Hmong pushed into Burma, Thailand, and Laos. While Hmong settlements were eventually established in the Laotian provinces of Sam Neua, Luang Prabang, and Phong Saly, it was the Hmong presence in Xieng Khouang—with its strategic proximity to North Vietnam, its mountainous terrain so ideal for guerrilla activity, and its soil so suitable for profitable opium poppy cultivation—that would eventually ensnare the Hmong in a series of relationships with Western global powers that would forever change their history and culture.

"We Do Not See You": Hmong in the French Colonial Context

When the Hmong arrived in Laos, they found a land governed not by any of the numerous ethnic groups in the country but by the colonial French. While the French had taken the trouble to conquer Laos, they had come to regard it as little more than a backwater and potential passageway to China. The French had hopes that the Mekong River, which travels through southern Laos, could provide a navigable channel to southwestern China and allow them to establish a "river empire" of trade and profits, thus providing access to a vast market that had been dominated by the British (McCoy 1970, 69–71). Beyond this, Laos held little interest for the French. The country had seemingly few natural resources to exploit, and French colonial officials did not view a Lao posting as a desirable career move. For example, while some forty thousand French competed for jobs administering the three provinces of Vietnam, only a hundred French officials were sent to Laos (McCoy 1970, 67). Day-to-day affairs of the colony were largely managed not by the French but by Vietnamese bureaucrats and by the Chinese merchants who for centuries had been managing the retail and wholesale trades in Laos (Chan 1994, 6).

Given their apathy, it is hardly surprising that the French made little effort to develop Laos. Few roads and railways were built, and in six decades not a single high school was constructed in the entire colony. By 1940, only seven thousand Laotian students were attending primary schools in a colony of approximately one million people (McCoy 1970, 83). Yang (1993) writes that the French educational and social policy was to create an aristocracy of peoples, with a highly trained elite at the top and the minority ethnic peoples, including the Hmong, kept at the bottom in a condition of "intellectual inferiority" (83).

Since few profits were to be made through exploitation of natural resources, French authorities in Laos resorted to raising revenues through taxation and forced labor. The French levied a head tax on all males between the ages of sixteen and twenty; taxed the sale of opium, alcohol, and salt; demanded corvée labor from local villagers, including the Hmong; and established a government monopoly on opium (Chan 1994, 7). French authorities offered little in return for such predations, and ethnic minorities in Laos lived in conditions that McCoy (1970) described as "little better than slavery" (80). A French priest on the scene described his government's relationship with the Hmong in this way: "We have been twenty-five years in the Meo country and we don't know a word of their language, we are unable to have interpreters, nor (Meo) schools, military (conscripts) or administrators. . . . The Meo say, 'We do not see you.'" (Quoted in Gunn 1990, 158.)

To consolidate their control, the French skillfully manipulated existing ethnic hierarchies, granting some minority groups the power to tax others and thereby enrich themselves in the process. In Vietnam, for example, the Hmong were taxed by ethnic Tai mandarins who demanded five Indochinese piastres or two hundred grams of opium per household—amounts greatly in excess of what the French themselves demanded (Gunn 1990, 153). The Hmong in the area rebelled, demanding direct access to French administrators as a way of escaping Tai extortion. In this way, the French could act as mediators capable of alleviating the very abuses for which they were responsible.

Demands upon minority peoples ultimately provoked rebellions against French governance, including a bloody and protracted Hmong revolt from 1919–1921 (Gunn 1990, 151–160; Mottin 1980, 42–43; Stuart-

Fox 1986, 15–16). The uprising was led by a messianic figure named Pa Chai Vue, who proclaimed himself the *Chao Fa,* or the ancient Hmong King, and called for the establishment of an independent Hmong kingdom in northern Vietnam. Pa Chai's revolt quickly spread, aided in part by propaganda tracts that may or may not have been composed in the sacred script purportedly promised by God to the Hmong people (Gunn 1990, 156; Smalley, Vang, and Yang 1990, 10). After two years of bitter fighting, the French suppressed the revolt, which they called the Guerre du Fou, or "War of the Insane," by using pacification techniques that would be adopted decades later by the U.S. military in Vietnam. These included destroying crops and sequestering villagers in "protected areas" where they could not feed or otherwise support the insurgents.

Although Pa Chai's uprising was ultimately crushed, the French were not eager to repeat their experiences with the Hmong and so elected to establish a system of *tassengs,* or administrative districts, that would be governed by the Hmong themselves. The system granted Hmong leaders a degree of autonomy but also encouraged rivalry and competition among clans for the position of district chief, which could be lucrative. The opium trade had expanded rapidly under French governance and by 1899 accounted for 15 to 40 percent of the colonial budget (Chan 1994, 9). Since the Hmong region of Xieng Khouang was the only legal place in French Indochina for opium cultivation, the district chief brokered all the opium sold in the region. In seeking to consolidate their control over the Hmong, the French played clan against clan, pitting two of the most powerful Hmong clans, the Ly and the Lo, against each another. This feud, abetted by the French, would ultimately have consequences not only for the Franco-Hmong relationship, but also for the entire history of the Hmong people in Laos.

The story of this feud is not a simple one. With both the Lo and the Ly clans vying for the coveted post of district chief of the Nong Het district of Xieng Khouang, the French ultimately sided with the Ly clan and appointed Touby Lyfoung as chief. By doing so, the French broke the promise they had made to the Lo clan that they would appoint Touby's rival, Faydang Lobliayao. McCoy (1972, 82–85) argues that the French favored Touby over Faydang because of the former's colonial education—he was one of the first Hmong to graduate from a French lycée, in 1939—and because he was unusually effective in increasing Hmong opium production at the outbreak of World War II, thereby increasing French colonial profits. In appointing Touby to the post, however, the French made a lasting enemy of Faydang, who would later align himself and his followers with the communist Pathet Lao movement during the Vietnam War.[6]

With the fall of France to Germany in 1941, Vichy France signed a treaty with Japan that allowed the French to retain administrative control of Laos but permitted Japanese troops to move freely though the countryside (Chan 1994, 17). While Faydang's men served the Japanese as guides and informers, Touby's *Meo Maquis* aligned themselves with the French (Lee 1982). When Japan surrendered in 1945, commandos of the "Free French" movement began parachuting into Hmong territory to gather intelligence and prepare for the recolonization of their former holdings. They were aided in these efforts by Touby, who had set up secret bases and assisted French counterinsurgency against the Japanese. For his efforts Touby was promoted by the French from *tasseng* to *Chao Moung*, or regional governor, and one of his half-brothers was given Touby's former position of *tasseng*.

Faydang responded by organizing the Meo Resistance League, one of the first Hmong nationalist movements, and by making contact with Ho Chi Minh's Viet Minh, who were fighting against the restoration of French colonialism in Vietnam (Lee 1982). Faydang would eventually serve as vice president of the nationalist *Neo Lao Hak Sat* (Lao Patriotic Front) and as the highest-ranking Hmong in the government of the communist Lao People's Democratic Republic (Chan 1994, 11; Lee 1982, 202).

Gary Yia Lee (1982, 201–202) has written that the split between the Ly and Lo clans—between what would later be thought of as the "CIA Army" and the "communist" Hmong—was less about ideology than about personal rivalries and grievances that predated the arrival of the French. The anthropologist and missionary G. Linwood Barney (1967), one of the inventors of the Romanized Popular Alphabet, supported this view, observing that "whatever Touby's men do, Faydang's must do the opposite" (275). Whatever the motivations, it seems clear, as McCoy (1972, 85) has observed, that a conflict between two Hmong clans that might once have been handled at the village level was escalated by French and, later, American political interests into a rupture of irreparable and ultimately tragic dimensions.

L'Armée Clandestine: The Hmong and the CIA

When General Vo Nguyen Giap's Viet Minh forces defeated the French at Dien Bien Phu, the struggle against communism in Southeast Asia assumed primary importance for the United States. American Cold War policy was framed by the so-called "domino theory," the belief that if one country were to "fall" to communism, its neighbors would tumble after it. After Dien Bien Phu, Laos was identified as a key domino. President

Dwight D. Eisenhower warned that "if Laos were lost, the rest of Southeast Asia would follow and the gateway to India would be opened" (quoted in Castle 1993, 10). To prevent such an outcome, the United States began to involve itself more directly in Laotian civil and military affairs, taking measures to ensure what it portrayed as the survival of "free world" nations in the region (Castle 1993, 11). These machinations would within a decade entangle the Hmong in a decimating war.

The American involvement with Laos had in fact begun well before the departure of the French in 1954. The United States had been sending economic aid to Laos since 1951, and by 1953 it was paying as much as 70 percent of the costs of the French war in Vietnam and Laos (Dommen 1964, 35). After the French withdrawal, the United States responded by taking steps to prevent further communist gains. Internationally, it distanced itself from the Geneva agreements in which Laos was declared a neutral and independent country. Regionally, the United States began a rapid military buildup in Thailand, which Washington policymakers wanted to make "the focal point of U.S. covert and psychological operations in Southeast Asia" (U.S. Department of Defense, quoted in Castle 1993, 12). And within Laos itself, the U.S. government continued to increase economic and military aid to the RLG.

Despite such measures, the Americans found it difficult to control events in Laos. The Laotian civil war breaking out between rightist, royalist, neutralist, and communist forces was complex and often thwarted U.S. efforts to shape Laotian politics. For example, an ambitious $3 million development project known as "Operation Booster Shot" was intended to influence the 1958 Laotian national elections on behalf of pro-American right-wing candidates. The program funded a variety of high-profile public works projects, along with air drops of food and medical supplies throughout the countryside. In spite of these efforts, the communist *Neo Lao Hak Sat* party and its allies won thirteen of twenty-one seats—an unexpected defeat that dismayed U.S. policymakers (Chan 1994, 25–26).

Nor were developments on the military front any more encouraging. Despite the 1954 Geneva agreements, the Eisenhower administration had decided to provide military aid to the RLG. The best way to build Laotian military capability, U.S. policymakers believed, was to provide military training and pay the salaries of all troops and officers of the Force Armée Royale (FAR), the RLG army. However, corruption was endemic and the United States had difficulty transforming FAR into an effective military presence. Meanwhile, the Pathet Lao and North Vietnamese continued to make gains, taking more and more of the Plain of Jars in Xieng Khouang, where the majority of the Hmong population had settled. Frustrated by their inability to control events and increasingly worried by growing communist advances in the north, American officials sought other means by which to influence Laotian affairs. One of these was a plan to establish an indigenous military force trained and supervised by the CIA that could carry out covert operations against communist forces. This indigenous military force would consist primarily of Hmong villagers.

Recruitment began in 1961, when the CIA sent case officers into the Laotian mountains to make contact with Hmong leaders (Castle 1993, 38). According to Edward G. Lansdale, the famous U.S. covert operative who was the subject of Graham Greene's Vietnam novel *The Quiet American,* the CIA hoped the Hmong would provide "an early warning, trip-wire sort of thing with these tribes in the mountains getting intelligence on North Vietnamese movement [and sealing] off the mountain infiltration routes from China and North Vietnam" (quoted in McCoy 1972, 265). To this effect, CIA case officers accompanied by Thai paramilitaries traveled by helicopter from village to village, recruiting Hmong clansmen to join the war against communism. Hmong villagers were told, "The Vietnamese will take your land. We [the United States] will give you the means to fight and defend your homes" (quoted in Castle 1993, 38).

What the Hmong were promised in return is still subject to dispute. Gareth Porter (1970) writes, "The Meo were reportedly promised an autonomous Meo state in return for helping the right wing fight the Pathet Lao" (183), thus reviving the revolutionary dream of Pa Chai Vue. Stephen Reder published interviews with older Hmong men—military veterans—who recalled a similar pledge.

> In 1960, five Americans came from the CIA and had us sign documents. We couldn't write, so we put our handprints on it instead. It said: "You help us, you hide us. We will fight the communists and if we lose and you don't have anywhere to go, we will give you a radio, a saw, an axe so you can cut trees and live in the forest. If you go into the jungle, we'll drop rice." I was involved with this for ten years. (1985b, 18)

One of the key supporters of the CIA recruitment effort was Vang Pao, a Hmong military officer in FAR who had fought alongside the French and earned their admiration. Charismatic and ambitious, Vang Pao would eventually be promoted to general and appointed military commander of Region II, consisting of the Lao provinces of Xieng Khouang and Sam Neua, where most of the Hmong population lived. In this role, Vang Pao would eclipse Touby as the paramount Hmong leader on the U.S. side and become the commander of L'Armée Clandestine, the so-called "Secret

Army" of the CIA. In the early days of the CIA recruitment effort, Vang Pao played a critical role in enlisting the support of Hmong villagers for the U.S. side, often dispensing money and material goods provided by the CIA (Lee 1982, 202). As the war intensified, villagers were conscripted or threatened with reprisals if they declined to join Vang Pao's army. Yang Lee Xiong, a Hmong man I interviewed, recalled it this way.

> At this time, the Hmong Army sent a Hmong colonel and an American to come to our village. I did not know the American's name.... They came and said we must join the army. If we did not join the army, then they will arrest us and put us in jail at Long Cheng. So everyone joined. There was nothing we could do. We had to do it. If we did not do it then there was only one choice of being arrested and jailed. So we had to do it.

Hmong recruits were trained to gather intelligence on North Vietnamese troop movements, harass communist forces moving from North to South Vietnam along the Ho Chi Minh Trail, and rescue U.S. pilots shot down by Laotian or Vietnamese gunners. Hmong soldiers also guarded key military installations, such as the navigational system on the mountain ridge at Phou Pha Thi. Almost a thousand Hmong soldiers guarded the ridge, from which U.S. Air Force bombers dropped 350,000 tons of bombs on Laos and another 500,000 tons on Vietnam over a period of two years (Castle 1993, 96). As the war escalated, so did the role of L'Armée Clandestine. Under the leadership of Vang Pao, the "Secret Army" was transformed into a fully equipped modern army and sent into set-piece battles against regular North Vietnamese troops. By 1962, L'Armée Clandestine had grown to an estimated 14,000–18,000 men. By 1969, Vang Pao's troops numbered some 40,000 soldiers and constituted the main military force for fighting communism in Laos (Chan 1994, 32).

The expansion of L'Armée Clandestine reflected the wider escalation of the war into Laos. As the United States vainly sought to disrupt the traffic of men and materials moving down the Ho Chi Minh Trail, it subjected Laos to increasingly destructive bombing attacks. In 1970, the Committee of Concerned Asian Scholars estimated that U.S. aircraft were conducting 17,000 to 27,000 bombing raids per month in communist areas of Laos, sometimes carrying out 800 sorties in a single day, "dropping napalm, phosphorus, and antipersonnel bombs... on everything, buffaloes, cows, schools, temples, houses and people (Lewallen 1971, 40, quoted in Lee 1990). A bombing campaign that had begun in secret in 1964 eventually dropped over two million tons of bombs on Laos in the 1960s (Stevenson 1972).

The bombings completely disrupted life in the northeastern region of Laos, killing tens of thousands of Hmong and turning hundreds of thousands more into refugees in their own country. Lee (1982) estimates that the war resulted in 370,000 people being displaced within Laos. Approximately 32 percent of these were Hmong, and in some regions the percentage was even higher. In Xieng Khouang Province, for example, Hmong refugees totaled 70 percent of the 155,000 displaced people. As the war progressed, so many Hmong soldiers were killed that replacements had to be brought in from hill tribes in Thailand and other parts of Laos to replenish Vang Pao's forces (Chan 1994, 40). By one estimate, 12,000 Hmong were killed in the war (Lee 1982), while another maintains that 17,000 Hmong troops and 50,000 Hmong civilians died in the conflict (Chan 1994, 40). By 1968, the casualties were such that Hmong children were being drafted to fight. Edgar "Pop" Buell, a retired Indiana farmer who was in Laos on behalf of International Voluntary Services but who also assisted the CIA, summed up the situation this way: "A short time ago we rounded up three hundred fresh recruits. Thirty percent were fourteen years old or less, and ten of them were only ten years old. Another 30 percent were fifteen or sixteen. The remaining 40 percent were forty-five or over. Where were the ones in between? I'll tell you—they're all dead" (quoted in McCoy 1972, 281).[7]

Despite the frenetic pace of the bombings, the communists continued to make gains. By 1970, an estimated 67,000 North Vietnamese soldiers had entered Laos, and Hmong forces were losing ground they had previously captured. By the late 1960s, the Plain of Jars was in possession of the North Vietnamese and Pathet Lao. Backed by CIA air support, Vang Pao staged destructive counterattacks, retaking the city of Xieng Khouang and recapturing much of the Plain of Jars. The gains were temporary. With the onset of the dry season in Laos, which provided greater mobility for supply convoys and mechanized infantry, the North Vietnamese struck back, forcing Vang Pao's forces to retreat.

When President Richard Nixon announced in 1973 that the United States had been conducting secret talks with the Vietnamese, the Pathet Lao offered to negotiate a compromise with the RLG. The coalition government that resulted included several high-ranking Hmong, including Touby Lyfoung, who served as deputy minister for posts and telegraphs. But by 1975 the coalition government had been overthrown and the Laotian monarchy abolished. The communist-led Lao People's Democratic Republic took control of the government.

On May 13, 1975, Vang Pao and his staff were evacuated from Long Cheng by U.S. transport planes. Some forty thousand Hmong began to follow Vang Pao out of the country, crossing the Mekong and taking refuge in Thailand. Those who stayed behind, especially Hmong and ethnic Laotians who had allied with the United States, were sent to "re-education camps," where many reportedly died of starvation and sickness. Touby Lyfoung, the Hmong leader and former protégé of the French, is said to have died of malaria at a re-education camp in Sam Neua.

Thousands of Hmong attempted to flee the country. While many reached Thailand, many others died: some from disease, others from attacks along the way, still others by drowning in the Mekong River as they tried to reach the Thai border. Virtually every adult Hmong I interviewed for this project told harrowing stories of the flight from Laos. Some spoke of leaving behind homes and family members, others of the trauma of seeing a parent, sibling, or child die from illness, gunshot, or drowning.

Those who did arrive in Thailand were incarcerated in refugee camps, where they might remain for months or even years. The decision whether to emigrate to the West was difficult. Letters and audiocassette tapes that reached the camps from the first wave of Hmong refugees who had resettled in the United States told of cars, homes, and free schools for children, but also told of urban violence, poverty, and racism. Many Hmong adults feared that if they migrated to the United States or other Western countries they would never learn the new language, find employment, or be able to raise their children in ways consistent with Hmong values. As a result, many Hmong delayed their departures from Thailand, hoping for a change in the political situation in Laos. Such hesitations notwithstanding, by the early 1980s some fifty thousand Hmong refugees had been resettled in the United States (Chan 1994, 49).

For those who did emigrate, isolation and depression became new enemies. Hmong men who once held positions of prestige and power found themselves having to contend with the evolving social dynamics of their transplanted communities, including changes in Hmong leadership patterns, gender relations, parenting styles, and even spiritual practices. Former leaders became dependent upon their children to communicate with schools, social service agencies, and other representatives of what many perceived as a hostile majority culture. The result, for some, was lost status and a loss of confidence in their abilities. "The older ones," a younger Hmong man told me, "they are like birds who have lost the trees."

For other Hmong, however, resettlement in the United States brought new opportunities for personal and social redefinition. In interviews conducted for this project, several younger Hmong acknowledged the terrible costs of the war but also suggested that it brought Hmong people into greater contact with the industrialized world, affording their children better chances for education and economic advancement. Hmong women, in particular, have enjoyed increased opportunities for education and personal independence in the United States, a theme we will take up in chapter 6.

Aftermath of War: Lost Books and Broken Promises

Why did the Hmong become involved with the CIA? What did they hope to gain? What promises were made to them in return for their participation? The popular narrative is that the Hmong were a "fiercely independent" people with an intense dislike of communism. When asked by CIA operatives in Laos whether he would fight for the U.S. side, Vang Pao reportedly answered, "For me, I can't live with communism. I must either leave or fight. I prefer to fight" (in Hamilton-Merritt 1993, 89). Despite this tidy narrative of congruence with American goals in Southeast Asia, however, scholars suggest multiple motives for the Hmong participation in the war.

One theory is that the Hmong fought to maintain their political advantages in Laos, where their relationships with the French had brought material prosperity and recognition in a country where Hmong people had been discriminated against by the Lao elite (see Reder 1985a). Lee (1982) cites economic motives, noting that "because of salaries offered and lack of employment opportunities in other fields" Hmong men took the opportunity to become soldiers. McCoy (1972), meanwhile, has argued that the Hmong were victims of their own rapacious leaders, principally Vang Pao, whom McCoy represents as a major drug lord intent on amassing great personal wealth through the manipulation of the opium trade. Finally, there is D. Gareth Porter's (1970) claim that the Hmong fought with the idea that they would be rewarded with an independent kingdom in northern Laos.

Ultimately, no single reason emerges for Hmong participation in the war. Rather, their involvement appears to stem from a combination of family grievances, historical alignments, economic necessities, personal ambitions, threats of violence, and the skillful manipulation of all of these factors by French and American authorities. Whatever the causes, there is among many Hmong a conviction that their involvement in the war was part of a wider agreement with the U.S. government. Many Hmong believe, as previously noted, that the U.S. government would provide for them in the unlikely event that America lost the war. A Hmong veteran interviewed by Reder recalled the U.S. "contract" with the Hmong: "The Americans in Laos had an agreement, a contract with us: 'You help us fight for your country, and if you can't win, we will take you with us and we will help you live.'...This is true about the contract. I have read it. I was a teacher in

Laos, and they gave the paper to every teacher. Vang Pao signed it. It said, You fight, and if we don't win we'll take you with us" (1985a, 19).

As of today, no documents have ever been produced to support this claim. No U.S. government or military source has emerged with copies of the letters or contracts validating the Hmong position. Whether or not such promises were ever written down, however, there is a profound and unhappy irony in the equation of a written "contract" with the survival of the Hmong. The lost CIA contract recalls another set of vanished writings that were associated with the loss of a homeland and subsequent exile: the Hmong books lost so long ago in China that fell into the river, or were eaten by horses as the Hmong slept, or were eaten by the Hmong themselves, who were starving. In both instances, the Hmong linked the loss of writing to the loss of the country: China in the ancient narrative, Laos in the modern version. In China, the lost writing was said to explain why the Hmong are a stateless people in Southeast Asia. In Laos, the lost contract is thought to explain the status of the Hmong as international refugees. For many Hmong, it would seem, the absence of writing is very much a part of their historical legacy, explaining much of their history and their status in the world today. Narratives of literacy are enmeshed with narratives of origin, and the history of Hmong reading and writing is crucially situated in the wider historical sweep of events.

CHAPTER 2

Rumors, Ropes, and Redemptions

Hmong Writing Systems in China and Laos

The absence of a writing system for the majority of Hmong did not signify...
a lack of interest.... the Hmong dreamed of a writing system, delivered from
on high, which would be their very own.
—J. Lemoine, "Les Ecritures du Hmong"

William A. Smalley (1996) observed that while the practice of writing in
Hmong life is comparatively new, beginning in the late 1950s in Laos, the
role of writing in Hmong culture is very old, reaching back to the beginnings of recorded Hmong history in China. Smalley is referring to the fact
that while the majority of Hmong in Southeast Asia and the United States
learned to read and write only within the last forty years, the Hmong as a
culture have long been aware of the writing systems of the more politically
powerful societies around them, including the Chinese, the Vietnamese,
the Lao, and the Thai. Smalley calls this "awareness without writing" and
argues that writing in traditional Hmong narratives has symbolized political independence, ethnic identity, and supernatural power.

We have seen, for example, how Hmong narratives link the loss of a
writing system to the death of the Hmong king and the exile of the Hmong
from their homelands in China. In such stories, the absence of writing
is connected to the political subjugation of the Hmong and their identity
as a stateless people. Other Hmong literacy narratives connect writing to
supernatural powers that can transform individual and collective destinies
(Johnson 1992, 371, discussed in Smalley 1996, 1). In one such narrative,
the boy *Maum Nyaj Lwj* (mao nya lue) and his mother are traveling through
the forest when they encounter a tiger. The boy writes something on a
piece of paper, throws it in the tiger's mouth, and the tiger disappears. The
boy later makes a river and cliff disappear in the same way. Comment-
ing upon the different roles assigned to writing in Western and Hmong
cultures, Smalley (1996, 2) has observed that while Western missionaries
thought of writing as something that "helps people to learn, makes communication possible over long distances, preserves records, and provides
entertainment," the Hmong have at different times in their history repre-

sented writing as having magical or spiritual properties and as being central to their political and cultural revivification.

Far from being a "preliterate" culture, if we interpret that term to mean, as in Ong 1982, "cultures totally untouched by any knowledge of writing or print" (11), the Hmong have experienced diverse forms of literacy in multiple languages over the last century. Smalley, Vang, and Yang (1990, 149) have documented at least fourteen attempts to create a writing system for the Hmong language over the last hundred years, at least six of which are still in use. These systems were created by Western missionaries, who used literacy as a tool for spreading Christian doctrine; by governments in China and Southeast Asia, which viewed literacy as a means for diminishing ethnicity and promoting national identity; and by Hmong people themselves, who have produced at least seven independent writing systems for their language in the last forty years, most of which have been linked to complex political and cosmological visions.

Each of these systems, whether missionary, governmental, or spiritual, can be understood as a rhetoric, a symbolic narrative offering readers and writers of the system a prescribed way of understanding themselves and their place in a larger social and economic narrative. A Chinese Miao learning to read and write in a nineteenth-century Christian missionary alphabet, for example, was encouraged to situate himself within a larger narrative and take up psychic residence within what the nineteenth-century Protestant missionary William H. Hudspeth (1937, quoted in Tapp 1989, 124) called "the incomparable story that Jesus loved the Miao." A Laotian Hmong woman learning to read and write fifty or one hundred years later in one of the Hmong scripts linked to political redemption, would have been invited to inhabit an altogether different narrative, one with radically different messages about history, politics, and religion.

Writing systems in this way can be understood as arguments through which readers and writers are influenced—by the choice of the materials printed in the writing system, the way the writing system is taught, and the status and prestige attaching to the people who teach the system—to identify themselves with a particular institution or cultural group. Because learning to read and write can be such a transformative experience, writing systems can have formidable persuasive power for those who learn to use them. Thus we may say that writing systems function, as the Russian critic M. M. Bakhtin (1981) has written of language, "not as a system of abstract grammatical categories, but rather...as...ideologically saturated...as a world view" (271). Readers and writers are invited to define themselves through the writing systems they use, by the reading and writing practices attached to these systems, and by the values these practices express. In this way does a writing system impose what Burke (1966) has called a "terministic screen," or a selection of reality that deflects competing or opposing versions of reality.

This chapter presents an overview of Hmong writing systems in China and Laos over the last century. The chapter considers the sources of the aforementioned scripts, the values attached to them, and their effects upon the people who learned them. A review of the writing systems used in the past provides a fuller context for understanding Hmong reading and writing practices in the present, as well as for understanding the values that the Hmong have ascribed to writing over the last century.

A few preliminary points: when I speak of "writing" in this chapter, I do not limit myself to the modern sense of the word, in which writing is largely equated with the use of an alphabet (Harris 1986, 37). Rather, "writing" in this context applies not only to alphabetic, but also to syllabic, pictographic, and mnemotechnic systems used by the Hmong in China and Laos. This chapter does not address the linguistic or technical features of these systems but focuses instead upon what I see as their inherent ideologies and their rhetorical effects upon readers and writers. The guiding questions in this chapter are as follows: what values were implicit in the adoption of a given writing system? What conceptions of self and the world did the systems offer to those who used them? In what ways were these offerings accepted, refused, or transformed by Hmong readers and writers?[1]

Dream of the Lost Books: Miao-Hmong Literacy Narratives

The history of Hmong writing begins, as we have seen, not with writing but with stories of writing—with narratives that provide the basis for Hmong beliefs about literacy.[2] Such narratives were widespread in Hmong oral traditions and have been recorded by travelers, missionaries, anthropologists, and linguists. The basic plot has been discussed: long ago in China, the Hmong had a kingdom, king, and a writing system, all of which were lost owing to the perfidy and ruthlessness of the Chinese. As a result, the Hmong were exiled from their homelands, deprived of their king, and became a stateless minority people. They also became a people without writing. In the variants to the story, as in the following version from Tapp 1989, the Hmong "book" is lost, stolen, or eaten.

> This is why we Hmong have no books. It was like this. Long, long ago,
> Hmong were the eldest sons. They went to the field to make a living

for themselves, but they did not, could not, study books. According to the elders, a long time ago, everybody moved, and crossed the great waters. The *Mab Suav,* meaning the Chinese and others, carried their books across on their heads, so they would be able to learn letters. But we Hmong were so afraid of our books getting wet that we could not do that, and we were hungry, so we ate them all up. That is the reason why now we can only be clever inside, in our hearts and only remember in our hearts, not in books. That was in China, where I have heard the Hmong still have books. (122)

Still other versions of the story have the Hmong stitching their writing into women's clothes to preserve it as they fled the Chinese, as in this account from the Chinese scholar Jiang Yingliang (in Enwall 1994, 47–48).

[The Miao] say that the Miao ancestor was Chiyou, and, originally, five thousand years ago, he lived in the area of the Yellow River basin. After being defeated by the Yellow Emperor he led his people to the south. While he was leading his people to the south, it was impractical to carry the books the people had, and he feared that the writing would be forgotten after the migration. Therefore, he ordered the women to embroider the writing onto the corners of their dresses and the edgings of their skirts. Thus the Miao writing was preserved.

Despite these travails, the Hmong book is not lost forever. The narratives holds that God will send a new king, a *Huab Tais* (hua tai), to liberate the Hmong from their oppressors and return them to their homelands. And with the king, God will send a writing system to validate the king's authority. In this way, the Hmong will be restored to their former status as a people with a nation, king, and writing system of their own.

In such narratives, the Hmong are a dispossessed and marginal people whose status has been fixed by more powerful peoples with their own kings, armies, and writing systems. Writing is associated in these narratives, as in Levi-Strauss, with the exercise of political violence and power. Tapp (1989) suggests that the Hmong have developed an especially strong awareness of writing because they have for centuries been in competition with the Chinese, a culture that Tapp describes as one of the most literate in world history. The myths of the lost Hmong writing, Tapp contends, express the economic and political deprivations of a minority people surrounded by more powerful states possessing writing.

Beyond this, the Hmong literacy narratives are an expression of ethnic identity (Enwall 1994, 162–163; Smalley 1996; Tapp 1989). Enwall (1994,

163), for instance, contends that the Miao have a predilection for writing and are unwilling to borrow such a crucial marker of ethnic identity from another people. To do so, Enwall argues, would be a sign of cultural inferiority. Tapp (1989, 121–130) argues that the "myth of the lost writing" has been central to Hmong definitions of identity, explaining for successive generations of Hmong their status and social position in the host country. And Smalley (1996, 3) concludes that for the Hmong, writing functions as a "symbol of identity," affirming Hmong values in a way that could never be expressed in a borrowed writing system. The history of Hmong literacy, then, begins not with pictographs, syllabaries, or alphabets, but with stories and dreams of writing.

Rumors, Ropes, and Rebellions: Early Miao-Hmong Writing Systems

Before they began using alphabetic or syllabic communication systems, Hmong people employed mnemotechnic forms of communication, such as rope knots and notched sticks (Enwall 1994, 56; Lemoine 1972, 131–138). Jacques Lemoine called these *écritures traditionelles,* or "traditional writings," and states that their use in world cultures can be traced to the Paleolithic era. The earliest mention of such systems among the Miao are found in nineteenth-century Chinese accounts, as in this excerpt from *Sketches of the Miau-tsze* (1859): "The people of this tribe have no knowledge of any written language. For records of events they use pieces of carved or notched wood" (trans. E. C. Bridgeman, quoted in Enwall 1994, 56). Lemoine avers that notched-stick communication was highly conventionalized and could be understood by others who knew how to read the markings. Using examples from Sayaboury Province in Laos, Lemoine illustrates that the number and placement of the notches could communicate information about finances, war, or general news that could be understood across distances. Three notches on a stick, for example, indicated a "friendly greeting" to the reader and an invitation to visit the sender; five or six notches on the stick referred to a financial matter; nine or ten notches signaled that a man had been condemned to death (1972, 134). Lemoine states that the use of such systems has continued in modern France, where bakers notch sticks to record sales of bread and credit records.

Other examples of what Ong (1982) called *"Aides-mémoire"* included the use of knots on grass strings; rough carvings on wooden boards or steles; charcoal drawings of objects such as men, horses, and roads; and the use of feathers and ashes to communicate urgency in political and military matters (Enwall 1994, 56–58; Lemoine 1972, 131–137). Enwall suggests that mnemonic systems represent an intermediary stage between the Hmong literacy narratives and writing systems using letters or other printed symbols.

While mnemotechnic systems may have been a transitional form of writing, there is a sense in which they, too, illustrate the rhetorical character of literacy, or the ways in which a writing system can offer a conception of identity and position. This is seen most clearly in the changing uses and meanings assigned to one kind of mnemotechnic literacy, the use of "feather letters," in China and Laos. A "feather letter" was a long stick to which a feather or other material object such as a pepper was attached. Feather letters were used by the Miao primarily in times of rebellion and revolt against the Chinese. Chen Shirou explains.

> [A "feather letter"] was a long wood stick, about one inch thick, one end was split, and there were inserted two feathers, a piece of fuse . . . , and two red peppers. This was said to be a Miao emergency message: the feather means emergency, the pepper means that the enemy is strong and the fuse means that the enemy already opened fire. If somebody received such a "feather letter," he would bring armed troops and come to their support. (1957, 3, quoted in Enwall 1994, 57)

So feather letters were a Miao system of communication, used principally during times of war. In Laos, however, the same technology acquired a radically different meaning after it had been appropriated by Lao government officials for communicating with the Hmong. Vue Lee Mai, an elderly Hmong man whom I interviewed, recalled his father receiving feather letters from Laotian village officials in the early 1950s.

> At the beginning, we Hmong did not know how to read and write, and when the local governor would tell us that they urgently needed some food or other things right away, they would put chicken blood, chicken feathers, a piece of ash on the letter. . . . This meant that the situation was hot—an emergency—and that we must find these things for them right away.
>
> Sometimes they wanted money, for example, tax money; sometimes they wanted food to eat; sometimes they collected meat. For example, in each village they would want one cow to be delivered to them right away, so the governor can send it to the soldiers to eat. Each month they would collect one cow, or rice from each village. If we did not send these things to them, then they will make it as hot as the items on the envelope, or they will cut your throat, or make it as hot as fire burning.

Thus did the feather letters that were used in China to organize rebellions against the central government become, in Laos, a means through which the government might communicate its demands for taxes, corvée labor, or other forms of tribute from the Hmong. Feathers, peppers, and ashes were no longer symbols of resistance and rebellion. Instead, they had become a technology for subordinating to Laotian political authority. While the chicken feathers, ashes, peppers, and fuses may not be "writing" in the strict sense of the word, they can be understood as *signs,* that is, as physical objects that have become "ideologically decorated" (Volosinov 1973, p. 10) or laden with meaning in specific contexts. The feathers, ashes, and fuses, then, took their meanings from the rhetorical environments in which they were used.

Widespread Like the Floodwaters: Writing and Rumors of Writing

The first accounts of a Miao writing system using printed characters come from Chinese travelers, soldiers, and scholars who either reported seeing Miao engaged in the act of writing or hearing rumors of such activity from others. None of these reports have ever been confirmed and none of the scripts survive. Still, the clues are tantalizing and illustrate some of the meanings that writing may have had for the Hmong in China and, later, in Laos.

In the seventeenth century, for example, the Chinese traveler Lu Ciyun (in Enwall 1994, 59) stated that he had seen examples of Miao writing in his sojourns through the region of Dongqi. Lu Ciyun produced two documents in this writing that were said to be songs and which were written in a script that was unlike Chinese. Western and Chinese scholars, however, are undecided as to whether Lu Ciyun had found Miao writing or a writing system belonging to another ethnic group. Albert Terrien de Lacouperie (1886, in Enwall 1994, 60) thought Lu Ciyun had discovered a sample of Yao writing, while the French missionary Paul Vial (1890, in Enwall 1994, 60) supposed that the writing was from the Chongia or Chajen people. Enwall agrees that the writing discovered by Lu Ciyun might actually have been used by the Yao or Yi peoples, although he does not dismiss the possibility that the writing may have belonged to a Miao group. In sum, the earliest recorded account of Miao writing may have described a writing system that was not Miao at all.

The next reported Miao writing system was mentioned in the *Boaqing fuzhi,* a nineteenth-century history of Baoqing, in Hunan Province.

The *Boaqing fuzhi* mentions a 1740 decree outlawing Miao writing, which was said to be widespread and taught to children in Miao schools in the Chengbu region. This writing was said to be in the seal character style and created in western Hunan province. That the writing may have been widely distributed is suggested by the fact that the Chinese authorities saw it as a threat and ordered its destruction. "We can see that the Miao writing of Chengbu was widespread like floodwaters and beasts of prey," Jiang Yongxing has written. "It made the Qing court fear" (quoted in Enwall 1994, 65).

After the Miao rebellion associated with this writing was suppressed, the Chinese authorities took control of local schools and banned the use of the system. No known samples of the writing survived, although in 1984 Miao villagers in the Chengbu region produced a stele, or rough carved board, with samples of what was said to be this same eighteenth-century Miao writing system. The villagers showed the stele to a Chinese cultural worker one evening, but when the worker returned to the village the next morning the stele was gone. As no samples of this script have ever reappeared, it cannot be said whether the writing was an ancient Miao alphabet or whether, indeed, it ever existed at all. The writing described in the *Boaqing fuzhi* might have belonged to another ethnic group, or it might have been a derivation of Chinese.

A third report of a Miao writing system, thought to have originated in the nineteenth century, emerged in 1949 when the Chinese scholar Wen You received a letter from a woman who had recently visited the Guizhou Province of China. The woman wrote that she had collected stone rubbings of what she believed to be an original writing system created by Miao living on the top of Leigongshan Mountain in Guizhou. The Miao stone was damaged, but the woman had obtained a piece of it and mailed rubbings of the characters to Wen You; in time, fifty-eight characters were collected (Wen 1938, in Enwall 1994, 70). According to the legends of the area, the Miao in the region had once had a king and possessed a carved stone with an inscription that nobody could read. The writing may have been used to record the history of the Miao in the region or may have been a form of "shaman writing," known only to local shamans (Enwall 1994, 71). Wen You speculates that the Leigongshan stele writing might have been associated with one Yang Dahe, a "religious rebel" who in addition to writing may have manufactured coins and printed money as part of a "false royal court" (in Enwall 1994, 67–72). Wen You concluded that the writing was indeed Miao, though Enwall states that the evidence is inconclusive.

Another account from China comes from a French military officer named d'Ollone who, between 1906 and 1909, reported the existence of a writing system belonging to a Miao group in southern China who spoke a language similar to Green Hmong in Laos (Enwall 1994, 77; Lemoine 1972, 137). This writing was copied for d'Ollone by a man who agreed to reveal the writing in exchange for d'Ollone's assistance in a legal affair. The characters of this system were unfamiliar to d'Ollone, with some resembling Chinese and others altogether different from the Chinese script. After copying the alphabet, the man told d'Ollone of a village where he might find books in this previously unknown script. But when d'Ollone reached the village after several days of walking through the mountains, he was told by villagers that no such books or writing system had ever existed (Lemoine 1972, 137). Since no other examples of this writing have ever been found, there is considerable controversy over d'Ollone's claims.

The Hmong in Laos were also reputed to have their own writing. A writing system supposedly representing the Hmong language was reportedly shown to Western missionaries living in Xieng Khouang Province of Laos during the 1950s. According to Lemoine (1972, 131–132), these "mysterious manuscripts" appeared to be related to Chinese. Unfortunately, the missionaries did not read Chinese and, "loyal to their pastoral tasks," as Lemoine discreetly puts it, did not think the manuscripts worth saving.

Did the Miao or Hmong have their own writing system in China or in Laos? The evidence is inconclusive. There may have been writing; there may have been only rumors of writing. What was thought to be Miao or Hmong writing may have been Chinese writing, or Yao writing, or may have never existed at all. Although we can only speculate as to whether an indigenous Hmong writing system ever existed, we can see for a fact how travelers, soldiers, and missionaries associated Miao-Hmong writing, whether real or legendary, with secrecy, rebellion, and religion. Hmong writing, in these accounts, was subversive and potentially menacing: it "made the Qing court fear." In this sense, writing—or its strongly embraced ideal—may have served as a marker of identity for the early Miao and Hmong, offering them a material or conceptual artifact, as the case may have been, through which to express their resistance to and independence from more powerful, literate peoples.

"The Great Demand These Crowds Made": Missionary Scripts in China and Laos

Setting aside the narratives, notched sticks, and rumors of scripts, Miao and Hmong writing, in the sense of syllabic and alphabetic literacy practices, began with the arrival of Western missionaries who created alphabets for the Miao in China and for the Hmong in Laos.[3] Unlike the writings imagined in the Hmong literacy narratives, the missionary scripts were not conceived to promote the causes of Hmong ethnic identity or political enfranchisement. Rather, these alphabets were created as a technology for spreading Christian doctrine and transforming the spiritual lives of those who learned the foreign scripts. Missionary alphabets therefore offered a fundamentally different conception of literacy from those previously imagined or devised by the Hmong and offered, as well, a new conception of the self and one's place and role in the world.

The Pollard Script

The most successful of the missionary scripts in China was created by Samuel Pollard, an English Protestant who in 1904 started a mission for the A-Hmao people, a Miao group living in southern China whose language is related to Hmong (Enwall 1994, 104–116; Smalley, Vang, and Yang 1990, 149–150). Shortly after establishing his mission, Pollard set up a school for the A-Hmao and began teaching Christian doctrine. Frustrated by the language barriers separating him from his students, he began experimenting with a written representation of the A-Hmao language. "Miao here every day. Trying to get out their language. So different to preach to them owing to not knowing their language. Have tried hard to get the word 'prayer' from them but have not succeeded. Neither the word for *sin*. . . . Translating 'Jesus loves me' with them. The class is 'PART TEACHING & PART LEARN-ING.' When I catch a word I put it down" (in Enwall 1994, 104).

Because he felt the Miao were "low down on the intellectual scale" and "ignorant" (Enwall 1994, 170), Pollard tried to make his writing system as simple as possible. The best way to do this, he believed, was to make the system phonetic so that learners could easily grasp sound-symbol correspondences. Basing his ideas to some extent upon the syllabary developed by the missionary James Evans for the Cree people in Canada, Pollard did not use Latin letters for his script but instead created new graphemes, adapting these in part from Evans (Enwall 1994, 171). Pollard's efforts were overwhelmingly successful. By 1949, an estimated 34,500 Miao had learned the script, and an additional 5,000 Sichuan Miao, a group related to the Hmong of Laos, had learned a separate Pollard script designed especially for them by the end of the same year (Enwall 1994, 216). Enwall calls Pollard's mission "the most spectacular missionary achievement in the whole of Southwest China" (1994, 104).

Why was the Pollard mission so successful? Why did it attract so many converts, and how did the alphabet achieve its "spectacular" success? The reasons for any religious conversion are complex, and we must be cautious when considering cause-and-effect relationships. For those who teach Christian doctrine, the power of the message explains why non-Christians, such as the A-Hmao, convert to the Christian faith. The spiritual truths of doctrine are revealed and embraced. Others emphasize the social and economic conditions that influence the spread of Christian doctrine. Tapp (1989), for example, has observed that missionary work in China and Southeast Asia has traditionally been directed at the minority peoples, such as the Hmong, whose marginalized social positions are thought to make them more receptive to the new faith than members of the dominant majority. In Pollard's case, he not only taught bible classes, but also advocated for the land rights of Miao people and promoted health care reforms such as mass smallpox inoculations. The Pollard mission was responsible for building schools and dispensaries for Miao, who had received no such attentions from the Chinese. Tapp (1989, 92) argues that these actions must have had a profound effect upon a minority people in desperate social and economic straits and likely rendered them more receptive to the teachings of the Western missionaries.

Beyond social and economic factors, however, there was another powerful inducement for Miao people to embrace the foreign faith: literacy. Tapp (1989) has written that the acceptance of Christianity among the Miao "did not arise solely from a degraded impoverished people clutching at foreign straws of succour, nor even from their desire to hear more of this strange 'King' who loved the Miao" (125). Rather, he argues, the fervor with which Christianity was embraced by the Miao had to do with the belief that the Pollard bible and other printed materials represented the lost Hmong "book," the writing that had been eaten by horses, sewn into dresses, or washed away in the river. "The great demand these crowds made," Pollard wrote, "was for *books*" (in Tapp 1989, 94). The missionary William Hudspeth described the effect of Pollard's alphabet upon the Miao.

> Before the Pollard Script, books and a library were unknown. The great majority of these tribesmen had never handled even a sheet of writing paper or a pen. They had heard that once upon a time there were books: a tribal legend described how, long ago the Miao lived on the north side of the Yangtze River, but the conquering Chinese came and drove them from their land and homes. Coming to the river and possessing no boats they debated what should be done with the books and in the end they strapped them to their shoulders and swam across, but the water ran so swiftly and the river was so wide, that the books were washed away and the river swallowed them.

This was the story. When the British and Foreign Bible Society sent the first gospels and these had been distributed the legend grew—that once upon a time lost books had been found, found in the white man's country, and they told the incomparable story that Jesus loved the Miao. Only the imagination can conceive what this meant to these hillmen, some of whom travelled for days to view the books. (1937, quoted in Tapp 1989, 124)

Hudspeth's account suggests the intermingling of Miao and Christian beliefs, as Miao incorporated Christian teachings into their own narratives of identity, position, and spirituality. While traditional Miao beliefs may have been utterly incompatible with strict Protestant orthodoxy, Christian and Miao doctrines nevertheless commingled with one another, penetrated and shaped one another, often to the dismay of the missionaries. Pollard writes with consternation of "old wizards" and "singing women" who prophesied the arrival of Christ and the deliverance of the Miao.

Similar forms of intermingling would take place in Laos in the 1950s, after the introduction of Christianity by Protestant and Catholic groups. In one instance, three Hmong men declared themselves to be the "Meo trinity" and began traveling through Hmong villages performing exorcisms and destroying Hmong shaman altars and other tokens of the traditional religion. Some years later, during the Vietnam War in the 1960s, rumors circulated that Jesus Christ had returned to Earth wearing American army fatigues, driving a jeep and distributing rifles to Hmong soldiers (in Tapp 1989). In these sacred visions we see how older and newer ideologies can inform and change one another, particularly in desperate social and political circumstances such as those experienced by the Miao in China and, later, by the Hmong in Laos. For the Miao and the Hmong, literacy was at the nexus of these encounters.

The Pollard system was not the only missionary script designed for the Hmong language. Another such system, one that was developed in Laos and would eventually transcend its missionary origins to become even more influential than the Pollard Script, was the Romanized Popular Alphabet (RPA).

The Romanized Popular Alphabet

Designed in Laos in the late 1950s, the RPA was the product of three Western missionaries—William A. Smalley, G. Linwood Barney, and Fr. Yves Bertrais—along with their Hmong assistants. As explained by Smalley (personal interview, June 28, 1997), Barney was originally posted to Laos by the Christian and Missionary Alliance (CAMA) to do missionary work and create a writing system for the Hmong language. Smalley was in Laos at the time working on a writing system for the Khmu language, also on behalf of CAMA. Barney wrote to Smalley with a number of technical questions, and the two men collaborated on the Hmong system. They then met with Father Bertrais, a Catholic missionary who was working independently on his own Hmong writing system, which turned out to be very close to the one Smalley and Barney had produced. The three men resolved what differences they had in representing the Hmong language and produced what became the RPA, an alphabet for *Hmoob Dawb,* or White Hmong.

In the RPA, the sounds of the Hmong language are represented by letters of the Romanized alphabet, which allowed for an orthography that could easily be typed, printed, and taught in the Laotian highlands. Romanized letters represented both the large number of consonant sounds—White Hmong has thirty-six—and the vowel sounds of the language (Ranard 2004, 44–45). So, for example, the Hmong words for "spleen," "ball," and "throw" were written with Romanized characters as *"po," "pob,"* and *"pov,"* respectively. The complex system of initial consonant clusters in Hmong could also result in more complicated spellings, such as *"txwv"* (to rebuke) (Heimbach 1969). Additionally, consonants were used in the final syllable position to represent the seven tones of the Hmong language.[4] For example, the tonal marker "b" indicates a high tone and is added to the Hmong word *"po"* to create *"pob"* (ball); the tonal marker "v" indicates a rising tone and is added to *"po"* to spell *"pov"* (throw); the tonal marker "m" indicates a low glottalized tone and is added to *"po"* to spell *"pom"* (see), and so on. The relatively straightforward nature of this alphabet, and the fact that it could be reproduced on Western typewriters, contributed to the ease with which it was disseminated and learned.

Initially, distribution of the RPA was limited to Christian converts and was used to translate religious materials and to teach other Hmong to read and write in their own language. With the escalation of the Vietnam War, however, and the subsequent decades of dislocation of the Hmong, the need for a communicative technology that could be easily learned and used by Hmong people became more acute. The RPA met this need. And while the RPA never assumed the same place in Hmong mythology as the Pollard Script, it has gained acceptance among Christian and non-Christian Hmong across the world, becoming the most widely used Hmong-language alphabet in the long history of Hmong writing. Today, the RPA is used to publish not only religious materials but also other Hmong-language texts such as community newsletters, novels and poetry, academic writings, and diverse forms of Web-based materials. Much of the RPA's growth can be attributed to the American war in Vietnam, which changed the course of Hmong life in Laos and gave new life and new meanings to the RPA. But credit to the RPA's central role in Hmong life also belongs to Fr. Yves Betrais, who has sponsored numerous published writings in the RPA on such topics as marriage, death, love songs, and histories (Tapp 2004).

Little of this growth was foreseen by one of the architects of the RPA, William A. Smalley. When Smalley left Laos in the 1950s, few Hmong were using the new system, and he assumed the RPA would eventually be replaced by written Lao and forgotten. When I interviewed him at his home in 1997, Smalley said that he thought the new writing system that he helped create might become a cultural as well as a religious tool, a means "to help people use the resources of their own language in ways that are suitable for the modern world." Smalley assumed that the RPA would soon be forgotten as Hmong people learned Laotian and were integrated into the Laotian economy. What he had not foreseen, he said, was the war that would cause tens of thousands of Hmong to leave their homes, resettle around the world, and make the RPA a necessary communicative tool for Hmong refugees scattered across the world. "We didn't foresee that," Smalley said. "We didn't plan the CIA." Despite the modest assumptions Smalley made a half century ago, the writing system he helped devise has played a major part in the historical development of Hmong literacy. We will discuss its uses and meanings in greater detail in chapter 4.

"Counterfeit Writing": Other Missionary Scripts

The Pollard Script and the RPA were not the only missionary scripts designed for the Hmong language. Other efforts include the Savina Romanized Alphabet, developed by the French missionary F. M. Savina and used to publish the first Hmong dictionary in Laos; the Trung Alphabet, created by the Vietnamese missionary C. K. Trung and used to publish the Gospel of St. Mark in 1932; and the Homer-Dixon Romanized Alphabet, developed in 1939, in which a primer and music pamphlet were published in 1941. Beyond the publication of these materials, however, there is no evidence that these writing systems were accepted or used by the Hmong for whom they were designed (See Smalley, Vang, and Yang 1990, 149–163).

Yet another set of missionary scripts, the Whitelock Thai-based and Whitelock Lao-based alphabets, were created in the 1960s after the RLG informed the Christian and Missionary Alliance that the government no longer wanted Hmong people to learn the RPA, which was thought to promote ideas of Hmong separatism (Smalley, personal interview, June 28,

1997). Shortly afterward, the Protestant mission in Laos was closed down, and the missionaries left Laos—although Catholic missionaries under the direction of Father Bertrais, who remained in Laos, continued to print materials in the script. Subsequently, the missionary Doris Whitelock designed Hmong writing systems based on characters from the Lao and Thai languages. Neither system achieved a following among Hmong people. Indeed, both scripts ignited controversy when some Hmong rejected them on the grounds that the Hmong already had "their own" writing system, the RPA, which they considered the "Hmong Alphabet," while the Whitelock system was considered a "Lao counterfeit" (Smalley, personal interview, June 28, 1997).

Imagined Citizens: Government-Sponsored Writing Systems

Yet another source of writing systems developed for the Hmong language has been the governments of nations in which the Hmong have lived.[5] Typically, these scripts were adaptations of the writing systems used by the dominant majority population. In Vietnam, for example, the Vietnamese Romanized Alphabet used conventions from the Vietnamese alphabet to represent the Hmong language. In China, an alphabet based upon the Pinyin system was created for the Miao language. And during the Vietnam War, the Pathet Lao developed their own Lao-based script for teaching Hmong-language literacy; it represented the communist alternative to the RPA, which was identified with the West and capitalism.

In general, these competing systems sought to bring the ethnic minority Hmong closer to the ideology and aspirations of the sponsoring nation or faction and to reduce the sense of Hmong ethnicity. In this sense, government-devised writing systems for the Hmong recall Benedict Anderson's (1983) concept of the "imagined community" of the nation-state. Anderson argues that beyond the village level, human communities are as much imagined as real in that most members of a community will never meet most of the other members face-to-face. To create the psychic and social conditions for nationhood and to induce human beings to identify with and sacrifice for the community, a bond must be established among disparate and self-interested individuals. Anderson contends that the main vehicle for the building of the modern nation was print-capitalism, which resulted in the creation of the literate elite classes that would rule the nation-state and the subsequent development, through printed materials, of a national consciousness.

In the case of the Hmong, government-sponsored literacies invoked rhetorics of nationhood that were intended to induce linguistic and cultural identification with the majority population. In some cases, the government-sponsored script was meant to be a bridge between the Hmong language and literacy in the national language. In other instances, government-sponsored writing systems in the Hmong language were meant to reduce the possibility that the Hmong would use literacy to develop nationalist and possibly separatist aspirations of their own, which, as we have seen, may well have happened in China. Government-sponsored writing systems can be seen as an attempt to encourage the Hmong to identify with a narrative of civic and political unity, even when the material realities of most Hmong people in these nations placed them at the margins of civic life. That few of these systems achieved much of a following may indicate the unwillingness of many Hmong to abandon the idea that their language should have its own writing system, even if the system was designed by foreigners, as was the case with the RPA.

Return of the *Huab Tais:* Hmong Messianic Writing Systems

Perhaps no form of literacy better expresses the importance of writing to the Hmong than the messianic writing systems created by various Hmong prophets over the last century. Smalley (1996) has identified seven such systems and has suggested that there may be no other instances in history in which so many writing systems were developed for a language by its native speakers.[6] Each of the systems connected writing to the cultural, political, and spiritual rebirth of the Hmong people, and each, in this sense, can be viewed as a material embodiment of the ancient Hmong literacy narrative prophesying that the Hmong king would return and deliver the lost writing system to the Hmong people. Beyond this, each of the Hmong messianic systems, as was true of missionary and government scripts, was rhetorical in the sense that it conveyed a conception of the universe and the place of the Hmong within it. The universe posited in the messianic scripts, however, revolved around neither Jesus Christ nor any government. Rather, these scripts offered a message of political and spiritual revivification rooted in Hmong cultural values.

An example of this was the writing system that may have been associated with Pa Chai Vue's uprising against the French in the early twentieth century. Leading a war that the French called "la Révolte du Fou," or the "War of the Insane," Pa Chai Vue considered himself a messiah and called for the establishment of an independent Hmong kingdom at Dien Bien Phu. While relatively little is known of this war, there is some evidence that Pa Chai may have developed a writing system and used it to further his revolt. The French historian Isabelle Alleton (1981), for example, writes that Hmong rebel leaders distributed written tracts in all the Hmong villages that had not yet risen against the French. These tracts or letters were said to urge the Hmong to take up arms against the French "under pain of reprisals" (35). Alleton goes on to say that Pa Chai sent letters to the villages announcing himself as the ancient Hmong king and that he distributed magic squares of cloth inscribed with unfamiliar characters that would protect them in battle. In a separate account related in Tapp (1989, 130) Pa Chai was said to have met "four madmen who knew how to write" upon his return from heaven. Pa Chai reportedly transmitted his divine instructions to these men by means of a single character. There are also claims that on his deathbed Pa Chai left his wife a mystical writing engraved on copper (Tapp 1989).

While none of this writing has survived, if it ever existed, there are Hmong today who claim to have seen Pa Chai's writing. When asked to recall the first time he had ever seen written language, Lue Vang Pao, an elderly Hmong man I interviewed, remembered a time in childhood when Pa Chai Vue's soldiers entered his village and gathered the villagers together to teach them about the origins of the earth, the loss of the Hmong kingdom, and the causes of the war.

> I saw the Pa Chai [soldiers]. They were crazy, and they were fighting in that war. I saw their writings also. Those writings, they were Hmong writings. They made them by cutting bamboo and boiling it, then pounding it, then scooping it up into a cloth. They then peeled the skin from it, and put it into stacks, and then they used chicken feathers to write on it. They used an ink, *teem nqaj* [teng nka], which is mixed into a thick liquid solution, and then they used chicken feathers to write.
>
> And when they had finished writing, they explained in detail from the beginning when the world was flooded with water, to explaining about the Hmong king, to explaining everything. They explained all those things in their writings.

Pao kept no copies of this writing, and no other examples of it are known to exist. However, if Pa Chai's writing, like the Hmong literacy narratives, exists more as myth than material fact, the same cannot be said of the *Phaj Hauj* (pa how) system, created by Shong Lue Yang, the Hmong *Niam Ntawv* (nea ndow), or "Mother of Writing." Shong Lue's system was without doubt the most widespread, sophisticated, and important of the

Hmong spiritual systems created to date.[7] Shong Lue Yang was a Hmong farmer born in Vietnam who apparently never learned to read or write in any language. In the months between May and September 1959, however, he produced a new and original writing system for the Hmong language that he called the *Phaj Hauj*. He also created a separate writing system for the Khmu, a minority people in Laos whose language is different from Hmong. Shong Lue explained to his followers that one day he heard a loud voice telling him that he should make special opium-smoking equipment, build a round house, and prepare offerings of candles and flowers. Finally, the voice told him to make ink and paper from an indigo plant and bamboo and light a pipe of opium. Shortly afterward, two men appeared and began to teach him the alphabet. The men came every night until Shong Lue had learned the alphabet. The men were sons of God who told Shong Lue that he, too, was a son of God and that he had been returned to earth to teach the *Phaj Hauj* to the Hmong.

The *Phaj Hauj* was unlike any previous writing system designed for the Hmong language. Among its features were unique letter shapes and novel ways of representing the vowel and tonal values of the Hmong language. Moreover, the *Phaj Hauj* was a phonological system, which made it distinctive among writing systems developed for language without writing. While there are numerous cases of syllabaries developed for languages without writing, including the Bamum script created by King Njoya in early twentieth-century Cameroon, the Alaska script devised by Uyaqoq between 1910 and 1905, and the Ndjuka script invented by Afaka of Dutch Guinea in 1916 (Daniels 1996, 583–584), the *Phaj Hauj* was not a syllabary but a phonological system, meaning that it represented every phonological unit in the Hmong language.[8]

The linguist Martha Ratliff (1996, 619) has called the match between the *Phaj Hauj* and the spoken Hmong language "perfect," and Smalley has written of the script that it "matches the spoken Hmong language as perfectly as writing systems ever match a spoken language" (Smalley, Vang, and Yang 1990, 172). Shong Lue Yang would go on to revise his *Phaj Hauj* system three times throughout his life, refining it significantly in each stage. In speaking to Shong Lue's audacious intellectual achievement, Smalley has remarked that a man who apparently did not know how to read and write in any language should produce a writing system as sophisticated as the *Phaj Hauj* is remarkable enough, but that the same man should produce two separate systems for two different languages, one in Hmong and another in Khmu, is little short of astonishing.

Shong Lue Yang's message resonated among ordinary Hmong and provoked anxiety among political leaders on both the communist and rightist sides during the Vietnam War. After being exiled from Vietnam by the North Vietnamese, who suspected him of being a CIA spy, Yang was imprisoned for three years by Vang Pao's forces in 1967, who thought his alphabet might contain Soviet or Chinese influences. After escaping from prison, Yang went into hiding in the jungles, where he continued to teach the *Phaj Hauj*. In February 1971, at the age of forty-one, Shong Lue and his wife, Bau, were assassinated by members of Vang Pao's forces disguised as communist soldiers. Shong Lue's death did not put an end to the writing system, however. More people continued learning it in Laos, where it became associated with the *Chao Fa*, or "Lord of the Sky," military resistance movement against the communists after the withdrawal of U.S. military forces from Southeast Asia. Later the alphabet would be taught in Thai refugee camps and, later still, in the United States. Smalley, Vang, and Yang (1990) estimated that more than 7,600 people have learned to read and write in the *Phaj Hauj*.

Like Pa Chai Vue's writing, if it in fact existed, Shong Lue Yang's *Phaj Hau* offered an identity and place in the universe to those who learned it. Created in the chaos of the Vietnam War, when Hmong social structures were collapsing under the combined pressures of communist incursions and American bombings, the *Phaj Hauj* expressed a highly complex message of Hmong unity, reconciliation, and spiritual rebirth. Smalley (in Smalley, Vang, and Yang 1990) has written that "the heart of Shong Lue Yang's message was harmony, cooperation, elimination of division among the Hmong people so that their culture could be preserved and their potential could be realized" (181). The writing system presented the Hmong with a conception of themselves as united, sovereign, and spiritually redeemed. The *Phaj Hauj* was more than a writing system for its users; it was, in addition, a guide to moral life and religious salvation. It was, in the language of this book, a rhetorical undertaking, a way for the Hmong to represent themselves symbolically and to inhabit a complex but coherent ideology.

Yet another Hmong spiritual system was discovered in the 1980s in the Chiang Kham refugee camp in Thailand.[9] A Hmong refugee named Ga Va Her approached a field officer of the United Nations High Commissioner for Refugees (UNHCR) and revealed that he was the proprietor of a sacred alphabet that was unknown to the outside world. Although nonbelievers were not supposed to be shown materials written in the alphabet, the difficult situation of the Hmong in Chiang Kham had persuaded Her that he should share the texts in his possession with UNHCR officials to preserve them. This writing system became known as the Sayaboury Alphabet, so named for the Laotian province that had been home to Her and his followers before their migration.

Ga Va Her gave the field officer, Nina Wimuttikosol, eight large volumes of writing plus a ninth volume containing elaborate maps and drawings. Among the materials were an alphabet primer, a set of religious guidelines, instructions for future Hmong administrators, and designs for the buildings, transportation systems, and currency that were to be used by Hmong leaders in the future. A separate volume contained moral instructions for the Hmong and emphasized the need for the Hmong to overcome factionalism so that they could escape poverty and political subservience. Her disclosed that the writing had been revealed by the god Ia Bi Mi Nu over eight centuries ago and that the system was called the *Ntawv Pauj Txwn* (ndow pa tzuh), which Smalley and Wimuttisokol (1998) translate as the "original, primeval Hmong writing" (10).

As with other spiritual writing systems, the Sayaboury Alphabet was unique. For example, all words appear to be represented by only five letters, the first two always identical. Another unique element of the Sayaboury is that it includes characters representing nonspeech sounds, such as the intonation used for chanting, the sound for calling chickens, the sound for shooting chickens, and others. Like the *Phaj Hauj,* the Sayaboury system appears to be intimately connected to Hmong beliefs about political, spiritual, and ethnic identity. And like the *Phaj Hauj,* it conceived of literacy, specifically the possession of an original and unique Hmong-language writing system, as central to the expression of these identities.

The Rhetoric of Writing Systems

The history of Hmong writing systems, this chapter suggests, can be read as a history of rhetorics that have sought to shape Hmong values, beliefs, and cultural practices over the last century. Each of these writing systems offered the Hmong a particular narrative, a competing story of the world and available identities, whether those of Miao rebels, Christian believers, citizens of the state, or mystics possessed of a secret and transcendent knowledge. In many cases, Hmong people embraced more than one of these identities, defining themselves through the sounds and symbols of multiple languages, literacies, and ideologies. Hmong people in the twentieth century, for example, may have learned to write their own language in the characters of the Lao and Thai alphabets, in the Romanized letters of the RPA, in the mystical characters of the *Phauj Hauj,* or in all four of these. While each of these systems offered a particular set of characters for representing the sounds of the Hmong language, what mattered was the ideology of the system and how it invited readers and writers to see the world and conceive of themselves. The writing systems were technical accomplishments, certainly; more important, they were also rhetorics conferring notions of self and society.

Beyond examining the rhetorical nature of the scripts aimed at or produced by the Hmong, this chapter raises serious empirical questions about the conception of the Hmong as "preliterate" people. While it is true that most Hmong refugees came to the United States without knowing how to read and write, as we have seen, it is equally true that the Hmong have had a long, complicated, and often intense engagement with multiple forms of literacy, each with its own functions and meanings. However, the problem of Hmong "preliteracy" is not merely an empirical one. More profoundly, it is a conceptual problem, one with implications not only for the Hmong, but for all peoples who do not practice reading and writing on a widespread basis. Just as a writing system suggests a particular identity and way of seeing the world, so, too, does the narrative of "preliteracy" offer a set of identities and positions to nonreaders and nonwriters. And these identities and positions are both reductive and damaging to those who suffer them, a claim I explore in the next chapter

CHAPTER 3

Never to Hold a Pencil

The Problem with "Preliteracy"

The word is a possession of man generally, whereas writing belongs exclusively to Culture-men.
  —O. Spengler, *The Decline of the West, volume II*

An understanding of literacy must begin with non-literacy.
  —E. A. Havelock, "The Coming of Literate Communication
    to Western Culture"

Tou Vang, a Hmong woman who came to the United States as a political refugee in 1989, was born in the village of Moung Seng in the mountains of northern Laos in the mid-1920s. Her parents were farmers, Vang recalled, who grew corn, rice, and sugarcane, supplementing the modest family income by raising and selling horses. Neither of her parents had attended school, Vang remembered, nor had any of her four brothers. In fact, no one in the family could read or write. When I asked her about her childhood, Vang spoke mostly of the long hours of work that defined daily life in Moung Seng.

> We just did farmwork, mainly. We got up the first crow of the rooster, at
> approximately three a.m., and prepared the fire, cooked, then pounded
> the rice until we saw the sky lighten a little bit. Then we fed the pigs and
> chickens, and after that I prepared lunch for the field work. We worked
> in the fields until it was dusk, and then we would pick a green vegetable
> plant to feed to the pigs. After that we would cut wood for the fire, and
> then we would go home.

The constancy of this life began to change in the late 1950s and early 1960s, when the CIA began recruiting and training Hmong men to fight as guerrillas during the Vietnam War. While the outcome of this partnership would ultimately prove catastrophic for the Hmong, the Hmong-CIA alliance initially worked to the benefit of many Hmong people, providing access to financial resources, new technologies, and government services that had been previously unavailable. One of these services was public schooling, which in the 1960s became widely available for the first time in Hmong villages such as Moung Yew, where Tou Vang had moved with her husband and six children. Before the war, Vang explained, there had never been a school in her village, and few people knew how to read and write. With the escalation of the war, however, more schools were built in Hmong villages, and Hmong children began attending school in greater numbers than at any time in Hmong history (Weinberg 1997, 185).

Although Vang did not attend school herself, the beginning of her children's education served as her introduction to written language. Prior to this, Vang said, she had heard of writing but had never actually seen it. She knew that the Laotian people had a written language and that they used this "to collect money, to do business, and to write letters." But Vang had never seen these letters or any other form of writing. The first time she remembers actually seeing words on paper was when she began taking her children to the new village school. "They allowed people to come and teach reading and writing in our village, and that is how I learned about it. I took the children to school there, and I saw them giving the children paper to write on... and the teacher opened the book and said, 'This is what we will teach your child.' That was all I saw, and then I went back to work in the fields."

Schooling in Moung Yew lasted for approximately eight years, or until the violence of the war began to make normal life impossible. As the fighting increased and U.S. bombing strikes over Laos created massive population displacement, the social structure in the countryside began to disintegrate.[1] As Vang put it, "the country broke apart." When the North Vietnamese army and their Pathet Lao allies ultimately overwhelmed CIA-supported Hmong forces around Moung Yew, the area fell under North Vietnamese control.

The next several months saw a series of forced relocations as Tou Vang and her family moved from place to place to escape the fighting. They finally arrived at the Hmong base at Long Cheng, the headquarters for CIA-Hmong military operations, where they would remain until 1975, when the United States abandoned its military efforts in Vietnam and thus its support of the Hmong army. The family subsequently spent three years in the jungles fighting alongside Hmong resistance forces before crossing the Mekong River and entering Thailand as political refugees. Although all of her children would eventually go to school in Thailand or in the United States, Vang herself never learned to read and write. "Even now, as an adult," she said, "I have never held a pencil."

—•◦•—

The concept of "preliteracy" has long held a singular fascination for Western academics, many of whom have looked to the presence or absence of literacy to explain a truly astonishing range of human behaviors and conditions. Niko Besnier (1995) traces the Western preoccupation with "preliteracy" to the nineteenth century and the formative years of anthropology, when the absence or presence of writing was seen as the "pivot" or "determinant of differences" between "civilized" and "primitive" cultures, between conceptions of "us" and "them" (1). From such nineteenth-century attitudes emerged the familiar collection of dichotomies meant to evoke the differences between cultures with and without writing—dichotomies that have survived, in ever-changing vestments, until the present day: "primitive" versus "logical" (Levy-Bruhl 1923), "mythical" versus "historical" (Goody and Watt 1968), "contextualized" versus "autonomous" (Olson 1977), "situational" versus "abstract" (Ong 1982), and so forth (see Brandt 1990, 13–32). The "Great Divide" theories associated with Jack Goody (1986, 1968; Goody and Watt 1968), Eric Havelock (1988, 1982, 1963), and Walter Ong (1982) may be understood as a twentieth-century expression of the nineteenth-century tradition.

In "Great Divide" theory, the presence or absence of alphabetic literacy within cultures was seen to be central to the evolution of human cognition, as well as to the development of democracy, history, and philosophy. Jack Goody and Ian Watt (1968), for example, wrote that the discovery of alphabetic literacy in Greece heralded among other things "a change from mythical to logico-empirical modes of thought" (12), while Ong (1982) suggested that literacy is "absolutely necessary for the development not only of science but also of history, philosophy, explicative understanding of literature and of any art, and indeed for the explanation of language (including oral speech) itself" (15). David Olson (1977) was perhaps the most categorical, declaring that "speech makes us human and literacy makes us civilized" (257). To be without literacy, in this line of thinking, is to be illogical, ahistorical, irrational, and uncivilized.

While literacy scholars have generally rejected the "Great Divide" and similar expressions of what Ruth Finnegan (1994) calls "technological determinism" (see also Street 1984), the concept of "preliteracy" retains its allure for anthropologists, historians, and educators, especially those writing about non-Western cultures in which reading and writing are not widespread, such as that of the Hmong. Takaki (1989), for example, has said of Hmong refugees in the United States that "they came from a pre-literate culture; they do not understand how signs and letters can carry meanings. The concept of written words and language is unfamiliar" (463). Similarly, Christina Hvitfeldt (1986) states that Hmong in Thailand "continue to live in traditional preliterate societies in remote mountain areas" (27), while Robert Shuter (1985) argues that the Hmong are a "predominantly preliterate culture...essentially an oral people" (103).

I think of "preliteracy" as a rhetoric, as a symbolic narrative offering an identity and social position to those who participate in it. In the rhetoric of preliteracy, members of cultures in which writing is not widely practiced are offered the identity of "people-without-writing" and are subsequently located in the nineteenth-century narrative that associated the absence of literacy with ignorance, primitiveness, and a semi-barbaric state of development. In such a rhetoric, preliteracy is more than an empirical category; it is a narrative of cultural values that ranks cultures on the basis of an ascending scale based on the possession and use of literacy.

Beyond what it suggests about human beings, the rhetoric of preliteracy also serves to mystify the forces that promote or constrain literacy development. Typically, preliteracy is represented as a characteristic of societies, cultures, and individuals. The problem with this conception is the way in which it locates the absence of writing within the boundaries of the society, culture, or individual while neglecting the contacts and connections that have influenced the historical development of literacy. To say, for example, that the Hmong are a preliterate people is to suggest that the widespread absence of reading and writing is an internal characteristic of Hmong culture, an expression of inherent Hmong practices, preferences, and values. In such a reading, the external relations that have in various ways contributed to the widespread absence of literacy are either ignored or left unstated. "Preliteracy" thus becomes a way of talking about supposedly bounded cultures and individuals rather than about the histories of relations among cultures, states, economies, and armies that influence all aspects of cultural development, including the dissemination or suppression of literacy.

The literacy experiences of the Hmong, however, compel us to take another look at the concept of preliteracy. Specifically, the Hmong experience suggests that the presence or absence of writing among certain peoples is not an expression of mentalities, values, or attitudes, but rather is the outcome of historical encounters and relations among peoples, especially among peoples of unequal power. Reconsidering the story of Tou Vang and other Hmong, we can see how the condition of preliteracy is more properly regarded as a product of historical circumstances and intercultural collisions that are largely beyond the control of societies judged to be preliterate.

In this chapter I explore those historical circumstances as they were experienced by the Hmong and the effects of these upon their literacy development. Drawing upon the testimonies I have collected, as well as published ethnographies and histories, I argue that the origins of Hmong preliteracy have less to do with cultural practices and preferences than with 1) Hmong political and economic relations with the majority population in China, 2) French and Laotian educational policies that systematically neglected the education of Hmong children, and 3) the military alliance between the Hmong leadership and the CIA during the Vietnam War, which resulted in what I think of as the "literacy paradox," in which more Hmong were exposed to education than ever before in their history, and yet the result was not widespread literacy but the destruction of literate possibilities for the majority of Hmong in Laos. All of these external factors, I argue, constitute what Eric Wolf (1982) called "that wider field of force," or the nexus of cultural, political, material, and symbolic interactions that resulted in the widespread absence of reading and writing skills in much of Hmong society into the late twentieth century.

Two Readings of Tou Vang's Story:
"Preliteracy" as Rhetorical Narrative

One way to read Tou Vang's story is to place it in the wider cultural narrative of "preliteracy"—a term that has resisted exact definition and yet retains its sway in scholarly and popular literature dealing with cultures, such as the Hmong, in which writing is not widely practiced. Let us consider the term briefly.

A review of the literature suggests that conceptions of preliteracy generally fall into one of two camps, which I think of as the *extreme* and the *qualified* accounts. In the extreme account, "preliteracy" refers to cultures in which writing is thought to be altogether unknown, an activity about which members of the preliterate culture are thought to have no knowledge at all. Ong (1982) provides a definition of extreme preliteracy, which he calls "primary orality," when he writes of cultures "totally untouched by any knowledge of writing or print" (11). In this version, the members of a culture lack a writing system and have no sense that written symbols might carry meaning, convey information, record history, or provide aesthetic pleasure. For most literate people, such a concept is difficult to fathom, and Ong concedes that "fully literate persons can only with great difficulty imagine what a primary oral culture is like" (31).[2]

In the qualified account of preliteracy, a given culture may have its own writing system, and the members of the culture may even practice writing to a limited extent. Nevertheless, these same people do not, in this narrative, regard literacy as an essential element of their lives nor see its absence as particularly compelling. Smalley (1976a) sums up the state of qualified preliteracy when he writes that in a preliterate culture "a child can be born and grow up, an adult can live and die, without a strong need to read and write. He can live a normal existence within his own community without feeling that he is in any way culturally deprived by lack of ability to communicate through marks made on paper. Life as he knows it does not include reading and writing as a major component" (2). The qualified account of preliteracy is the more flexible definition and is generally the one used to describe contemporary preliterate cultures such as the Hmong.

This account of a qualified preliteracy would seemingly describe the world and life experiences of Tou Vang. As Vang herself explained, she had little knowledge of literacy as a young woman coming of age in Laos. She grew up in an agricultural family in which neither parents nor siblings knew how to write. She did not attend school, did not see written language until she was in her forties, and arrived in Thailand as a refugee who, in her own words, had "never held a pencil."

For many academics, the preliteracy of Vang and other Hmong has been the most significant feature of Hmong life, a defining characteristic thought to have implications for Hmong cognition, communication, and educational development. Recalling the rhetoric of the "Great Divide," studies of the Hmong have referenced preliteracy or orality in examining features of Hmong cognitive development (Timm 1997), communicative patterns (Shuter 1985), learning styles (Hvitfeldt 1986; Marshall 1991), and literacy acquisition (Walker-Moffat 1995).

Much of the work ascribing stronger or weaker degrees of causality to Hmong preliteracy has come from the field of education, where the widespread absence of writing in Hmong culture is thought to have implications for the success or failure of Hmong students in U.S. schools. Helaine Marshall (1991), for example, attributed the difficulty of many Hmong students in progressing beyond high school to students' "residual orality," which causes students to "memorize, repeat, spend extensive periods of time attempting to master large amounts of material"—strategies that do not, Marshall contended, help students learn academic literacy skills. Hvitfeldt (1986) suggested that the "shared cultural meanings" of Hmong adult students—meanings shaped in part by their "preliterate, pre-technical society"—have restricted Hmong "cognitive and social flexibility" and caused difficulties for Hmong learners and their teachers in U.S. classrooms (76). Shuter (1985), meanwhile, argued that the preliterate Hmong have a communicative style shared by "oral people," in which "words *cannot* be disconnected from deeds and events, and peoples *cannot* be separated from social context" (104, emphases added). Shuter related this "central world view" to the difficulty that some adult Hmong encounter in learning English in the United States.

> In schools [Hmong adults] encounter definitions and detailed explana-
> tions of words, words that are disconnected from objects and about
> concepts they cannot see and touch: this is an abstract, categorical
> world detached from situation and nature. As a result, many older
> Hmong become frustrated and drop out of school, particularly the men
> who appear to have less experience with detail and tolerate it less than
> Hmong women. (1985, 106)

Such analyses are problematic on multiple levels. For one thing, they are empirically misleading, as chapter 2 demonstrates. Beyond this, they assign a striking prominence to literacy at the expense of history and social context. Hmong high school students must "spend extensive peri-ods of time attempting to master large amounts of material" not because they are studying academic content in a new language, but because they have an "oral" orientation and thus attempt to memorize rather than ana-lyze school lessons and assignments. Similarly, the failure of some Hmong adults to learn a second language is attributed to their "preliterate" back-grounds, which cause them to become "frustrated and drop out of school," rather than to the mental and emotional stress of being forcibly displaced from their homeland and exiled to a new and alien culture. In this view, the tumultuous Hmong experiences of warfare and exile disappear from the equation, counting for less than the presence or absence of written lan-guage. So it is with the rhetoric of preliteracy, in which virtually all traces of process, struggle, and history are expunged.

A related problem is the way in which preliteracy becomes the basis for classroom prescriptions. Since much educational research is applied, meaning that it is intended to help classroom teachers by providing guid-ance with pedagogy and curriculum, education scholars writing about the Hmong have been inclined to suggest teaching approaches thought to be suited to the supposedly preliterate condition of Hmong students. This is not to say that all such prescriptions are necessarily inimical to good teaching. In fact, such recommendations often suggest positive and useful ways of teaching Hmong and other non-English-speaking students. Marshall (1991), for example, suggested using "the native language and content from the native culture" in classroom activities with Hmong stu-dents (21), and Hvitfeldt (1986) advised that educators develop "some understanding of the ways in which Hmong cultural knowledge influences classroom behavior" (74). Nonetheless, even the most general and seemingly innocuous advice is grounded in a specific conception: the Hmong student as preliterate. And this opens the way to a deeper set of problems.

A rhetoric, I have argued, offers its constituents an identity and a position within a larger historical narrative. The narrative of preliteracy, as we have seen, is one in which the absence of writing has historically been associated with ignorance and primitivism. While contemporary researchers would no doubt categorically reject such echoes in their own work, what Besnier (1995) called "the historical persistence of this nineteenth century preoccupation" (1) continues to linger. Even contemporary conceptions of preliteracy, in other words, contain trace elements—and sometimes more than trace elements—of the essentializing attitudes of the past.

How else to explain, for example, the assertions by Hvitfeldt (1992), in a study of academic writing by Malaysian students, that "people whose orientation is predominantly oral have difficulty distinguishing between a conclusion that is logical and one with which they tend to agree" (33)? How otherwise to account for Ong's (1994) contention that African-American students have difficulties with conventional logic because these students retain much of their "primary oral culture" in which "intensive analysis is not practiced" (141)? How else to interpret Shuter's (1985) apparent certainty about what "oral people" can and cannot do? Whatever the intentions of these analyses, they betray a deeply ethnocentric view of thought and logic that seemingly does not allow for difference from standard Western practices.

In essence, the rhetoric of preliteracy offers a deficit theory, one that is built upon the categories of knowing and not knowing, ability and *dis*ability. The category of "literate" speaks to having a specific form of knowledge and a mastery of skills, while the category of "preliterate" implies ignorance of this knowledge and the absence of these same skills. "Literacy" becomes the unmarked and normal term, while "preliteracy" and its variants serve as the marked and abnormal terms.

The key point here is that the explanation for success or failure is located within students and their cultures and not in the historical forces that have shaped cultural behaviors. So, for example, when Hvitfeldt (1986) writes that "many of the Hmong, Lahu, Lisu, and Akha hilltribe peoples [in Thailand] continue to live as traditional preliterate societies in remote mountain areas" (27), the issues of *why* certain peoples have remained "traditional," *how* they have remained "preliterate" in the modern world, and *what* historical relationships have consigned them to living in "remote mountain areas" where they may not have access to literacy are generally outside the scope of inquiry. In this way does the rhetoric of preliteracy function as another of Burke's "terministic screens," or language that asserts a version of reality while screening out alternative conceptions of the world.

At this point, I would like to offer a second way of reading Tou Vang's story, one that locates the presence or absence of writing within a wider field of historical relations. In this reading, to say that Vang was preliterate because she was raised in a culture in which literacy was largely unavailable is to say less about her than about the economic conditions in Laos that left Hmong people few options for supporting themselves beyond subsistence farming. Similarly, to point out that Vang never attended public school is to speak not of her motivation but of the educational policies that denied schooling to most Hmong in nineteenth- and twentieth-century Laos. And to observe, finally, that Vang arrived in Thailand as a preliterate refugee, an adult who "never held a pencil," is to reflect not only upon the vicissitudes of her life, but also upon the extreme violence and civic disruption of a war that made normal activities such as schooling all but impossible. Ultimately, the fact that Vang has not learned to read and write may tell us less about her choices, desires, and values than about the social, economic, and military relationships in which the Hmong were enmeshed over the last two centuries.

Read this way, Tou Vang's story suggests a different way of thinking about the literacy development of cultures and individuals. In this reading, the understanding of literacy development begins not with the assessment of individual abilities, which is the practice followed in most U.S. schools, nor with the analysis of seemingly bounded cultures, which is where many ethnographic studies begin. While not discounting the relevance of these, this alternative reading of Vang's story begins by considering the histories of social, political, and material contacts that have worked to define individuals and cultures and have shaped the ways in which literacy is obtained or denied. Perhaps the best way to illustrate this is to turn to the Hmong experience generally, looking at the ways in which the concept of preliteracy can be understood as an expression of Hmong entanglements over the centuries with the Chinese, French, Laotian, and American governments.

Mountains, Schooling, and the CIA: The Relations of Hmong "Preliteracy"

What little we know of the Miao in China suggests that they were a rebellious people who resisted Chinese efforts to assimilate them and who, as a result, were often forced to relocate in an effort to escape cultural and political domination. The ancient Chinese history, the *Shu Ching,* for example, tells of the Miao people being pushed from the central Yangtze plains in 2700 BCE to the mountains of northwestern Kansu (Cooper 1984, 16). The ethnographer William Geddes (1976) sketches a similar migration, contending that the Miao were forced out of the valleys of the Yangtze and Yellow Rivers some time between 2700 and 2300 BCE and subsequently driven into the mountains. The French historian Jean Mottin (1980) suggests that the Miao were the aggressors, attacking Chinese settlers who were moving into Hmong territories in the third century BCE. The reasons for these ancient conflicts are unclear, though they probably had to do with competition for land and resources. Whatever the causes, the Hmong appear to have been driven from fertile river valleys into less arable mountain regions, where they began to make the adaptations that we now equate with "traditional" Hmong culture. Geddes explains,

> [The Hmong] are tied to the mountains by their whole way of life. Love of the countryside may play a part. Their physical constitution may do so also. Competition for land and political circumstances may do so. But more important is their ecological adaptation worked out over hundreds, and possibly thousands of years. They have developed an economy suited to their mountain environment, which acts as the core of their total culture. (1976, 31–32)

The culture that developed in the mountains of southern China apparently did not include literacy. As we have seen, the Miao did not have their own writing system, or at least none has been documented. Moreover, Hmong in China apparently did not learn to read and write in other languages, including the language of the dominant Chinese, which may have been viewed as a tool for assimilating Miao culture and therefore rebuffed. Another possible explanation for the absence of writing in Miao culture is geographical. The military campaigns that pushed the Miao into the mountains would have meant that they were remote from Chinese cities and isolated from what Brandt (2001) calls "sponsors of literacy," such as schools. Distant from the sources of written language, and for much of their history at war with the culture that might have fostered reading and writing, the Miao in China may have had few opportunities to develop a literate tradition.[3]

Still another possible factor in the literacy development of the Miao was the introduction of maize into the Chinese diet. The anthropologist Robert Cooper (1984) has speculated that Chinese wars against the Miao might well have been related to Chinese population growth stimulated by the introduction of the maize crop in the sixteenth century. Prior to the introduction of maize, Cooper writes, the population of China had been rising gradually, from 50 million in the first century BCE to 100 million in 1200 to 150 million in 1600—a gain of approximately 100 million people in 1,600 years. After the introduction of maize, however, the Chinese population surged from 150 million to 430 million in 1800, a gain of 280 million in just 200 years (19–20). The surge in population would have resulted in, among other things, a need for more arable land and may have increased military pressure upon peoples residing on such lands, such as the Miao.

Cooper acknowledges that it is uncertain whether the introduction of maize was responsible for this increase in the Chinese population, or whether maize was adopted as an alimentary solution to a population increase caused by other factors. Nor does Cooper claim that it is certain that the Manchu campaign against the Miao was a response to an increase in the Chinese population. Other factors may have played a greater role, such as the desire by the Manchus to control Miao opium-growing areas. Even such speculation, however, underscores the entangled nature of literacy relations. If indeed the introduction of maize led to a Chinese population spike, this would have led to a desire for more land, leading to wars against the peoples possessing that land, leading to the Miao migration to the mountains and their increased isolation from written language. In this scenario, Miao "preliteracy" would have indirectly resulted from the successful cultivation of a particular form of grain.

When Chinese military pressure in the nineteenth century became acute, thousands of Miao began migrating to Southeast Asia—to Vietnam, Laos, and Thailand, where they would become known as the "Meo," then as the "Hmong." In these countries, they established themselves in remote highland regions, as they had done in China, and resumed the cultural and economic practices that had sustained them previously—practices that, as before, militated against the development of written language. For example, the distance of Hmong villages from Laotian population centers meant that the Hmong were once again remote from conventional sponsors of literacy. Added to this, the Hmong practice of swidden, or "slash and burn," agriculture required long hours of work each day, leaving little time for literacy instruction even if it were available. Vue Lee Mai recalled the situation when he was growing up in Laos in the 1920s: "I didn't have any time to learn how to read and write. If you lived in the countryside, there was no time at all. If you went to do that thing, I mean learn to read and write, you won't have anything to eat."

Pao Lee had similar recollections. He explained that in the 1940s families were so focused on survival that they often felt ambivalent about having their children attend school. Lee recalled that his parents were reluctant to see him leave his village to attend a Laotian school several miles distant. "In Hmong culture, the parents worried about work—the farm, the ricefields, the field, the pigs, cows, and chickens.... They worried about how to raise their families...to not be hungry. In my country, in 1945, in 1947, so many people were hungry."

This is not to suggest that the Hmong had no interest in reading and writing. Indeed, we shall hear testimonies from Hmong who often went to difficult, if not extraordinary, lengths to obtain schooling for themselves and their children. But the testimonies do indicate that for many Hmong in the early twentieth century literacy and schooling were of necessity a secondary concern and difficult to obtain under any circumstances.

The sources of Hmong preliteracy thus appear to be manifold, albeit speculative: antagonism toward the literate power seeking to subjugate them; geographical isolation from literacy sponsors; and economic conditions that made literacy a luxury beyond the reach of most ordinary people. Taken together, however, these factors draw the locus of Hmong preliteracy away from Hmong cultural practices and preferences and locate it in the relationship of the Hmong with more powerful states and peoples.

Yet even if these speculations give us some ideas about the sources of Hmong preliteracy, they do not sufficiently explain how the widespread absence of writing in Hmong culture was maintained throughout the nineteenth century and well into the twentieth century. To understand this, we must examine the educational policies of the colonial French and Royal Laotian governments.

"Foreigners and Parasites": "Preliteracy" as Educational Policy

The relative isolation of the Hmong in the highlands of Laos might not have had the effects it did upon Hmong literacy development had the French or Laotian governments made any serious effort to provide schooling in these villages. In fact, neither the French nor Lao made any such effort. From the time the Hmong began arriving in Laos, the education of Hmong children was neglected, first by the colonial French administration that ruled Laos from the mid-nineteenth century until the 1950s, and then by the Royal Laotian Government that succeeded the French.

Prior to the coming of the French, neither the Hmong nor the majority Laotian peoples had any systematic exposure to formal schooling in the Western sense. The education of Lao children took place in *wats*, or pagodas, with Buddhist *bonzes* serving as the teachers (Phommasouvanh 1973, 39). The Hmong received no formal schooling at all but were educated in the context of home and village (Bliatout et al. 1988, 15–30). After the establishment of a secular school system by the French in 1917, however, education in Laos began to shift from pagoda schools to government classrooms, and more Lao began receiving a French-style education, but only Lao of a certain class. The number of Lao children who had access to this education was minuscule. Alfred McCoy (1970, 83) has written that in six decades of French rule not a single high school was constructed in the entire colony and that by 1940 only seven thousand Laotian students were attending primary schools in a colony of approximately one million people. According to Hmong scholar Yang Dao (1993, 83), the French favored a system that would prepare a small cadre of elite "indigenous" bureaucrats to administer the colonial government.

Hmong children were even less likely to attend school than children of the Laotian majority. Only after persistent requests from the Hmong leadership to French colonial administration was a single school for the Hmong opened in Nong Het in 1939, and only a token few Hmong students were sent abroad to receive educational training in Vietnam or France (Yang 1993). The handful of Hmong who did receive some education was expected to use their skills to administer to French interests, just as Lao and Vietnamese students had been trained to serve as bureaucrats in the colonial administration.

Nor did the educational situation change much after Laotian independence from the French in 1953. In the educational system sponsored by the RLG, students from the wealthiest classes were favored over students from low-income sectors of Laotian society. This meant that the vast majority of people in Laos received little or no formal education. Bounlieng Phommasouvanh's 1973 study of the Laotian educational system showed that while students from the wealthiest classes constituted only .16 percent of the total Lao population in 1968–1969, they totaled 24 percent of the enrollment in Lao schools. The poorest classes, in contrast, accounted for 98 percent of the total population but made up only .4 percent of school attendees (114–118).

While the Laotian ruling classes were far from blameless in this situation, it is worth noting that Lao educational policies of the time mirrored French educational traditions. Daniel P. Resnick and Lauren B. Resnick (1977) have pointed out that the French educational system in the eighteenth century was profoundly elitist, reserved for the aristocracy and bourgeoisie, while the masses were offered a less intellectually demanding curriculum designed to foster patriotism. In this sense, the Laotian educational system in the twentieth century might be seen as yet another disfiguring legacy of colonialism, with implications for all the peoples of Laos, including the Hmong.

Whatever the lineage of the policies, minority peoples such as the Hmong continued to be excluded from Lao schools in what Meyer Weinberg (1997) calls "disproportionately large numbers" (179), meaning that the overwhelming majority of Hmong had no access to public schools. While the Lao accounted for roughly half the population of Laos in the 1950s, they made up 88 percent of the enrollment in secular schools. The Hmong, in contrast, accounted for less than 4 percent of the school population, even though they constituted around 8 percent of the total population of Laos (Weinberg 1997, 179). By the early 1960s a two-tier educational system was firmly in place. While the children of the wealthy, urbanized, French-educated Lao elite received access to the best education, the vast majority of children in Laos, including the Hmong, received limited schooling or none at all (Halpern and Kunstadter 1967, 239).[4]

Chia Xer Lor recalled that there were schools where he lived as a boy in the 1940s, but they were for Laotian children, not Hmong.

> At that time from my father's generation back, in Laos, there was no school. The Laotians had a few schools, but they were for Laotians, and they did not want to enroll the Hmong. The Laotians only accepted their own children. From my father's generation back, no Hmong knew how to read and write. Up in the highlands there was no reading or writing. It was not until 1955, when I was twenty years old, that we went to school. I was one of the first to go to school in our part of the country.

The disregard for Hmong education in independent Laos reflected the antipathy felt by factions of Lao society toward the Hmong. Many Lao distrusted the Hmong minority population, especially as the Hmong grew more powerful in the 1960s as a result of their military alliance with the CIA. The prejudices felt by some Lao toward the Hmong were illustrated in a 1964 letter written by a Lao government official: "The Meo have no right to work as officials in the Ministry of Justice. They are foreigners. Living in the mountains, they are too ignorant to work with the Lao. To be worthy of the name, Laos must be ruled and governed by the Lao. The Meo have no country; they live as parasites on Laos" (quoted in Yang 1993, 30).

Hmong students who did manage to enroll in Lao schools were educated not in their native language, but in Laotian, meaning that for the first twelve to eighteen months of their schooling many students could not speak, read, or write in the language of instruction (Smalley 1985, 248). Beyond the obvious linguistic and educational difficulties resulting from this policy were its psychological costs. Requiring Hmong students to attend school in what was essentially a foreign language, Yang (1993) wrote, "actually engenders feelings of alienation from [Hmong students'] own culture and runs the risk of creating uprooted individuals with no true cultural home" (99). While the Educational Reform Act of 1962 stipulated that students should be educated in their native languages, this was in most cases more an ideal than a reality (Yang 1993, 99).[5]

In spite of these difficulties, or perhaps because of them, many Hmong families continued to advocate for education, in some cases building their own schools and hiring teachers where the government failed to provide. Education was desired for both material and psychological reasons. Schooling was seen as essential to social and economic advancement in Laos, which many Hmong defined as a position as a government official or teacher (see Tapp 1989, 123). Hmong adults who had not learned to read and write themselves often took steps to see that their children would receive an education. Moua Vang Her, a fifty-nine-year-old Hmong man, recalled his father admonishing him to learn to read and write.

> So around that time my father came back home from the war, and he told me, "Son, you have to listen to me now. I see other people's fathers and sons, and they are all reading and writing, and they have good jobs and they make good money. And they don't go to the front and fight. Now there is still time for you to learn from me. No matter if there is no school here, you can still learn from me. And I will teach you whenever we have time. In the morning or afternoon, anytime that I am free. I have two books. I have a first-grade book, and I have a third grade book for reading. I don't have a second-grade book. But no matter what I have, I will teach you. And you, from now on you do not play too much, and you have to stick to what I tell you, and you have to learn. Anytime that I am free, you have to learn from me. Whatever you cannot read, I have to teach you.

Beyond its material significance, literacy had a psychological value. Literacy and education were seen by the Hmong as a means by which they might achieve a measure of respect from the majority Lao, at least some of whom, as we have seen, regarded the Hmong as inferiors. Learning to read and write was not only an escape from the punishing manual labor of agricultural life, but also a way of asserting the social and intellectual equality of the Hmong with the Lao. Pa Toua Thao, a Hmong man who began first grade in 1949, when he was nineteen years old, explained, "If you did not know how to read and write, the Laotians would not give you very much respect. But if you knew how to read and write like them...then they gave you more respect. This is why it is very important for you to go to school....If you were able to learn how to read and write, you could become a teacher or become an official in the city. Then they would accept you."

Such testimony makes clear that Hmong preliteracy in Laos must be seen, at least in part, as a consequence of French and Laotian educational policies in the late nineteenth and early twentieth centuries that denied schooling to the Hmong and suppressed their literacy development. To say that Hmong literacy was "suppressed" does not mean that restrictions against Hmong education were codified in law, as in the nineteenth-century United States, where teaching slaves to read was punishable by whipping and imprisonment (Cornelius 1991). Rather, French and Lao educational policies inhibited the development of Hmong literacy simply by neglecting the education of Hmong children. So while it may have been true, as Smalley (1976) has written, that a Hmong person in twentieth-century Laos could "live a normal existence within his own community without feeling that he is in any way culturally deprived by lack of ability to communicate through marks made on paper" (2), we should at least acknowledge the extent to which this "normal existence" was a consequence of state policies that worked to deny Hmong students access to the education that might have encouraged them to question what was considered "normal." As Tou Vang expressed it, "We thought we would have liked to go to school, but there was no place to go. We Hmong did not have a teacher, did not have a school. You only planned to go farm the fields so you can have rice to eat; so you have a farm and land so you can eat and have clothes to wear. You only tend to your life. We did not know about that other kind of life back then."

"Preliteracy" and the CIA: The Destruction of Literate Possibilities

If the absence of schooling under the French and Laotian administrations prolonged Hmong preliteracy, the alliance with the CIA effectively ended the possibility of widespread literacy development for the Hmong in Laos. The paradox is that the Hmong alliance with the CIA would result in more village schools being built and more Hmong being exposed to formal schooling than at any time in Hmong history. Thousands of Hmong children would learn to read and write elementary Laotian in these American-funded schools. Yet the end result of the Hmong alliance with the U.S. government would not be widespread literacy, but the abandonment of village schools, the devastation of villages, and the deaths of tens of thousands of Hmong men, women, and children. This violence did not merely forestall literate possibilities for the majority of the Hmong in Laos, as the French and Laotian neglect had done, but destroyed them outright.

In the beginning, as the United States deepened its military involvement in Laos and the Hmong military contribution became more vital to U.S. interests, the educational opportunities available to the Hmong increased dramatically. Beginning in the 1960s, the U.S. Agency for International Development (USAID), a development and propaganda arm of the U.S. government, financed an intensive school construction program for Hmong students in the context of a "nation-building" effort designed to support U.S. goals in Laos (Castle 1993, 59–60). Under the direction of Edgar "Pop" Buell, the retired Indiana farmer who had come to Laos under the auspices of the International Voluntary Services, USAID built almost three hundred elementary schools, nine junior high schools, two senior high schools, and a teacher training school (Schanche 1970, 93). Yang's (1993) study of Hmong schooling rates in Laos during this period reported that Hmong enrollment in the village schools rose from fifteen hundred students in 1960 to ten thousand by 1969 (98).

The bright promise of public education, however, would not be realized in the Laotian highlands. As the intensity of the war increased, so did U.S. bombings of Laos. While these attacks were meant to punish Vietnamese and Laotian communist forces, they had a devastating effect on the civilian population. The air attacks obliterated villages and forced families to abandon their homes, farms, and animals. The number of refugees within Laos multiplied as the Hmong and other Laotian peoples sought refuge from a staggering aerial assault, the likes of which "no people in history," Fred Branfman (1972) wrote, "had ever before been subjected" (17).

Given the destruction, education became largely an afterthought. Where schooling did take place, it was often carried out in areas where the fighting was frequent. Pao Lee, who served as a teacher-soldier in the Hmong army, recalled,

> It was very hard to teach. There was a lot of fighting. So hard that you
> had to carry your weapons to class with you. Yes, there was constant
> fighting all the time. You lived with it. You would lay your guns nearby
> and teach. You would lay them across the desk. You had your radio also,

and you carried it all the time. You took your guns there, your radio there, your ammunition, grenades. You took everything there. Whenever you would hear gunfire outside the classroom, then you would go check it out. It was like that.

While such arrangements allowed for some primary education, classes were continually disrupted as families moved from place to place to escape the fighting. Christopher Xiong's experience in the 1960s was typical.

The first school I attended was in a military base. And that's where I went to school for three years.... And then because of the war, the communist soldiers were coming near to the military base. And my brother and his family ... moved to another village. So I then came back and joined with them and then I attended school for a couple more years. And then I was in third grade, I believe ... when that region was taken over by the communist soldiers. So counting from my preschool, I guess I attended school for four or five years. I can't remember how many years for sure because of the war, but I was in third grade when we left that region of the province. And then we had to escape for several days and nights to reach a safer place.

Pa Tou Thao, who turned forty-two in 1997, recalled similar patterns of movement and resettlement during the war.

After my father was killed in the war, we had to live at our grandparents'. Every kid in my family continued to go to school because my dad had been the one who encouraged us to go to school.... But, you know, in the northern part of Laos they fought a lot at that time ... so you had to move from place to place.... So that's kind of like, you didn't graduate exactly in the same city, you know. You studied about a year, a couple of years in this city and then, now they were fighting again in that city, and you had to move to another city and start again.

In some cases, relocations would mean the end of schooling altogether. This was the case for Bee Lor, whose education in Laos came to an end when his family took refuge in a military encampment where no schools had been built. "We lived in a village called Pha Lue. They had a school there. They went from kindergarten to fourth grade.... I went to kindergarten in Pha Lue for one year. And then, yeah, we lost the country, and then I had to go to some place, to another village. And after that we never had the chance to go to school again."

For many students, the patterns of fighting and relocation could exact an emotional toll, further impeding education. Neng Vang, who was a grade school student in the 1960s, recalled his memories of this period.

> As a student, the war was pretty much in our minds and the teacher talked a lot about it. And, for example, overnight you can hear the sounds of machine guns in some of the villages. And then in early morning, the teacher would tell us that this village has been lost, and that village has lost, and that village has lost, and that many people got killed according to the news that the teacher could get.
>
> We were very concerned, and we were always thinking, "Why in our country is there fighting for days or months, and we have no chance to get ourselves an education, and continue on with our education?" So what I saw in all my life was that we always moved from place to place, village to village. We never had any real chance to stay in the same place year round and continue with our education. So we were very concerned about the war, and every student would be talking about the war.... We felt that war was taking away all the opportunities that we dreamed about.

Instead of being sent to school, Hmong youth were sent into battle. Even when students were enrolled in school, they faced the possibility of being forcibly removed and pressed into military service. Neng Vang recalled seeing fellow students taken for the military as they walked to school.

> So [the soldiers] just caught the students and threw them in the trucks. They had two to three trucks. I saw them pull over the students, and many of the students cried and cried, but they couldn't do anything because the government were positively the rulers. Whoever tried to escape would get into trouble. The parents ... learned what had happened, so they went to the school to complain to the school superintendent. But he couldn't do anything. He said it was an order from the government.

Tou Meng Vang was one of those who went into the army as a child. He was not forced to join the military, he told me, but left his village in 1963 when the communists arrived and began killing the adult Hmong males who lived there. Vang fled to a temporary resettlement area and was given a job cooking for the soldiers and patrolling the perimeter of the settlement at night. He lived in a cave that he and a group of other boys had dug out of a muddy hillside near the top of a mountain. In return for his service to the military, he was allowed to attend classes taught by Hmong soldiers. But he attended classes, he said, only after he grew accustomed to the war that was taking place around him.

> You know, sometimes we were sad because we thought about our parents. But we lived away from our parents. We saw people die every day. We saw people get injured every day. We lived high on a mountain. Very cold, and very windy, and rainy, you know, and it's really hard for you to cook, and you were hungry. And you have no clothes, and you wear your soldier clothes, and you were serving the soldiers, serving the CIA at that time. We never knew what kind of game that we were playing, you know. And then you were fighting every day, hearing the sound of weapons, you know. Fighting at night you saw the flashing of the lights of the gun, the weapon's round. And you saw people killed every day. Sometimes you were scared, but we saw that for months and months, and years, and it just looked like a normal thing. And people died just like animals, and people got injured or were crying, or suffering, and it just looked simple, you know. It's just like that. They killed each other, our friends, cousins, they all died.... They never found a way to go to school but served in the army and fought directly with the communists, and they all died.

These testimonies illuminate the literacy paradox created by the Hmong-CIA alliance, in which more Hmong students were exposed to education than ever before in Hmong history, yet the result was not the advent of widespread literacy but instead destruction, death, and the end of literate possibilities in Laos for the majority of Hmong aligned with the CIA. Beyond that, the testimonies illustrate the ways in which the absence of literacy, which is reflexively called "preliteracy," is less a characteristic of individual initiative or cultural practices than it is an outcome of intersecting forces and pressures that shape the lives of individuals and direct the fates of seemingly bounded cultures.

The Rhetoric of "Preliteracy"

In the rhetorical conception of literacy, one does not think of the absence of written language without thinking of its presence, and of the multiple connections uniting both. Literacy and preliteracy are connected, features of the same landscape, points along what the philosopher of language

V. N. Volosinov (1973) called the "territory shared" (86). An understanding of literacy begins, therefore, not with the assessment of individual abilities, which is the practice followed in most U.S. schools, nor with the analysis of seemingly bounded cultures, which is where many ethnographic studies begin and end. While not discounting the relevance of these, a rhetorical approach to literacy, or in this case, preliteracy, begins by considering the histories of social, political, and material contacts among peoples, and the symbolic resources—the rhetorics—used by elite powers to shape identities and social possibilities, including the possibility of learning to read and write.

Other Gods and Countries

Hmong Literacy Development in Laos

All identity is individual, but there is no individual identity that is not historical.
>—E. Balibar, "The Nation Form: History and Ideology"

Reading, as a phrase would have it, was not just reading; it was the reading of something.
>—L. Soltow and E. Stevens, *The Rise of Literacy and the Common School in the United States*

While the literacy development of the Hmong people was inhibited by an array of powerful forces in China and Laos, there nevertheless existed in twentieth-century Laos several equally potent forces that worked to promote Hmong reading and writing. Perhaps the most influential of these were the Lao village schools, the Hmong military, and missionary Christianity, all of which assumed an increasingly prominent role in Hmong life with the escalation of the war. These sponsors of literacy, as Brandt would call them, not only offered the Hmong the opportunity to learn to read and write, but offered, as well, an identity and a framework for understanding the world. Each of these literacy sponsors, in other words, taught reading and writing in the context of a broader rhetoric, a symbolic and ideological narrative that used literacy as a means to shape thought and influence actions.

To be a Hmong student in a Lao village school in the 1960s and 1970s, for example, during a time when the survival of the Lao nation was threatened by civil war, was to learn not just the mechanical skills for reading and writing in the Lao language; rather, to be a student at a Lao village school was to be offered an identity as a Laotian citizen and a place within a Laotian national hierarchy. Hmong students in Lao village schools were trained to see Lao values as their values, the Lao king as their king, and the Lao nation as their own. So might the Hmong come to accept themselves as Lao and be called upon by the Royal Laotian Government to make sacrifices for the nation to the extremes of fighting and dying. In this way was learning to read and write in the Lao language organized by what I call the *rhetoric of Lao schooling.*

The Hmong military, in turn, offered a selected number of Hmong a context in which to practice the reading and writing skills they had learned in the village schools. As L'Armée Clandestine continued to grow throughout the 1960s, the bureaucratic apparatus required to manage this force grew correspondingly. One result of this was a new class of person in Hmong society, a kind of military scribe called the *tus sauv ntawv* (tu shau n-dow)—literally, the "one who writes"—whose duties included bookkeeping, correspondence, report writing, and map making. For these individuals, reading and writing practices were shaped by what I have labeled the *rhetoric of military literacy,* which offered the scribes both a set of templates for their writing and a way of understanding the war and their place within it.

The missionary schools offered yet another form of literacy practice to Hmong learners, one that diverged radically from those taught in village schools and practiced in the army. While the Lao schools and the Hmong military taught reading and writing in the Lao language, Christian bible classes taught literacy in the Hmong language, albeit in the roman characters of the writing system designed by Western missionaries. Beyond this, while the rhetorics of Lao schools and the military encouraged loyalty to the Lao state and the Hmong army, the *rhetoric of missionary literacy* promoted acts of reading and writing that transcended secular institutions and invited the Hmong to identify themselves with the doctrines of an alien God.

This chapter examines how the rhetorics of Lao schooling, Hmong military literacy, and missionary Christianity shaped the ways in which Hmong people learned to read and write in Laos. These rhetorics shaped Hmong literacy development by determining the materials used for teaching, the topics written about, the teaching methods practiced, and, ultimately, the meanings attached to written language. Hmong people learning to read and write in the context of these rhetorics were therefore taught more than a set of practical mechanical skills; beyond these, they were taught divergent ways of understanding themselves and their places in the increasingly violent and uncertain world of twentieth-century Laos.

These rhetorics were not, of course, mutually exclusive. Hmong people learned to read and write in multiple contexts, for different purposes, and in different scripts. Beyond this, while the competing rhetorics of literacy in Laos offered powerfully shaping conceptions of self and the world, there is no sense in which these rhetorics determined Hmong identities or rendered readers and writers powerless to challenge, respond, or re-imagine the institutional rhetorics offered to them. To be called upon by a rhetoric is not necessarily to accept its proffered identity to the exclusion of others. Rather, the Hmong experience of multiple literacies in Laos demonstrates the agency and resourcefulness of individual agents—readers and writers—in directing the ends and meanings of their literacy training. In letters, journals, songbooks, and fragments of autobiography, Hmong learners appropriated the literacy skills they had learned and used these to assert their own conceptions of identity, culture, and history—conceptions that were at times in conflict with those learned in the village schools, in the military, or in Christian bible classes. To illustrate, let us turn to the rhetorics shaping the literacy experiences of the Hmong in Laos, beginning with the rhetoric of Lao schooling.[1]

"Once Our Laotian Race in Asia": The Rhetoric of Lao Schooling

Hmong students at the elementary school at Na Wae in 1971 began each morning by lining up outside the classroom so the teacher could inspect their fingernails.[2] Like all Hmong students, Chia Vue was expected to wear her uniform to class, cut her hair short, and keep her fingernails neatly trimmed. Students whose nails were dirty or too long had their fingers "punched" as many as ten times with a long stick. If a student arrived late to class, as Chia Vue once did, that student was made to run around the school building three times as a penalty. After morning inspection, students stood at attention as the teacher raised the Lao flag and led the class in singing the Lao national anthem.

Classes were held in a one-room, roofed bamboo building that had been constructed by residents of Na Wae. Inside, students sat four and five abreast at long wooden desks facing a chalkboard, where the teacher stood. The class numbered about twenty students. The teacher was a Hmong man but spoke only Lao in class. At first Chia Vue understood very little but said she would "listen and just catch whatever I could." Students were given notebooks, pencils, and, books, all unusual in a Hmong village classroom where books and educational materials were typically in short supply.

In class, Vue studied math, science, social studies, art, and music. The principal teaching method was memorization, and students who failed to memorize and recite correctly were apt to receive a minor corporal punishment. Vue recalled, "I remember that . . . we had to memorize a story, and every morning we had to come up front and read the story to the teacher without looking at the paper. If someone didn't remember their story, that person had to kneel down in front of the class."

Writing assignments were generally limited to copying sentences the teacher had written on the board. When students did write, they composed short essays on topics suggested by the teacher. Vue remembered few of these assignments, although she vaguely recalled writing an essay about where her village was located relative to the rest of Laos. Compositions were turned in to the teacher, who corrected for grammar and spelling.

The end of every class day was the same. Students would file outside the building and stand at attention in a circle around the flagpole. As the teacher lowered the flag, the students would sing, for the second time that day, the words to the Laotian national anthem.

> Once our Laotian race in Asia highly honoured stood,
> And at that time the folk of Laos were united in love.
> Today they love their race and rally around their chiefs.
> They guard the land and the religion of their ancestors.
> They will resist each foe who may oppress them or invade
> And such invaders will be met with battle unto death.
> They'll restore the fame of Laos and through ills united stand.[3]

The role of public schooling in reproducing existing social hierarchies and arrangements has long been acknowledged by sociologists, educators, and historians. While the traditional view of schooling is that it functions as a prerequisite to the functioning of a healthy democracy, more critical historical analyses have foregrounded the role of schooling in "impos[ing] the values of one social group upon another, that is…as a form of social control" (Soltow and Stevens 1981, 11). In this view, the socially progressive function of schooling is but one use among many and not always the primary one. Harvey J. Graff (1987) argues that if school literacy in nineteenth-century United States was used to promote political liberation, it was equally a means for imposing "order, cultural hegemony, work preparation, assimilation and adaptation, and installation of a pan-Protestant morality" (340). Society was to be shaped and students socialized by means of what one historian called "the whip of the word" (Harrison 1971, 35, in Soltow and Stevens 1981, 21). Studies of schooling in the twentieth century have complicated this conception by representing schooling not as a site of domination but rather as a ground of struggle in which students, parents, teachers, and other community members contend over issues of learning, teaching, literacy, and ideology.[4]

In the Hmong context, education in the village schools was an outcome of both necessity and calculation, reflecting the military and political circumstances of the day. As noted previously, schools in Hmong villages were funded by the United States in response to demands by Hmong leadership, which gained greater leverage as its role expanded during the Vietnam War. Yet while village schools were funded by the United States, they were under the governance of the Laotian Ministry of Education, which set policies regarding curricula, pedagogy, and language of instruction (Yang 1993, 98–99). This meant that schools were intended to teach Hmong children to read and write Laotian, to integrate the Hmong into the majority culture, and to inculcate ideals of citizenship and national identification into students.

What Lao village schooling was apparently not intended to do, at least from the perspective of the RLG, was engender abstract thinking or critical inquiry that might potentially be destabilizing and contrary to the goals of the government. We have seen, for example, in the daily routines of Chia Vue's school day—from the material conditions in which she studied, to the discouragement of thought implied in daily recitations, to the linguistic hierarchies enforced in the classroom, to the mandatory gestures of identity in singing the Lao national anthem twice daily—the educational practices through which critical thinking was discouraged and the primacy of the Lao state proclaimed. In this way were education and literacy, including teaching methods, language practices, and the meanings of written language, shaped by the rhetoric of Lao schooling, which emphasized allegiance to the RLG and identification with its political worldview. Yet it is equally clear from the testimonies that Hmong students were never passive recipients of a dominant code that left no room for resistance or reinterpretation, but used their newly acquired literacy skills for social and cultural purposes of their own. These diverse and at times contradictory agendas for literacy become evident as we listen to the Hmong testimonies and what they tell us about learning to read and write in the Lao village classroom.

Stones as Chalk: The Material World
of Hmong Education

Materially, Hmong village schools in the 1960s and 1970s were characterized by simple construction, too few teachers, and a chronic shortage of such basic educational supplies as paper, pencils, chalk, and books. These conditions limited what teachers and students might accomplish in the classroom and influenced pedagogical choices, particularly as these pertained to reading and writing. The dearth of writing materials, for example, meant that reading was generally emphasized over writing and that students and teachers, if they did wish to write, had to be ingenious in obtaining the necessary supplies. Pa Toua Thao's recollection of his time in school is typical.

> In our country, the school had no chalkboard so everyone had to go cut and make these large pieces of plywood and connect them together. Then we used ashes—pieces of burned wood, like charcoal—to smear them black. Then you took these white rocks from the nearby cliffs and burned them until they begin to melt; then you placed them in the water. Once they became crystallized and turned into white powder, then you took some bamboos, small bamboo shoots the size of your fingers, and you would pour the white powder into the bamboo shoots. What you got were these long sticks of chalk to be used for writing on the blackboard.

Ger Hang, who attended a Lao village school as a child, also recalled the shortages of writing materials.

> I remember the school did not have that many notebooks; therefore we had to write on a small piece of cardboard about eight and a half by eleven. Also, we didn't have pens and pencils. So we had to use chalk, and write with that, you know? And at the first grade you just started learning the alphabet. And so you would write on the cardboard, and after you wrote it, you would read it. And then after that then you erased it, and then you would write something different.[5]

The teaching of reading was equally compromised by the shortage of books. Tou Meng Vang, for example, recalled the dearth of reading materials in his elementary school. "[In our school], we didn't have anything at all. Just notebooks in the hand and just one pencil, that's it. You didn't have any books to read. You didn't have any textbook, nothing at all.... We had nothing. No textbook, no dictionary, nothing."

The absence of writing materials, shortages of books, and other limitations of the village schools expressed in material terms the wider set of political and economic relationships of the minority Hmong to the ruling Laotian majority, as well as the value placed upon Hmong education by the Laotian state. The conditions of the Lao village schools were not simply material, then, but also ideological. As Volosinov (1973) wrote, "Every phenomenon functioning as an ideological sign has some kind of material embodiment, whether in sound, physical mass, color, movements of the body, or the like.... A sign is a phenomenon of the material world" (11). In this reading, the physical conditions of Hmong schools were the "material embodiment" of the prevailing ideological signs. The material conditions expressed relationships of power, authority, and hierarchy. Accepting this, we may go further: the material conditions of schooling in the highlands of Laos were also rhetorical; that is, they conferred identities and positions upon students and their families. They offered the Hmong the collective identity of a subordinate people. More, they communicated to Hmong families something of the value and possibilities of their literacy training, just as the material conditions of American inner-city schools speak to the values and possibilities of education for millions of minority children in the United States (Kozol 1991). Hmong students who made their own chalk, wrote on cardboard squares, and memorized words because there were no books in which to read them were learning more than simple coping skills; they were learning, as well, the priorities given to their literacy training and the intended meaning of education for Hmong people in Laos.[6]

Recite and Copy: Teaching Methods in the Lao Village School

Beyond their rhetorical meanings, the material conditions of the village schools shaped everyday teaching practices. The shortage of books, as we have just seen, made dictation and recitation the principal teaching methods, meaning that students were given few assignments, if any, calling for reasoning or abstract thinking. Instead, rote learning prevailed as the principal teaching strategy in the classroom, as students copied down passages the teacher had dictated or written on the board. Tou Meng Vang remembered,

> [In my school, you did] memorizing and a lot of reciting, up to four
> pages of reciting. So all the learning had to be done in memorizing or
> reciting the lesson.... We memorized poetry. We memorized the lesson
> of the day, like the lesson about history....
>
> The teacher wrote the lesson on the board because we didn't have
> textbooks. The textbook was only for the teacher, so he wrote things on
> the board. The time that I am thinking about is when I was in third grade
> and fourth grade, and we didn't have enough textbooks to pass around,
> so the teacher wrote and we copied.... You had to make sure that you
> copied it right because you could be punished too if you didn't do things
> right.

Doua Vang, a Hmong man now in his fifties, recalled a similar classroom regimen.

> We didn't have books and the teacher would write on the blackboard.
> Then we would copy what the teacher had written onto our papers
> and try to read it in class a couple of times. And then you went home,
> you would read what you have copied in school. And then the next
> day...each student would present, you know, by reading to the teachers
> to see if you are able to read what you have learned.

If students could not remember their assignments, Neng Vang explained, they were disciplined.

> The teachers would be writing on the board, and we would be copying it
> down. I think the reason for this was because the teachers did not have
> enough textbooks for everybody. So if the teacher had only one copy,
> then when we got to a unit, the teacher had to write it on the board and
> everybody copied it down and took it home to study.
> At that time, going to school in our country, if you missed one word
> you received one punishment, you would get hit by a stick one time. If
> you made two mistakes, you got two sticks. So because of this everyone
> had to study very hard, and we were very good in dictation and writing
> compositions. We were very eager to study hard, and everyone wanted to
> do it perfectly. If during dictation you did not do it perfectly, you got hit.

The emphasis on recitation, rote learning, and corporal punishment has been historically typical of schooling directed toward the socialization of economically subordinate or colonized peoples. Lawrence Stone (1968) has written that the schooling of the poor in nineteenth-century England was characterized by "a stuffy and overcrowded classroom...the indiscriminate use of physical punishment to enforce discipline...[and] a curriculum based on the most mechanical type of rote learning of material which had no conceivable relevance to [students'] life experience in the past or their life experience in the future" (117). Brian Street (1995) has similarly noted how in the Christian mission schools of nineteenth-century Fiji, "texts were limited...writing materials were scarcely available...[and] teaching techniques involved chanting, repetition, and copying with little attempt to 'convey meaning to the mind of the student'" (93). And in the contemporary United States, Mike Rose (1989) has shown how students labeled "basic" or "remedial" can be isolated in "developmental centers" where they are given worksheets and atomistic grammatical exercises in place of assignments that call for extended discourse and critical analysis. The result, Rose says, is a "deep social and intellectual isolation from print" (211).

The pedagogies directed at poor children in England, Fijians in Christian mission schools, "developmental" students in the United States, and Hmong students in Lao villages can all be understood as examples of literacy used to promote socialization into the existing political order and to discourage critical analysis. In this sense, Hmong students who were punished "if you missed one word" were learning to remember more than vocabulary words or short readings; they were learning, as well, the authority of doctrine and its place in governing their intellectual lives. Hmong students and teachers in such classes might be said to have been practicing what Paulo Freire (1970) called "the banking concept" of education, in which thinking is discouraged and knowledge is deposited, like funds into a bank, into the supposedly unquestioning mind of the student. The pedagogical methods used for teaching literacy in these classes were not designed to offer students education for its own sake but were intended, as Soltow and Stevens (1981) wrote of schooling in the nineteenth-century common schools in the United States, to promote "access to a particular way of viewing the world and to a particular set of values" (22).

"Main Language for Everyone": Learning Lao in the Classroom

Beyond material conditions and teaching methods, an important tool for socialization in the Laotian village schools was the language of instruction. While the Educational Reform Act of 1962 called for the use of students' first language in the primary education of minority children, the reality was that minority students were expected to learn to read and write in the national language, Laotian, rather than in their home languages (Yang 1993, 98–99). Indeed, speaking the Hmong language was discouraged even if the teachers were Hmong. Vang Lee Xiong explained, "There were two teachers, a Lao and a Hmong person. But they didn't speak Hmong; mostly Lao. If you didn't know any Lao words, you just kept your mouth shut. If you were able to speak Lao, go ahead and speak. But if you cannot speak Lao you have to keep your mouth shut. If you spoke Hmong to them, they pretended they didn't know what you were saying."

This is not to suggest that the majority of Hmong students or their families resisted learning Lao or advocated for Hmong-language classrooms. For many, education in the Lao language was viewed as a necessary tool for economic advancement and for political participation on the national level (Yang 1993, 97). Indeed, Hmong students attending the Lao village schools inhabited two linguistic worlds: Hmong was the language of home and used for family, courtship, and ritual, while Laotian was the language of the public and used for government, business, and military affairs. Nua Lee, a Hmong man in his forties, explained, "Lao is the main language for everyone. So if you went to court, you had to speak in Lao. When people wrote letters, they wrote them in Lao. Whatever people did, the Laotians were in control of the country. So everyone who wants a good life must know how to speak in Lao."

For Blia Thao, a thirty-nine-year-old Hmong woman, learning Laotian was not only necessary to fulfill her ambition of becoming a nurse and improving her economic status, but was also a marker of social status. "In school we tried to speak Lao as much as we can. And at that time, people felt that if you can speak Lao, you are in a better class. It's like...if you don't speak Lao at all, then that means that you are in a very low class. If you speak Lao and have an education that means that you are in a high class.... You just felt that way and you wanted to fit in."

Not to know Lao, these testimonies suggest, meant that one did not communicate in the public language of the nation, did not participate in the possibilities for economic advancement, did not escape the stigma of speaking a minority language such as Hmong. Not to know Lao was in a sense not to exist, at least not in public life. Hmong people who wished to trade farm life for a position as a bureaucrat, teacher, or something else that would lead to what Nua Lee called "a good life" understood the necessity of becoming literate in the majority language. And yet while this training did have the effect of teaching a select number of Hmong the majority language and qualifying them, at least in theory, for positions within the Lao bureaucracy, the accompanying effect was to diminish the importance of Hmong language and literacy in the context of the classroom.

Kings and Moral Cultures: Writing in the Village Classroom

Perhaps the most overt manifestations of the rhetoric of Lao schooling were the writing assignments given to Hmong students. While writing, as we have seen, was not given the same emphasis as reading, Hmong interviewed for this project did recall being given writing assignments in their classrooms. In most cases, students remembered, these assignments addressed Laotian values, history, and culture. Lor Tong Cha, for instance, recalled studying Lao, the founding of the Lao nation, and the origins of Lao royal family.

> At that time we studied the Laotian language and studied Laotian history. We studied about the *Cauj Paj Nkoo* (chao pha nkong),[7] the Laotian king. We studied about the Laotian king and about the Laotian people. Mainly we studied about the Laotian people.... We studied about their rules, laws, and regulations; about how to speak Lao; how to make a living in Laos. All these things were taught in Laotian only.

Blia Thao remembered that writing assignments sometimes addressed the political situation in the country, including the role of the United States in Laotian affairs.

> For example, the teacher would have you take the textbook to read. After you are done reading, the teacher would keep the book. Then he would give you the topic to write and you would write it yourself. There are writings on such things as how the country of Laos developed to its present state. Is it true that history occurred like that? Why did the Americans come over to our country? These things I wrote about.

Vang Meng added, "I remember first grade when we mostly studied the Laotian language. And we read Lao and wrote Lao, but we had no Hmong class at all. No Hmong, just Laotian. And what we studied was the geography, and science, and moral cultures, and religions, and history of Laos."

Such testimonies suggest that learning to read and write in the village schools was not simply a matter of mastering the mechanics of deciphering and producing written symbols. Rather, to be a Hmong student in a Lao school during a time of civil war was to be offered a language and conceptual vocabulary through which to define oneself as constituent of the Laotian polity and be called upon by the government to make sacrifices on behalf of the nation in a time of civil war, even to the point of developing what Etienne Balibar (1991) has called "the capacity to confront death collectively" (94). This identification with the state was the aim of the rhetoric of Lao schooling, and it was this rhetoric that shaped students' education and literacy development.

In addition to what they express, rhetorics are distinguished by what they foreclose, by the possibilities they deny or conceal. Notably absent from the Hmong testimonies of schooling are recollections of reading or writing assignments that concerned Hmong language, history, or culture. "And we read Lao and wrote Lao, but we had no Hmong class at all," Meng

Vang related. "No Hmong, just Laotian." Hmong students did not study the history of the Hmong in Laos, or the Hmong emigration from China, or any of the diverse elements of Hmong culture, such as their religious practices or their artistry as storytellers, musicians, and silversmiths. No educational materials addressed these topics, nor were they part of school curricula. In this sense, Lao schools were not merely teaching reading and writing, but were also teaching students what not to read, write, or think. Asked if he ever wondered why he did not study the Hmong language in his elementary or secondary school in Laos, Christopher Xiong replied, "You know, come to think of it, we never thought about that. Because at that time I think we didn't quite value the Hmong language, the written language."

There are, of course, dangers to this sort of argument. In applying a conceptual framework as a means to account for the behaviors of a vast number of people over a span of decades, there is the risk of reducing the unruly varieties of individual motivations, tensions, and ambiguities into deceptively tidy and reductive categories. For example, although I have stressed the ways in which village schools used literacy as a tool for promoting Lao interests, it is also true that many Hmong identified themselves with the Lao state and were eager to study the Lao language. For these individuals, the chance to study in Lao schools was a necessary precursor to the economic advancement for the Hmong generally (Smalley 1985). Beyond this, there were the emotional ties that some Hmong had to Laos. By the 1960s, the Hmong had been living in Laos for almost a century. For many, Laos was "their country," and the Lao government, while not their own, was the one to which they had grown accustomed and accommodated themselves. Indeed, one of the Hmong phrases for Laos is *peb lub tebchaws* (pay lue tay chaw), which can be translated as "our country" (Trueba, Jacobs, and Kirton 1990, 26). For at least some Hmong, then, learning to read and write Lao might be seen as a means through which they could reach across the personal and public domains, advance themselves economically, play a role in national affairs, and yet still retain their identities as Hmong people. One rhetoric does not necessarily exclude others.

Yet while the purposes and outcomes of education are never entirely unitary or lacking in contradictions, it seems safe to say that Lao schooling was not intended to encourage a Hmong critique of existing social relations, specifically those pertaining to the political and economic status of the Hmong. Rather, schooling was a vehicle to promote loyalty to the government, diminish ethnic identity, and ultimately generate what Benedict Anderson (1983) has described as the "profound changes in consciousness" that make it possible for individuals to identify themselves with the "imagined community" of the nation. In the rhetoric of Lao schooling, the language, cultures, and traditions of the Hmong and other Laotian minority peoples seemingly had little place in domains of national life.

Rhetoric as "Rewriting": Appropriations of Lao Literacy

If the rhetoric of Lao schooling invited the Hmong to see themselves as Laotians and to adopt an ideology of Lao nationhood, it must also be said that Hmong students were not passive recipients of a dominant code but appropriated the literacy skills they had learned and used these to their own ends, whether for writing letters, keeping journals, or composing their histories. Chia Vue, for example, used the reading and writing skills she had learned in the Lao village schools to communicate with her distant family. As was true for many Hmong students, Vue was sent to a village far from home where she could attend school, her own village having none. To relieve the loneliness she sometimes felt, Vue used her Lao literacy skills to write what she called "simple letters" to her family, sharing details of her everyday experiences. "I would tell them that I missed them and whether I had a good day or a bad day at my school. I would tell them what we were doing on that day, maybe about things that were hard, or where we were getting our food. And I would ask them questions, 'And what are you doing there?'"

Lor Tong Cha was also a letter writer. For him, however, letter writing was a way to advocate for family members and friends who had been displaced and impoverished by the war. Lor used the literacy skills learned in a village school to write on behalf of those who had fled the fighting and taken refuge at the Hmong military base at Long Cheng, to which Lor himself had relocated. His letters, addressed to the political and military authorities who ran the camp, appealed for food and other material necessities. Lor explained,

> At this time there was a lot of fighting, so [my family's and friend's] ways of making a living and doing business had been disrupted.... I wrote to the military leaders or to those who watched over the village, for example the *Nai Koo* (nai kong) or the *Toj Xeem* (taw seng),[8] the city officials who were in charge of food distribution. I wrote mainly asking for rice and canned meat, the canned meat that they gave to the soldiers.
>
> I wrote because people wanted those things. They did not know how to write, so they would ask me to write for them. Most of these

people were relatives, brothers and sisters, those people who lived in or were from the same village; those people who were close to you. I learned how to write from these letters—because you wrote a lot.

Vue Lee Mai, a Hmong teacher whose own schooling was disrupted in the fourth grade, used his Lao literacy skills years after he had left Laos and resettled in the United States. Calling upon his experiences as a farmer, a soldier, and as a refugee, Vue began writing his autobiography in the Lao language, a document that recalled his place in recent Hmong history.

Then I wrote some stories about when we arrived in Thailand. Yes, I have written some. I wrote about our lives when we came to Thailand—how we crossed the Mekong River, what that was like, how poor we were. I wrote these down. . . .

I used the Lao language. I wrote about the life coming from Laos to Thailand, and how hard life was. How long was it before we arrived in Thailand? What happened when we arrived in Thailand? Those things, I have written them.

The things I wrote, I wanted to preserve them as hard copies, so when I die my children can find them to read and understand how their dad's and mom's lives were hard and difficult. Also, I wanted them to understand how our life was back then, and what caused us to be in America.

Freire (1970) has written that literacy represents a way of "reading the world," by which he means, as I understand him, the acts of reflection and action through which learners transform the world around them. People who learn to read, Freire argues, are capable of intervening in their own realities, transforming conditions of injustice or oppression. Having learned to use literacy in a particular way and for a particular purpose—to help them assimilate into the Lao state—Hmong writers nevertheless turned their new skills toward their own purposes, toward the personal, the pragmatic, the historical. One might argue that these writers had embarked on their own "readings of the world," using literacy as their means of interpretation. The letters, appeals, and historical writings we have sampled were not representative of any systematic resistance to the Lao majority or expression of Hmong identity. Yet these modest, everyday acts of reading and writing can perhaps be seen as "rewritings," or counter-rhetorics that more closely reflected the life experiences of the writers and suggested new meanings and possibilities for the literacy practices of the Hmong people in Laos.

The One Who Writes: The Rhetoric
of Military Literacy

Vang Lee joined the army in 1972 after his father had been killed in combat. He enlisted, Lee said, to take his father's place in the war and fight against communism in Laos. He was fourteen years old. As a soldier, Lee was resourceful, tough, and a natural leader. Eventually he would be given his own command and lead other men into combat. He was also literate. From 1969 to 1971, he had attended school in his village of Moung Mok, learning to read and write the Lao language. Shortly after joining the Hmong army, he was made a secretary to the battalion commander at Long Cheng. As secretary, Lee was responsible for writing letters, keeping records, filing reports, drawing maps, and summarizing intelligence gathered from the battlefield. He had access to paper and ballpoint pens, and he was introduced to the technologies of the typewriter and the telegraph. Later, Lee's position would require that he learn to read and write a very basic form of English, which he needed to communicate with the CIA agents running the military operations out of Long Cheng. But his main responsibility, Lee recalled, was to keep written records of men and materiel, including the numbers of those killed and wounded in battle. Lee recalled,

> When I was a soldier, I served as a secretary....I would write such
> things as, "Tonight, we fought each other, and how did we do?" I
> would keep records of how many people died, how many people were
> injured....Also the enemy, how many people did we see, exactly, die
> there in that battle? How many of them were injured and killed? And if
> we got grenades, or guns, or bullets from the enemy, I would write that
> down. We needed to report everything.

Literacy has long played a role in campaigns of warfare and conquest. From the handbook of drill and tactics written by the second-century Greek writer Tacitus, to the study of military fortifications and siege warfare by the sixteenth-century Italian Francesco Feretti, to the World War I officers' training manuals on how to prepare soldiers for trench warfare, literacy has been a means for analyzing theory and disseminating technical information to help soldiers fight and win wars.[9] As modern Western armies have come to rely upon increasingly sophisticated technologies, literacy has assumed an even greater importance. Officers and recruits alike must have the reading and writing skills necessary to comprehend complex textual materials. The significance of literacy to the contemporary U.S. Army, for example, is demonstrated by the resources devoted to the education of new recruits, whose literacy skills are carefully managed and measured (Sticht 1995). Indeed, one might argue that literacy is one of the most indispensable weapons in Western military arsenals.

Literacy was vitally important to L'Armée Clandestine. As the war in Vietnam escalated, the size and responsibilities of the "Secret Army" began to change. What began as an irregular guerrilla force charged with gathering intelligence and conducting hit-and-run attacks on selected targets eventually became a conventional army of some forty thousand soldiers engaging North Vietnamese troops in full-scale, logistically demanding battles on the Plain of Jars. Among the many consequences of this transformation of the Hmong force was the growth of a large and increasingly complex military bureaucracy, one that needed to keep records of payrolls, inventories, personnel, and casualties. And this, in turn, called for a new class of person in Hmong society, the *tus sau ntawv* (lit., the "one who writes"), a kind of military scribe who was responsible for carrying out the specialized literacy activities required by the expanding administrative apparatus of L'Armée Clandestine.

In most cases, the scribes did not learn their basic reading and writing skills in the "Secret Army." Rather, the army provided a context in which a select group of Hmong men could enhance the literacy skills they had learned elsewhere, usually in the village schools.[10] However, while military writing was built upon the skills learned in village classrooms, it generally surpassed these in terms of its literate and cognitive demands. While reading and writing in the village schools generally focused upon rote learning and recitation, military literacy was oriented toward practical, purposeful, and, in some cases, analytical ends. In addition, military duties also introduced a small number of Hmong to a functional form of English-language literacy that served as a necessary communicative tool for Hmong soldiers and their CIA sponsors. So while L'Armée Clandestine was not engaged in the systematic teaching of literacy, as were the village schools and Christian missionaries, the military did provide new and unfamiliar ways of using written language and so developed the existing skills of literate Hmong.[11]

The position of the scribe and its attendant literacy practices also offered a rhetorical identity, a way of understanding the war and the scribe's personal place within it. In what I call the *rhetoric of military literacy,* the scribes were offered the identities of clerks, managers, bureaucrats, and administrators. They were low-level functionaries whose knowledge of reading and writing was essential to the everyday operations of the war. More, their literacy practices told a kind of story about the war. Their writings were neither narratives of great deeds and puissant warriors nor heroic tales of carnage and suffering. Rather, the writings of the military scribes offered a narrative of war as an everyday reality, a series of almost mundane events that could be quantified and accounted for in the daily activities of list making, record keeping, and report writing. In this way could a war of staggering violence and destruction, one largely prosecuted and funded by a foreign power, be naturalized, invested with routine, given a sense of administrative inevitability. The widespread destruction of life and property was accounted for, if not explained, by the lists, letters, and ledgers produced by the scribe. Scribal literacy in this sense had two separate though related functions. Most immediately, it was a functional and administrative tool, used for communications and record keeping. Beyond this, however, scribal literacy served as a rhetorical instrument for managing and ultimately controlling the everyday meanings of the war.

As before, Hmong people who learned the skills specific to their scribal duties inevitably transformed the purposes and meanings of these skills. Scribes interviewed for this book spoke of using the literacy skills they had practiced in L'Armée Clandestine to keep their own journals, ledgers, and other records, and to compose histories recording their experiences as soldiers. Scribes kept these records and wrote these narratives for themselves, for their fellow soldiers, for their families, and for posterity. Their writings demonstrate how the rhetoric of military literacy, functional and clerical, could serve as a bridge to new forms of literacy practice and new expressions of written meanings: ones that went beyond those learned in the context of the "Secret Army." To better understand the experiences of the Hmong military scribes, let us consider their selection, their training, and their writings, official and personal.

Bureaucratic Universe: Literacies of the *Tus Sau Ntawv*

The military scribe was not a formal designation. There were no applications to fill out, no standardized tests to pass, no recommendations to solicit. Rather, Hmong soldiers who could already read and write Laotian were appointed as scribes by their commanders and charged with carrying out the specialized literacy tasks required by the military. The Hmong scholar Paoze Thao (personal communication, July 16, 1999) explained that there were actually three classes of military scribe, each with distinct duties: 1) the *tus sau ntawv* (the "one who writes"), who was mainly responsible for keeping records and writing letters; 2) the *nai sai* (nye sye), who was responsible for sending telegrams from the field to the base and providing military intelligence to base commanders; and 3) the *tug xib paub maim* (tue see pau my), who provided information to CIA and Hmong pilots attacking enemy positions or dropping military supplies and food to Hmong soldiers in the field. As the Hmong military veterans I interviewed did not observe distinctions among these scribal roles, but spoke in general terms of the *tus sau ntawv,* that is the practice followed in this chapter.

Once selected, scribes were typically stationed at one of the Hmong military bases and given a variety of writing tasks, all of which were related to the military mission. Much of the scribal writing was clerical: creating lists, compiling accounts, and keeping records of the human and material resources necessary for the prosecution of the war. Lor Tong Cha, for example, recalled that his duties as a scribe required that he keep personnel and payroll records.

> After I became a soldier, then I wrote for the soldiers. I became what you would call in this country a secretary. I was the person who wrote letters to help the soldiers, who recorded the soldiers' names into lists, who wrote whether they were good soldiers or not. . . . I made lists of the people who were receiving government money, what rank these people had, and what rank I and others had, things like this. Then I typed it into pages and saved them.[12]

Pa Toua Thao, another scribe, recalled similar duties.

> I wrote letters and kept records of the military personnel and their status. I kept records about the fighting and where people fought. So, I helped them write records and reports regarding these things. . . . In doing this, I came to keep records. I kept track of gun registration numbers. When there was a battle, I recorded how many guns were lost, how many guns were still at hand. I also kept records of the soldiers, how many came back from their leave, how many did not, how many soldiers were ill, and how many soldiers were in the base. I did these things.

As the fighting escalated and casualties mounted, the scribes also compiled lists of those killed and wounded in battle. Pa Toua Thao explained, "Regarding those reports . . . like when the soldiers went to war or when there was fighting, after the fighting they would radio back or return and report to us. Then I would have to write down as to how they fought, how many were killed, and how many survived."

Hmong military scribes also wrote letters on behalf of Hmong soldiers and their families. Typically, these letters were written for soldiers who wanted military leave but could not read or write themselves. In this case, they would request that the scribe write the letter for them, which would then be forwarded to the ranking officer responsible for approving or denying the request. Vue Lee Mai recalled, "The writing I did included writing permission letters for people who wanted to go home. If a person was injured, I had to write to the commanding officer asking permission for this person to go home. If a person was ill, the letter would ask permission for this person to stay in the back, away from the fighting for a little while. This is what I did."

When soldiers overstayed their leaves, the scribe would write another kind of letter, this one on behalf of the Hmong military command at the CIA headquarters at Long Cheng, reminding the person that it was time to return to the war. In this way, literacy took on a regulatory function, serving as a means through which the Hmong military commanders could communicate with and control the soldiers under their command. Xai Moua, another scribe, remembered it this way.

> Those soldiers who requested permission to go home, you would write letters for them asking.... But when the soldiers went home and did not return, then you would have to write letters ordering them to return. When someone did not return, I would write to him telling him that he has gone past his leave date and that he must return to work as before. If he did not come back after this letter requesting his return, then he must accept his punishment.... Most came back.

Military scribes also wrote letters requesting compensation on behalf of Hmong women whose husbands had been killed in combat. Vue Lee Mai explained that when a soldier was killed, his widow had to file paperwork to receive compensation from the Hmong military command. Since few women could read and write, the necessary paperwork was completed by the scribe. Vue explained,

> You had to keep records when soldiers died, and you had to apply for money from the high officials. You kept a record of when you applied for money for those who have died, or were wounded and were in the hospital. You wrote to help those families—wives and children—who had needs. The letter would explain as to whether the husband was killed by a gunshot, got hit by a mine, or just disappeared; these things you explained also.[13]

Such letters were not original compositions but were actually form letters printed in Thailand or Vientiane, the Laotian capital. The scribe was responsible for learning how to fill them out correctly in consultation with the widow or other family member. Vue explained, "Those forms would tell the soldier's name, service, rank, age, the city he lived in, the names of his mother and father, the name of his wife—this is what the form would say. Yes, they gave you a sample form and you filled out the form. They were already created; they left white areas for you to fill in."

If much of the scribal work was clerical, some writing tasks called for the exercise of more complex skills. Scribes were also expected to write summaries of battlefield reports sent to the base by Hmong commanders in the field and then send these summaries on to Hmong military intelligence. Such reports demanded the literate skills of restating, summarizing, and synthesizing information from multiple sources. Lor Tong Cha, for example, recalled writing reports that drew upon information sent from multiple locations on the battlefield. Lor explained that his commanding officer insisted that reports be syntactically and grammatically correct. If the reports were in any way inaccurate, Lor said, his commanding officer would return them with instructions that they be rewritten. "After I was done writing the reports then I would give them to Colonel C. . . . He has to check the reports, then you can send them. . . . He would check to see if the information was correct, if you wrote them correctly or not; he would finish correcting them in Laotian. And then he would approve whether or not you could send the report. . . . If it was not right then you must redo it."

Xai Moua also recalled receiving direct instruction on writing from his Hmong military superiors.

> When we learned how to write we were taught by the officers. They taught us that, if we were writing something to be telegraphed back to the main base—for example, if we did not have enough food—then we should write just a little bit, just the precise meanings. But we were also taught how to write a letter telling them that today we fought this many hours and this many of our soldiers died; or that we killed this many communists in this area. . . . We then became good in writing.

Being a military scribe also meant being introduced to technologies that were not widely used by other Hmong soldiers or civilians. Lor Tong Cha, for example, remembered being taught how to use a Lao-language typewriter for writing his reports. Xiong Kou, another scribe, learned a specialized military code for transmitting information between the field and the base and was taught to operate the electronic equipment necessary for transmitting and receiving messages in this code. Kou recounted,

Those who went to fight in the front would send telegraphed messages back to the base. These were very hard to translate. The messages were written in numbers. They had written numbers in groups of four; one group would be made up of four numbers. These would be written down [after they were received]. Then they would be translated into one line, one sentence at a time. Then they would be sent to General Vang Pao. General Vang Pao would send them to the appropriate offices, and each office would do its specific tasks accordingly.[14]

In general, scribes learned a specialized set of literacy functions and performed these on behalf of the Hmong military command. In this sense did the work of the Hmong military scribes recall what Eric Havelock (1963, cited in Ong 1982, 93) called the literacy "craftsmen" of ancient Greece, those whom "others might hire to write a letter or document as they might hire a stone-mason to build a house, or a shipwright to build a boat." Hmong scribes, however, did not work for the civilian population but for the Hmong military. Their writing served as a conduit for a form of institutional authority.[15]

There were also important social and regulatory purposes to scribal literacy. As Bernardo Gallego (1992) has explained, literacy functions as an instrument for social cohesion and helps to maintain social order "through the human record keeping system" (73). The writings of the *tus sau ntawv* —the lists, records, letters, reports—functioned in this way, serving as a means through which military authorities could regulate the Hmong military and civilian populations. François Furet and Jacques Ozouf (1982, 312, quoted in Gallego 1992, 73) have observed that "it is through the written word, as it short-circuits the barriers erected by the oral community, that each subject or citizen is recorded and defined by his social coordinates; born on such and such a date, of this father and that mother, in the town of X, occupying some specific profession, and so on." In the same way, the forms, lists, letters, and reports filled out by the military scribe "recorded and defined" Hmong soldiers and their families, locating them within the bureaucratic and rhetorical universe of the Hmong military and its CIA sponsors.

Alpha, Bravo, Charlie: Learning English as a Scribe

Most of the writing undertaken by scribes was in the Lao language, reflecting the literacy education the scribes had received in the village schools.

However, as more Hmong soldiers began working directly with U.S. military and CIA personnel, there arose a need for a common medium of communication. Since few Americans spoke Hmong, some Hmong soldiers began to learn specialized forms of English military jargon through which they could communicate at least in rudimentary fashion with CIA pilots. In this way did the war, and in particular the CIA presence at the military base at Long Cheng, introduce a small number of Hmong to the English language and English-language literacy, providing one historical starting point for what has become the primary spoken and written language for tens of thousands of Hmong men and women in the United States.[16] Xai Moua, for example, recalled that his introduction to English was the English-language materials he saw at the military base in Thailand. He used these materials to study the new language: "We saw that language, English, and we were curious. There were these books, which were written in English, with Thai and Lao on the other side. We bought them and studied them ourselves. If you knew someone who knew the language, you would go ask him to help you for a little while. There was no class for us to learn it."

The English learned by the Hmong scribes was functional and motivated by immediate needs. Hmong soldiers who undertook learning English, for example, often did so to communicate with U.S. pilots who were conducting bombing missions over Hmong territories in Laos or dropping supplies to Hmong soldiers in the field. Xai Moua recalled,

> So we bought [English] books to study, so that we could work with the pilots, the Americans, who came to work in our country. Where should he drop the bombs? Where should he drop the food? Where should he go pick up the dead people? Where should he go pick up the wounded people? All these things we studied, and we studied how to read map coordinates, so we can direct the airplanes to go land there.[17]

Vang Lee was also introduced to English literacy while working with CIA pilots in Laos. Vang remembered learning the linguistic code known as the "NATO phonetic alphabet" (formally the "international radiotelephony spelling alphabet"), in which common nouns replace letter names in long-distance communications such as radio transmissions (see O'Connor 1996, 791). Thus "A" becomes "Alpha," "B" becomes "Bravo," "C" becomes "Charlie," and so forth. Vang's first introduction to the letters of the English alphabet came from his exposure to this code. "For example . . . in the army, they used ABCs, right? In the army, they would say 'Alpha, Bravo, Charlie, Delta, Echo.' . . . They would say it like that. They would have a map. But on the map, they would just write an abbreviation, like 'Hotel' or 'Tango.'

Tango is 'T,' right? 'Tango' and 'Ouija,' these would be on the map. So when they told me, I learned how to read it." Vang explained that learning the code was necessary to ensure accurate communication between Hmong soldiers and CIA pilots. Clear communication, he said, could be a matter of life and death.

> Usually, we have to tell the pilots what map to look at, and we have to tell them the numbers, the coordinates. And they take a look at the map, and they want to know, "All right now, the enemy is here, right?" We would report the place where the enemy was surrounding us. But we would use the codes of the map, for example, FV or sometimes G or GF, sometimes U or G, like that. It depends what the map said, and where we were.
>
> Sometimes the map had six numbers, sometimes twelve numbers. And the people there, or the leader, they would know where the enemy is and they will call in the jets or the T-28 planes to bomb the enemy positions. In the army, the map was very important for us. If you gave the wrong coordinates to the pilot you would die. If the airplane dropped bombs on you because you gave them the wrong coordinates, you died right away....
>
> You know, one time, I can't remember exactly, I think it's one hundred or two hundred soldiers died when the battalion called in the wrong coordinates and they dropped bombs on our soldiers. Yeah. It was very hard for us. So they wanted the people who reported that information to know how to do it, and to report it exactly right.

In later years, after Vang had fled Laos and resettled in the United States, the English letters he learned in the context of his military training would provide his foundation for learning the Romanized Popular Alphabet (RPA), the missionary alphabet that uses the same Roman characters as the English alphabet, though assigning different phonetic values to each letter. The "ABCs" of the NATO code, in other words, provided a bridge to the sound and symbol correspondences of the RPA. In Vang's case, this meant that learning an unfamiliar military code while fighting a war financed by foreign interests eventually helped him to become literate in his own language, albeit in a writing system conceived and promoted by foreign missionaries.

Among other things, this remarkable complexity of literacies suggests the intertwining and mutually informing nature of rhetorics and rhetorical identities. The symbolic environments experienced by Lee Vang and other Hmong in L'Armée Clandestine were not self-contained or autonomous, but in constant interaction and tension with one another. The literacy of the village schools led some Hmong to positions as military scribes, which further exposed others to the possibilities of English literacy, which might then lead, in seeming paradox, back to literacy in one's native language. There was a profusion of literacies available to a selected number of Hmong in L'Armée Clandestine, a variety of writing systems that might be used to represent words, ideas, and worlds. There was, as well, a profusion of identities and positions available to the scribes. All the various literacies, the multiple representations of sounds, syllables, words, and sentences, offered invitations to adopt multiple identities within different and not always complementary hierarchies. Literacy was not an end in such dialogues, but rather a graphical means through which greater powers—the RLG, the CIA, Christian missionaries—might seek to impose constructions of the individual and the society, the nation and the state, the secular and the sacred. The military writing of Vang Lee in this sense represented a gathering place of competing symbols, rhetorics, and ideologies.

To participate in a rhetorical narrative is not, however, to be determined by it, and while the literacy practices of the scribes were shaped by the rhetoric of military literacy, this did not prevent them from later applying their writing skills to their own ends, both personal and historical. This was especially evident after the defeat of the CIA-backed Hmong forces in 1975, when former scribes began joining the Hmong resistance movement, the *Cob Fab* (chao fa), and turning the literacy skills they had practiced in the Hmong military toward new purposes and meanings. In doing so, scribes asserted alternative identities for themselves and expressed new understandings of their relationship to the institutions they had formerly served.

Resistance Literacies: Writing in the *Cob Fab*

In 1975, when the U.S. government ended its support of the "Secret Army" in Laos and withdrew from Vietnam, thousands of Hmong fled toward the Mekong River and sanctuary in Thailand. Not all Hmong, however, chose to leave immediately. Many remained behind, disappearing into remote jungles and mountains. There, they continued to resist the communist forces as members of the *Cob Fab*, the Hmong resistance.[18] Among those who joined were former military scribes, who found that the literacy skills they had honed in the Hmong army could be put to new uses in a different kind of war. To illustrate, let us consider the testimonies of two former scribes, Xai Moua and Vue Lee.

The Subversive Accountant: Xai Moua's Story

One military scribe who stayed behind after the collapse of L'Armée Clandestine was Xai Moua, who joined the military in 1961 at the age of twenty-five. Moua could read and write when he joined the army, having attended a Lao village school for three years. For about a year, he received military training in Thailand, then returned to Laos to perform a variety of military functions, including those of the scribe. In 1963, Moua began keeping a journal in the Laotian language to record his experiences as a soldier. He explained, "You would write.... Since you have gone into battle, where have you lived? What did you do? Where did the fighting take place? Did you shoot them or did they shoot you? How long did you fight before you got to come back home? How long did you get to stay away before you went back into the battlefield? These things, you kept in the journal."

Moua kept this journal for seventeen years, filling five notebooks with his accounting of battles, dates, places, and the names of the wounded and dead. When the Hmong army disbanded in 1975, Moua, fearful of giving himself away as a former military man, threw his notebooks "into the river" and fled into the jungle to join the resistance. There, he led a small company against Vietnamese and Laotian communist forces. As a *Cob Fab* commander, Moua began yet another journal: "We would put down, for example, 'Today we went to fight the communists. What time did we leave? What day did we attack their base? Did we win or lose? How many of us died? How many wounded? How many were missing? Or how many communists did we kill?' These things, we wrote them down."

Keeping lists of the dead and wounded had been part of Moua's work as a military scribe in the Hmong "Secret Army." In the resistance, however, these documents assumed a different set of meanings. While Moua's journal still represented an accounting of the war, a record of its daily events and expenses, the journal also functioned as a ledger of debts owed to the *Chao Fa,* an account that could someday be presented to Hmong military authorities or the CIA when the time finally came for Hmong families to be compensated for the losses of their sons, husbands, and other family members. As Moua explained,

> And when we fought and died, there was no money to pay to the
> soldier's parents, or to the soldier's widow. So we only wrote down the
> names, wrote down the dates, wrote down the times when the soldiers
> were killed. If in the event that we did not win the war, or if we lost the
> country, fine. But if we struggle and the general [Vang Pao] and others

returned due to our efforts, then we will take the parents and widows to the general and tell him that they are owed money.

Moua also used the scribal skills he had learned to write what were essentially IOUs to the civilian population supporting the *Cob Fab*. When he had fought as a soldier in Vang Pao's army, Moua said, weapons, ammunition, and especially food had been readily available. But after 1975, these same supplies were harder to come by. Food was a particular problem, as men fighting in the resistance found it difficult to plant and harvest crops. Consequently, Moua and other *Cob Fab* resistance fighters were forced to rely upon local villagers for rice and other provisions. Each time his men requisitioned food from Hmong citizens, Moua wrote a letter stating exactly the kind and amounts of food that had been taken. The villager was given this letter, which was to be redeemed for cash after Gen. Vang Pao returned. Moua stated,

> When we were fighting with the CIA and with General Vang Pao, we had airplanes; we had guns; we had food to eat; we had everything. . . . However, after Vang Pao fled and we went to live in the jungles, we didn't have anything to eat. . . . We would have to ask the general population, both Lao and Hmong, to give us rice to eat—to give us this many kilograms of rice, for example. But we didn't have any money. So we had to write on paper that "If we had money, we would pay you; but since we do not have any money, General Vang Pao will pay you when he returns." So we wrote these things down. If we came to buy a pig or ask for a pig to eat, we would write it down. We would write down, "If you give us your pig for the soldiers to eat, when the General returns he will pay you," or "When we have our country back, we will pay you." So we did these things.

Such comments suggest the changing role of literacy in the *Cob Fab*. While the former scribe Xai Moua was still carefully compiling lists, records, and accounts, using the same literacy skills he had practiced as a scribe serving in L'Armée Clandestine, these writings now took on new meanings. Previously, Moua had written on behalf of the Hmong military bureaucracy, carrying out the literacy tasks that would enable it to function efficiently. As a *Cob Fab,* however, he was writing on behalf of Hmong soldiers and civilians, using his literacy skills to create documents that were meant to support their claims upon the Hmong military and the CIA, should these institutions someday return to Laos. Moua's military literacy, in other words, was no longer exclusively the property of the institutions that had sponsored it; it now served Moua's fellow resistance fighters and the civilians who supported them.

Besides tallying the debts owed by the resistance to the civilian population that helped to sustain them, Moua's scribal writings also served as a form of insurance, verifying his claims and those of his men should these claims someday be challenged. In his words,

> We wanted to have records about our life, about what we did. The first thing was, if the government didn't care about us and didn't help us, or if the Americans do not want and help us, then we will have these writings to support us.... We kept these records so that one day if General Vang Pao didn't care about us, and if they were to deny us, we will have these writings when we talk with them. And if one day the CIA didn't want us and would not help us, we will have these writings when we talk with them.

As before, Moua was using the skills he had learned as a scribe in the Hmong military, but now his military literacy was transformed into a type of legal literacy, serving to indemnify Moua and his men against possible losses in the future. Moua's literacy was in this sense an act of faith—faith in the law-abiding nature of the authorities he had once served and faith in the power of literacy to legitimize the debts incurred by the *Cob Fab*. That Moua believed his journals would be accepted as corroborating evidence of his claims speaks both to his trust in literacy and the goodwill of his former paymasters in the Hmong army and the CIA. Yet the journals might also be interpreted as a quietly subversive gesture, a means by which Moua might someday contest the authority of the Hmong military bureaucracy and the CIA should they disavow or betray him.

In this sense Moua was asserting a new identity for himself and a new position relative to the Hmong military. He was still the Lao citizen fighting for his country, as he had learned to be in the village schools, and he was still a Hmong soldier-scribe, as he had been trained to become in L'Armée Clandestine. Yet now he was also a resistance fighter, an advocate for the local villagers, and a potential litigant prepared to challenge the authority of the Hmong military authorities and the CIA should this become necessary. So while Moua's literacy practices appeared on the surface to be consistent with his training as a military scribe—meticulously recording what soldier died on what date and the names of that soldier's wife and children, as well as other details of Moua's life in the resistance—the rhetorical meanings of these literacy practices had changed, as had the identities and positions they now offered Xai Moua.

Writing as Moral Lessons: The Writing of Vue Lee

Vue Lee joined the "Secret Army" in 1969, when he was sixteen years old, after two years of schooling in a Lao village school. He was sent to Thailand for training, where he learned Morse code and how to operate a telegraph. His first military assignment was to accompany Hmong troops into the field and send back information about enemy troop movements, either by telegraph or in written reports. "You had to write to the headquarters, telling them what's going on, you know, what is happening that day. You had to send that information back to headquarters. I used a telegraph when we had an emergency situation, you know, when the communists were too close. But when...the communists weren't too close, when they were far away, yeah, then you could write reports on paper."[19]

Lee was eventually promoted to officer rank and began keeping a journal of his activities. He continued to keep this journal, he said, after he joined the Hmong resistance.

> After 1969, I became a leader, what the Americans would call a lieutenant. I became a lieutenant, and I knew I should keep my records. So I wrote down...what I was doing in the army, and how my leaders, my bosses, how they treated me. I kept the journal from the time I was in the military through the time when we began to join the *Cob Fab.*...I wrote about once a week. And sometimes, depending on if I had something new to write about, or something I'm interested in, I would write that down also. I probably wrote about seventy pages.

Where Xai Moua wrote on behalf of Hmong civilians, his fellow *Cob Fab,* and himself, Lee wrote for posterity. He kept his journal, he explained, because he wanted his children to understand something of his life as a soldier. "I was trying to keep those records to show my kids, when my kids grew up, that what I did was good, and to help them understand my past life. And I wanted them to see that when you are young you might be poor, but your life can change in good ways." For Lee, the records of places, dates, and times noted in his journal—the application of his scribal literacy skills—were more than a spare account of his daily experiences. Rather, they represented the outlines of his personal history; they were notes on the lessons of his tumultuous life. As was also true for Xai Moua, the outward forms of Lee's literacy practices appeared the same—lists, dates, accountings—but their meanings had been transformed, as had the rhetorical identities suggested by literacy. No longer simply a military scribe, Lee's writings cast him in the roles of historian, teacher, and father-to-be.

Re-imagining the "Clerkly Skills"

The work of the scribe in L'Armée Clandestine called for the ability to create lists, fill out forms, and write reports, or to practice what Driver (1954, 62, 72, quoted in Goody and Watt 1968) called the mastery of the "clerkly skills." For Vue Lee and Xai Moua, however, the specialized literacy skills they had practiced as military scribes were eventually used in ways that went beyond such "clerkly skills." For Xai Moua, literacy offered a means through which to verify his past and indemnify his future, as well as those of the men under his command. For Vue Lee, writing was a way of explaining his past life and imparting lessons that might be studied in the future. The biographical writings of both writers demonstrate how writing can be used for purposes that may be at odds with the aims of the rhetoric through which it was taught, and how dominant rhetorics of literacy may be appropriated and adapted in even the most challenging circumstances.

Hmong military scribes did not, then, write for the purposes most commonly associated with literacy. They did not write to express their feelings, record their histories, or experience aesthetic pleasure—at least, not in their capacity as scribes. Rather, they wrote to facilitate the efficacious functioning of an expanding bureaucracy. Indeed, the scribes were a product of this bureaucracy, their positions authorized by it. Their literacy practices were neither solely the products of individual cognition nor an expression of Hmong cultural practices. Rather, they were an outcome of contests among global superpowers—contests that embroiled the United States in Southeast Asia, spurred the creation of a covert military force, transformed this force into a modern conventional army, and so created the need for the military scribes to generate their collections of lists, codes, ledgers, and accounts. The military writings of the scribes at Long Cheng, in this reading, can be seen, indirectly and at great remove, to be a result of struggle among Cold War powers competing for preeminence. And literacy development, seen from this perspective, is neither purely cultural, as in many ethnographic accounts, nor an individual act of mind. Rather, it is a product of institutional expressions of and struggles for power, material and symbolic, local and global, that shape the discrete acts of individual readers and writers.

In Christ There is No East or West: The Rhetoric of Missionary Literacy

Way back, only God existed; God, Fua Tai, made all things; last of all, He made man; He made him different from animals; He made man so that he could think, speak, reason, and act with a will; He made man to have fellowship with himself; man disobeyed God; this was the beginning of sin *(tsi);* God is without sin, and has nothing to do with sin; sin brought about physical death; sin caused separation between God and man; God promised man that He would provide a method by which this fellowship would be re-established and the guilt and penalty of sin could be removed from man; God promised to provide a Savior *(tu tvau)....All these things and many more details have been given to man in a book* [emphasis added]; it is in many languages; it is in Lao for you to read if you know Lao; if you believe in Jesus as your Savior from sin and its penalty, you may have your spirits removed, enter into fellowship with God by the Spirit, and be assured of living eternally with Christ.

—Christian message as it was preached over several hours in Hmong villages in Laos (from L. G. Barney, "Christianity: Innovation in Meo Culture")

Chang Lo recalled that he was introduced to Christianity in 1963, when an American Catholic priest came to Lo's village of Na Kuang. Lo was about ten years old at the time and living with his grandparents, who had taken him in after his father had been killed in the war. The priest visited once a month, teaching three nights a week in a schoolhouse that had been built for religious instruction by Hmong Christians living in Na Kuang. Lo recalled that the priest taught from materials that had been printed in the Hmong language—hymnals, prayer books, and Catholic bibles. The first prayer Lo learned to recite, he remembered, was printed in one of these books.

> The fathers had a book that talked about how to pray. So you tried to get an example from that book, and the priest would try to teach you what it said in that book. He would just help you a little bit, working step-by-step with you, you know.... I still remember some of those prayers. That first prayer that the Father taught me, he said it in Hmong, and it was—

> *Ntuj thov koj pab kuv tej dej num niaj hnub kom kuv tau dim ntawm tas puas tsav yam xwm txheej.*

> [Lord, I ask that you help me with everything that I do today; So that I might be free from all my burdens][20]

Christian missionary work in Laos began in the eighteenth century, when American Presbyterian missionaries, riding elephants from Thailand to China, paused long enough in Laos to establish a mission for the minority Khmu people (Smalley, personal interview, June 28, 1997). Missionary contacts with the Hmong were not established until 1925, when a mission operated by the Christian and Missionary Alliance (CAMA) was opened in northern Laos. Operating under the assumption, as Smalley explained, "that people should be reached in their own language" (personal interview, June 28, 1997), the missionaries printed a bible in an old Northern Thai script to distribute among the local population. Few Hmong could read this text, but it nevertheless presaged Christian efforts to proselytize the Hmong in their own language. Shortly after the establishment of the CAMA mission, Catholic priests opened their own mission in the capital city of Vientiane. Neither group was particularly successful in attracting Hmong converts, at least not initially, and with the outbreak World War II the Protestant mission was closed—not to reopen again until after the war (Barney 1957).

In May 1950, a Hmong shaman named Po Si (po she), who had learned of Jesus Christ from a Khmu convert, had a vision and began traveling from village to village with the message that the foreign missionaries spoke for the "true God," the Hmong *Fua Tai* (fua tai). Po Si's message caught on quickly in Hmong villages around Xieng Khouang, the provincial capital, and nearly a thousand Hmong converted in the space of a month. By 1953, some two thousand Hmong and a thousand Khmu people had converted. By 1957, there were approximately five to six thousand Christian converts in ninety-six villages, about 70 percent of whom were Hmong (Tapp 1989, 97). The conversion of the Hmong had begun in earnest and would continue in Laos through the 1970s and in refugee camps in Thailand and the United States after that.[21]

Why did so many Hmong become Christians? The answers are diverse. For G. Linwood Barney (1957), one of the creators of the RPA and a seminal figure in developing "the Meo Church," the Hmong shift from shamanism to the Christian faith was part of a pattern of cultural change in which "the old ways" were being exchanged for new ways of living that included wage labor, increased political awareness, education, and modern medical care. Some of these changes, Barney writes, were conducive to the acceptance of Christian beliefs.

One of these new ways of living was medical care, which had a particularly powerful influence—in effect, healing Hmong bodies while undermining traditional beliefs. The Hmong shaman Lue Vang Pao recalled that it was his introduction to Western medicine that caused him and his family to abandon shamanism and accept Christianity.

> At that time, we were in the war, bullets hit and went through the body
> like this. I did shaman ceremonies to help it but couldn't help it, so I
> took it to the doctors and had an operation. They fixed the stomach and
> intestines. Then I decided to let [my family] learn the new ways. They

learned new ways, then I decided not to practice and leave shamanism. I felt that that shamanism is only for those situations where no one was shot; then you can use shamanism to help. Otherwise, if someone shot you right here in the chest through to the other side or other areas, went right through, then your shaman spirits can't fix it. [The communists] shot and hit my brother-in-law. He was hit with two bullets on this side, right here through to the back of the body. I took him to the doctors to get it fixed and it finally healed. Then I left shamanism. The bells [and other shaman equipment], I left them far away at Ah Zae Doo.

Nicholas Tapp (1989) has offered another perspective, arguing that Hmong conversions to Christianity reflected the historical desire of the Hmong for literacy. Once again, the Christian bible was thought to have been the incarnation of the "lost book," restored by foreign missionaries to the Hmong of Laos, just as it had been restored a century earlier by Samuel Pollard to the Miao in China. In this view, the desire for literacy and the congruence of Christian doctrine with what Tapp calls "ideals of messianic leadership" that had been present in Hmong society at least since the time of the nineteenth-century revolutionary leader Pa Chai led many Hmong to embrace the new faith. From this perspective, Hmong became Christians, at least in part, to reclaim their literate birthright, the book that had been lost, as the stories had it, when it was eaten by horses, or fell into the river, or was eaten by the Hmong themselves, who were starving.

Nor can we overlook the reasons given by Hmong converts themselves, for whom Christianity was a new and radical way of living, one that offered a path to salvation through the teachings of Jesus Christ. In interviews I conducted, Hmong people explaining their conversions to the Christian faith spoke less of cultural changes or literacy, if they mentioned these at all, than they did of the revealed truths of Christ and his teachings. These individuals converted, as had converts around the world before them, because the Christian faith brought new meanings to their lives.

However diverse the array of reasons for Hmong people becoming Christian, there is no disputing the role of literacy in *facilitating* their conversions. Hmong converts were taught to sing from hymnals, read from prayer books, study from mimeographed catechisms. They were offered instruction in their homes, in makeshift classrooms, in churches built by traveling priests. Through these materials, practices, and scenes of literacy, Hmong learners were invited to define themselves as "Christians," learn a new language of sin and salvation, and identify themselves with a foreign religion. Missionary literacy in this sense was an enticement not simply to read and write, to decode and encode graphical forms, but was an inducement to reconstitute one's inner life in the symbols, tropes, and meanings of an alien faith. In this way were the literacy practices of Hmong Christians organized by the *rhetoric of missionary literacy,* which determined what Hmong students read, for what purposes, and toward what meanings. Reading and writing in this rhetoric were learned not for their own sake but to achieve individual redemption and attain a position in a divine hierarchy that transcended secular authorities.

An Alphabet of One's Own: Reading and Writing Practices in the RPA

In the 1950s and 1960s, Western missionaries were often itinerant figures, traveling from village to village, house to house, to preach the Western gospels and teach Hmong converts how to read the bible, prayer books, hymnals, and other religious materials. This meant that classes in the new faith were also classes in elementary literacy instruction, as students learned to read from Hmong-language primers or worksheets. Chang Lo recalled one such class.

> The priest came to see us maybe once a month. And he tried to teach. He had a blackboard to write down everything that you needed to learn in the Hmong language.... And then he taught us how to pray, and maybe one or two songs, and whatever was easy for people to learn and memorize. Most people memorized what they were taught.... And after that we would go home, and he would give us some handouts, some papers mostly in the Hmong language.... He would say what the word was, what the consonant was... or whatever, you know. So he tried to show you that. I remember that it didn't take me long at all to learn Hmong before I knew how to read and how to write that.

Gia Nhia Thao, a forty-three-year-old man, had similar memories.

> Catholic priests came to our town to talk about religion, and they also taught you how to read and write in Hmong. So that was the first time I learned Hmong. I learned from those priests. I was about twelve or thirteen.... Every Sunday the priest came to talk about religion, and then he gave some lessons, I remember, like one hour, to teach the children how to read and write. So after Mass all the old people went home, then the children stayed with the priest and he taught us how to read and write in Hmong.

As these testimonies make clear, missionaries were offering a radically different form of literacy than previously experienced by the Hmong of Laos. While the village schools offered literacy instruction in the swirling characters of the Laotian script, and while the military offered new ways of using this script, Christian missionaries offered something else altogether: literacy in the Hmong language, codified in the RPA. For many Hmong the chance to become literate in their own language was a compelling development, drawing people to the doctrines of the new faith. As Tou Vang Meng recalled it,

> I saw an alphabet book, a Hmong alphabet teaching book, that was created . . . by the fathers from the church. . . . Yes, and we went to church, and they read it, and they had those books. And I saw that those books were interesting, and I thought, you know, oh, this will be helpful. This is my language. This is my alphabet. I should know this. I should learn. Yes, when we became Christians, we first saw that written Hmong book. That's what attracted people, you know.

For the missionaries, Hmong-language literacy offered several distinct advantages in proselytizing the Hmong. For one thing, the Hmong-language alphabet allowed missionaries to print bibles, hymnals, prayer books, and other materials necessary for propagating the new religion. Also, printed materials in the Hmong language expedited the training of Hmong ministers, who could assist the missionaries as they traveled through villages to spread the Word of God. Finally, the RPA made it easier for the missionaries themselves as they endeavored to study and learn the Hmong language. Thus missionary linguists intent on spreading the Christian message appropriated the Hmong language, conceiving of it first, as linguists do, in terms of a system of sound and symbol correspondences that could be fixed on a page, then, as missionaries do, as an instrument for preaching the Word. From the perspective of the missionaries, literacy in the RPA was a practical and perhaps indispensable tool in converting the Hmong.[22]

Instruction in the new script emphasized reading over writing, a practice consistent with missionary literacy campaigns elsewhere. Writing of nineteenth-century missionary activity in Melanesia, for example, Brian Street has argued that missionary teachers wanted to produce readers who would passively consume missionary texts rather than learn to critique and challenge them. Consequently, writing instruction was "severely limited in terms both of the materials the mission was prepared to make available and the uses to which they were prepared to see them put" (Street 1995, 84). Street states that the restrictions placed on writing instruction reflected the understanding that writing involves "a greater degree of authorial control" on the part of the writer and may lead to forms of thought and action counter to those of the official or dominant rhetoric.

For a select number of Hmong, however, writing was vital to their Christian-sponsored literacy experience. Both the Protestant and Catholic missions recruited and trained acolytes who traveled throughout the countryside performing pastoral tasks on behalf of the priests or pastors. Chang Lo, for example, was fourteen years old when he moved to Vientiane to enroll in the French Catholic school and begin his training to become a catechist. While Lo took courses in history, science, and math, the primary focus of each school day was religious studies. Writing, Lo remembered, was central to this religious training.

> Mostly the writing was about religion. When you went to that school, you know, you had to prepare for what you were going to talk about the next day. . . . And when you studied the Bible, there would be a point that you would prepare to talk about the next day. And the priest would sit down and listen to what you were talking about, you know, and whether that was right or wrong. That's what you did a lot. So you did lots of writing, and a lot of studying.

Lo recalled that students worked with the priests to translate Roman Catholic concepts such as "sin," "penance," "redemption," and "everlasting life" into the Hmong language. This required that Hmong trainees and French priests collaborate in exploring the linguistic and philosophical resources of the Hmong language for the purpose of creating a Hmong metalanguage in which the doctrine of a foreign religion might be expressed. One example, Lo recalled, was the Christian concept of "angel." The translation that appeared in the French-published Hmong bible—*dab ntuj* (da ndu)—misleadingly invoked a "bad spirit" or evil person rather than a heavenly body. Lo and other trainees worked to find the Hmong words that would express the Christian concept more accurately.

> So we adapted Hmong words for the Catholic faith. And we did lots and lots and lots of writing, and then lots and lots of discussion about those things. . . . For example, Hmong people say, *"dab ntuj."* And when Hmong people think about *dab ntuj*, they think of something bad. *Dab* means bad people, bad spirits. The Hmong bible that was translated by the French priests talked about *dab ntuj*, but the Catholic priests didn't mean

dab ntuj the same way that Hmong people understand *dab ntuj*. The priests use *dab ntuj* when they wanted to talk about an angel. They said *dab ntuj,* and that was supposed to mean angel. Well, we had to adapt that one, so that it had no bad meanings for Hmong people. Instead, we said *ntuj cov ntshiab* [ndu cho nchia]. That made more sense to people. In the expression *ntuj cov ntshiab, "ntuj"* means the same thing as "heaven" or "God," and *cov ntshiab* refers to someone who is "very good"; it's not a bad meaning like a *dab*. That's an example of what we talked about, you know.

Hmong catechists in training also wrote sermons that they delivered to the priests. Afterward, the priests would comment on and evaluate the sermon. The discussions were linguistic as well as theological, as priests sought to understand Hmong expressions of Christian thought. Lo recalled a conversation he had with a Catholic priest after Lo had given a sermon on the concept of life after death.

Once I gave a talk, a sermon, about when Jesus died, you know, how he died that night then rose up in the morning. And I used lots of Hmong words to describe how Jesus rose up and went to heaven. And that was very interesting to one of the priests. He said, "I really didn't know those words in Hmong before. I learned those Hmong words from you." And the priest wanted to learn those words. The Hmong words were:

Sawv rov los muaj txoj sia nyob mus li

[Rise from the dead to live forever][23]

Students in Lo's catechism classes worked in groups, critiquing each other's writings in much in the same way that a writing group might operate in a typical college composition program in the United States. Lo recalled,

So we did a lot of writing. Sometimes we wrote new things, like a new song for the church. Sometimes we wrote about Hmong culture, about a wedding or a funeral, and what people are supposed to do and what they are not supposed to do. We had an instructor, but sometimes the students disagreed with one another, you know. So we had to have a writing group that worked together during class. And so the group members might say, "Well, why don't you go and you think about what you wrote. It's not right." So you had to write down what you think. Then you had to show it to other students.

Under the careful tutelage of the priests, Lo and other trainees studied the language and rituals of Hmong weddings, funerals, and other cultural events. One reason for this, Lo said, was to develop credibility when visiting Hmong villages. Knowledge of Hmong cultural practices was essential if catechists were to be taken seriously in the villages. There is, of course, an irony in Hmong youths studying their own cultural rituals under the guidance of Western priests, but Catholic missionaries were by and large serious students of Hmong language and culture. The French Catholic missionary Fr. Yves Bertrais, for example, not only helped create the Hmong alphabet, but also conducted numerous studies of Hmong cultural life, publishing a Hmong-French dictionary, several collections of Hmong songbooks, various Hmong-language health manuals, and many other materials (Tapp 2004).

Indeed, Tapp (1989) has argued that one difference between Catholic and Protestant missionaries in Laos was the tolerance of the former toward Hmong cultural practices. Catholic missionaries, according to Tapp, were much more willing to accommodate Hmong traditional practices than their Protestant counterparts. As a result, Catholics were better able to integrate Hmong cultural practices into their missionary teachings. As Chang Lo recalled it,

> The Catholics, we still keep part of the culture that's good. You know, that's why the catechists had to study so hard to understand that. We didn't study only the way of the Bible, you know, but we studied the Hmong way and culture too. You had to understand that there are good things about our culture that are not in the Bible. It's good whether it's the Catholic way or not, you know.... Because if you are a group, an ethnic group, you know, you need to carry on your culture too. It doesn't mean you have to throw everything away.

Yet not all elements of Hmong traditional practice were acceptable in the new doctrine. Hmong students were also taught to discard cultural traditions that were contrary to Catholic teachings, such as the practice of shamanism. In Lo's words,

> But if something was not right, we threw it away. One thing we threw out, for example, was shamanism. Shamans believed that when you had a baby, you had to call spirits in three days, but we don't do that anymore because we don't believe [in] so many spirits. Those kind of things, for example, we threw them away. And the way people believed in magic, we threw that away because we don't believe that people can do such things without God. Many things we threw away, you know.

Bakhtin (1981) wrote that "there are no 'neutral' words and forms—words and forms that can belong to 'no one'; language has been completely taken over, shot through with intentions and accents" (293). In that vein, we may say that the literacy of Hmong Christians was taken over by and shot through with the intentions, accents, and ideologies of Christian missionary rhetoric. Hmong spiritual life was to be remade in this rhetoric, verbally constituted by it, transformed by its intentions and accents. And yet as Chang Lo's experience demonstrates, rhetorics and the identities they construct are always in play, in patterns of movement, in shifting relationships and tensions. As Lo learned to read and write in his own language, his experiences were shaped by the imperatives of missionary rhetoric, which directed the content, purposes, and meanings of his literacy experiences, using these to offer him a new conception of himself and his relationship to God. Yet even as he internalized the Christian message and its tropes of sin, penance, and salvation, he brought Hmong idioms to these tropes, filling them with Hmong meanings and working with his missionary sponsors to create a language that might traverse the borders of two distinctly different rhetorics.

The uses of the RPA, moreover, were not restricted to negotiating the meanings of Christianity in the Hmong context. As Hmong people learned the new writing system, they began using it for their own purposes—composing letters, transcribing traditional songs, and authoring family histories. As compelling as the rhetoric of missionary literacy was for many Hmong, it did not ultimately constrain the uses of RPA, as we shall see.

Songbooks and Letters Home: Appropriations of Hmong Literacy

As knowledge of the RPA spread through Laos and, later, through the refugee camps of Thailand, it resonated in ways that went beyond the Christian message and spoke to deep cultural memories of the Hmong people and their desire for a writing system of their own. Over time, the system was transformed from a vehicle for spreading the Word of God to an emblem of Hmong identity and cultural independence. To put it another way, the letters and phonetic values of the RPA remained unchanged, but the rhetorics animating and giving meaning to these were transformed. Neng Vang, for example, who learned the Hmong alphabet from an older brother, recalled that when as a child he was sent to a school in a village far from home. He and other Hmong boys were lonely, Vang said, and so they wrote down

Hmong songs they could sing together after school. These were written in the Hmong language and collected in a notebook. "We used the Hmong writing when we went to school in Na Tou school district. This district was far away from our parents, and so everyone was really upset with that. We liked to sing Hmong folk songs. So we created a book of Hmong folk songs, we wrote them down in a book, so that we could sing them at that time. Oh, we wrote a lot."

Similarly, Ma Thao learned Hmong writing when she was about twelve years old and a student in the Catholic mission school in Vientiane. Thao used the new writing, she said, for letters to friends and family members but also to compose *kwv txhiaj* (kuh tziah), traditional Hmong folk songs dealing with themes of love and courtship. Thao got the idea of writing down *kwv txhiaj,* she said, from watching French priests who were transcribing and publishing Hmong songs and other cultural materials. Eventually, Thao said, she had compiled an entire book of *kwv txhiaj.*

> We would sing Hmong songs, the *kwv txhiaj* that the Fathers wrote
> down. They were the ones who wrote them. Then I wrote some, too.
> Because if I didn't write it then I wouldn't remember it, so I had to
> write. . . . If I wanted to sing about marriage, then I would write about
> that. And if I wanted to sing about dating, then I would write about that.
> Or I would write about the New Year, things like that. I didn't keep these
> writings, but we did have a book of them.

These testimonies are examples of how the Hmong writing system was used to transcribe existing oral materials, translating older cultural forms into the new medium of written language. However, Hmong people also used the new technology to create new compositions, mainly in the form of letters to friends and family living in distant villages. Neng Vang remembered that letters served both as a means of communication and a way of teaching himself the new writing: "Well, mostly we just used the Hmong alphabet to write letters or something. We did not have any teachers, you know, who gave us homework or taught us how to write. There were no teachers. So I just studied myself and wrote letters. I wrote letters to friends who were in my school, or I wrote letters to my parents, or to friends in my village."

Other Hmong wanted to learn the new system so that they might write letters to their wives or girlfriends. Many thousands of Hmong, Vang Lee Xiong explained, were separated from wives, families, and lovers by the war. Since most Hmong women did not read or write in the Lao language, letters written in Laotian had to be read aloud by a third party, a kind of literacy broker, and possibly translated from Lao to Hmong. This meant that private thoughts and feelings expressed in a letter to a spouse or lover had to be mediated by an outsider and perhaps translated from one language to another. Consequently, both men and women were motivated to learn the new Hmong writing system, which could be learned in nonschool settings and which offered couples the opportunity to communicate in their own language, in their own words, without the intercession of an outside reader. Several Hmong women interviewed for this project spoke of being motivated to learn the RPA after receiving courtship letters that they could not read themselves.

The informal nature of how the RPA was learned is exemplified by Vang Lee Xiong's introduction to the writing system. Xiong had attended a village school as a child, where he learned to read and write Laotian and a smattering of French. As his family was not Christian, he had little in the way of opportunities or motivation to learn the missionary script. He recalled, however, that at the Hmong military base at Long Cheng, where he was stationed as a soldier, a military radio station broadcast a daily mix of international and national news, traditional Hmong music, and propaganda. The station also broadcast brief personal messages written by Hmong soldiers, reading them aloud in the hope that family members would be listening in villages back home.[24] Xiong recalled,

> The announcer would say, "This is from Mr. Vang Lee Xiong. He would like to make this announcement to his parents to tell them that he is doing fine. And probably it will be another six months or another year before he will be able to come home for a visit. But please be informed that Vang Lee is okay. No illnesses." Almost every morning and every evening, they would make announcements like that on the radio.

Messages were typically read in the Hmong language, presumably because parents listening at home might not have understood Laotian, and soldiers were responsible for writing their own announcements. As Xiong could not read and write the RPA, he initially enlisted a female cousin to transcribe his messages. Eventually his cousin grew tired of this duty and prevailed upon Xiong to learn to read and write the RPA. He recounted,

> The first time I asked her to write a letter for me, [my cousin] was willing to help me write it. But the second time I asked her, about three to six months after the first time, she was mixing formula for her baby. So she asked me, "Do you know French?" I said, "Yes." She said, "Can you write in French?" I said, "Yes." She said, "If so, instead of letting me write

the letter for you every single time, let me teach you how to write." So I sat down and I thought, Why doesn't she help me again? But I grabbed a piece of paper and pencil, and...while she was preparing the formula for her child, I told her what I wanted to say in my letter. Then she helped me spell my sentences word by word. I knew some words. I wrote *kuv* [koo], meaning "I," and *koj* [kaw], meaning "you," and *mus* [moo], meaning "go." I wrote all the words I knew and then she helped me write the words I didn't know. Thirty minutes after I finished that letter, I was able to read and write Hmong clearly. Even now I use the method she taught me to teach other people.

Xiong's introduction to literacy in his own language illustrates how reading and writing in the RPA blended elements of interpersonal relationships, technological change, and missionary Christianity, each of which influenced the forms and purposes of literacy practice. Additionally, Xiong's experience illustrates how the RPA stimulated a popular literacy movement that took place outside the mediations of schools and other institutions. Unlike literacy in the Lao language, which was taught in school and used to create a national consciousness, literacy in the RPA was often learned informally, one to one, and was used for expressing the immediate, the personal, and in some cases the intimate.

Reflecting on the use of the RPA by the Hmong in the 1950s and 1960s, William A. Smalley told me that for a writing system to have value, there must be a reading public to support it. This means there must be primers, literacy campaigns, and enough printed materials in the system so that people have enough to read and develop a reading ethos. "We didn't know at that time," Smalley said, "that the Hmong already had a reading ethos, whether they could read or not."

Thai Transitions

Once they had crossed the Mekong River into Thailand, Hmong who fled Laos were incarcerated in one of the so-called "first asylum" camps: compounds located throughout Southeast Asia where refugees of the Vietnam War were confined while their applications for emigration to the West were evaluated. Such camps were hot, crowded, unsanitary, and often dangerous places. They frequently lacked adequate medical services, and refugees were at risk of being victimized, in some sites, by the military authorities supposedly protecting them. However, while refugees in other first asylum camps—the Vietnamese in Pulau Bidong, Malaysia; the Khmer in

Khao-I-Dang, Thailand; the ethnic Lao in Ban Napho, Thailand—were eager to leave the camps and begin their new lives in the West, the Hmong were initially reluctant to emigrate. Some Hmong believed the promises of military leaders such as Gen. Vang Pao that Hmong fighters would someday return to Laos and liberate the nation from the communists. Others were unwilling to leave behind family members, especially elderly parents and grandparents for whom the Thai camps, if not home, were nevertheless more familiar and closer to Laos than the United States (Robinson 1998, 121). Still others were dismayed by reports of America they received from friends and relatives who had emigrated. Letters and audiocassettes spoke of new opportunities but also of poverty, isolation, racism, and even sudden death while sleeping.[25] In the three and a half years following the war, only 5,000 Hmong chose to resettle in the United States, a relatively small number compared to the 6,000 Cambodians, 8,000 Laotians, and 130,000 Vietnamese who emigrated during that period (Hein 1995, 48). Indeed, while other Southeast Asians were being denied admission to countries in the West, only the Hmong were actually refusing the offer to resettle (Long 1993, in Hein 1995, 41–42).[26]

Of the first asylum camps housing Hmong refugees, the largest was Ban Vinai, a dusty, four-hundred-acre space in northern Thailand, which by the 1980s grew into a sealed city holding between 43,000 and 45,000 Hmong refugees (Long 1993). For many Hmong, literacy learning continued at Ban Vinai, where various missionary groups, voluntary agencies, and government authorities jostled to provide a veritable bazaar of services, doctrines, and literacies: Hmong-language literacy in the RPA in classes sponsored by missionary Christians; English-language literacy in classrooms run by voluntary agencies; Hmong-language literacy in the *Phaj Hauj* in classes organized by believers; and Thai-, Chinese-, and even French-language literacy in lessons offered by private teachers. Ndrua Thao, who arrived in Ban Vinai as a child and who would later earn a master's degree in ethnomusicology from a college in the United States, recalled the different languages and literacies he studied at the camp.

> I actually began studying French a little bit, mostly taught by my brother ... [and] I had a few French classes but it wasn't really a thrill for me. At the time I was really big into Chinese. ... It was the language that I picked up the easiest. Mostly I think that the grammatical structure is basically the same as the Hmong, and I can just learn the word, and speak it fluently. ... But then my brother said that I had to learn English because chances were that we might be coming to the United States.

For those who had the means, Ban Vinai featured numerous private schools and tutors. Even for those without financial resources, however, there were avenues for learning to read and write. Kou Lee recalls that he was about ten years old when he learned to read and write Hmong by listening outside the window to lessons being taught in one of these private schools.

> When I was in Laos I never went to school. But when I was in Thailand...I learned to read Hmong. I didn't have a chance to go to school either. They had a Hmong school. But to go there, you had to pay. And I didn't have the money because my mother was in Laos. My older brother was there but we didn't have the money so I just go stayed outside...because in Thailand they cut the window [but] they had no glass to block you—so you can see, you can listen....I stayed outside looking through the window and listening to the teaching. So after school was over I waited outside the school. And some of the students, when they got out, they tore out some of the papers on which they had written on the whole day. Some of them threw the papers away outside the school. I picked them up. I picked up their papers, and I read what they said. I tried to read and put it together. And I kept doing that, and I did learn how to write Hmong and read Hmong. That's how I did it. Just putting things together.

While Ban Vinai became a familiar and in some ways comforting place for many Hmong, it was not a permanent home. Although initially reluctant to emigrate to the West, the majority of Hmong refugees were eventually prompted by political circumstances and their own mounting apprehensions about the future to choose resettlement. For one thing, the dream of returning to Laos seemed more remote with each passing year. Communist governments in Laos and Vietnam were firmly entrenched, and years of sporadic Hmong resistance had produced little effect. Also, Thai authorities had come to regard the refugee populations as an unfair burden upon their nation and so began to make life in the camps as unappealing as possible, a strategy designed both to pressure those living in the camps to leave and to discourage new arrivals. In 1983, Thai officials closed Ban Vinai to new arrivals. Hmong who arrived after this time might be pushed back over the border or placed in austere holding centers with no chance for resettlement, a policy the Thai government called "humane deterrence" (Robinson 1998, 116–120).

More than any set of policies, however, perhaps the keenest incentive for the Hmong to resettle in a third country was the concern parents felt for the future of their children. Education at Ban Vinai was severely pro-scribed, and many parents made the difficult decision to leave Thailand in hopes of providing a better future for their children. Most emigrated to the United States. In 1980, some 27,200 Hmong left Thailand for the United States, a number that exceeded the first five years of Hmong departures combined, and departures continued at a steady pace in the years follow-ing. By 1992, approximately 88,200 Hmong had left the camps for the United States (Hein 1995, 47).

Before a refugee family, whether Hmong, Vietnamese, Cambodian, ethnic Laotian, or others, could be admitted to the United States, they were obliged to spend three to five months studying the English language and American culture at one of three "processing centers" funded by the United States. These were located in Bataan, Philippines; Phanat Nikhom, Thailand; and Galang, Indonesia. Most Hmong went to Phanat Nikhom, although a very small number were sent to the Philippine Refugee Pro-cessing Center. Donald Ranard and Margo Pfleger (1995) have written a retrospective on the language and literacy training in the processing cen-ters, while James W. Tollefson (1989) offered a sharp critique of these same programs, contending that they were aimed at training refugees for subor-dinate economic positions in the United States rather than offering mean-ingful language and literacy instruction.

As I had formerly worked in the Philippine center, which is where I first encountered the Hmong, I was curious to hear how Hmong people remembered their time in the processing centers. Few people interviewed for this project, however, spoke of this time in any detail. Indeed, most seemed to regard this period of their lives as incidental to their experiences in Laos or the United States. Perhaps this was because of the relatively short time refugees spent in Phanat Nikhom or Bataan, or perhaps because life in the centers, for better or worse, was largely free of the transfor-mative events that characterized life in Laos and, later, the United States. Whatever the reasons, the Hmong rarely mentioned their experiences in the processing centers.

Three Rhetorics

Rhetorics, I have argued, invite us to become and to belong. "We are invited by the rhetoric," as Black (1993) expressed it, "not simply to believe some-thing but to *be* something...solicited by the discourse to fulfill its blan-dishments with our very selves" (172). For the Hmong in Laos, three of the most powerful rhetorical invitations, as we have seen, were those of

Lao schooling, military bureaucracy, and missionary Christianity. Each of these offered literacy instruction, but they offered beyond that a distinctive identity and position within a larger institutional framework. Lao schools taught Hmong children to read and write, but also invited them to define themselves as Laotians, members of the "imagined community" of the nation. The Hmong "Secret Army" provided a number of Hmong men with an identity and a place in a larger military hierarchy. And Christian missionaries offered the Hmong the opportunity to read and write in their first language, though largely for the purpose of conforming Hmong spiritual life to an alien faith.

In each case, literacy was offered in the context of a shaping rhetoric that offered a distinct conception of reality. Yet while each of these rhetorics was powerful and pervasive, the testimonies affirm that rhetorical identities are not exclusive of one another. Hmong who became literate as Christians, as soldiers, and as students moved among these identities in negotiating the influences of competing institutions. Beyond this, while each of these rhetorics of literacy sought to shape aspects of language and thought, in each case the Hmong redirected the literate skills learned through participation in these rhetorical worlds to "unauthorized" forms of personal and cultural expression, first in Laos, and later, as we shall see in chapter 5, in the United States.

CHAPTER 5

Writing Hmong Americans

Reading and Writing in the United States

Perhaps as important as any other single factor in the success of the resettlement effort is the fact that Wausau's Hmongs [*sic*] have adopted an optimistic and even eager attitude toward their resettlement. They have not only accepted America as their new home, but have embraced it eagerly....When asked how well he felt the Hmongs have adjusted to their new home, one of the local clergymen...answered simply, "They're American."
—M. Kronenwetter, *Wisconsin Heartland*

In any term we can posit a world.
—K. Burke, *A Grammar of Motives*

Although neither she nor her family were Christians, Zer Lee explained, members of the Baptist congregation in Minnesota that had sponsored the Lee family came twice each week to take the family to church. Lee was twelve years old at the time and did not speak English well enough to understand the services or tell her Baptist sponsors that she felt, in her words, "really bored, without understanding anything."

Nevertheless, the Baptists continued to look after Lee and her family, helping them with shopping, housing, employment, education, and other material needs. Ultimately, as Lee put it, "we felt that these people, they are really loving." The Baptists also continued to take the family to bible classes, eventually finding a Hmong translator who could help teach Lee and other members of her family to read the English-language bibles that the Baptists had provided. In time, Lee began studying the Bible on her own, improving both her reading skills and her understanding of Christian doctrine. And this in turn led to profound transformations of her spiritual life: "And after I was able to read and write, I was able to read the Bible and understand why God created us and things like that. And then I decided that Jesus was my savior and I decided to ask him into my life. And then I became a Christian."

Bible class, of course, was not the only site where Zer Lee was learning to read and write in the United States. She also attended the local public school, where she was one of the few Hmong students enrolled. While her early experiences were difficult—"I was crying because it was so hard," Lee remembered—by the time she reached high school her English had improved to the point where she was reading academic materials, writing research papers, and learning many of the same rhetorical paradigms taught to students in public schools throughout the United States. "They taught you how you write your outline first. And then, they taught you how to jot down all your main ideas. They taught you how to write by placing all your points, all your good points, in your body. Then they taught you how to write the introduction and how to summarize in your last paragraph."

After graduating from high school and completing a year of community college in 1986, Lee married and moved with her husband to join family members in Wisconsin. Now literate in English and Hmong, Lee soon found a job as a social worker with a voluntary agency responsible for assisting Hmong families with resettlement concerns. The agency served as yet another site for Zer Lee's literacy development, as she became proficient in managing the paperwork required of her by the state and federal bureaucracies administering to the refugee population. As a social worker, Lee was expected to write letters to her clients in the Hmong and English languages, to translate agency documents from English to Hmong, and to help Hmong adults with the extensive paperwork that accompanied federal and state financial assistance. She explained,

> In writing letters to my clients, I have to do it in both English and Hmong.
> Usually I send them the Hmong version and then save the English
> version so that my supervisor can read it.... And I have translated
> some of the flyers that we have.... We have flyers that go out to parents,
> telling them about some future workshop or future parenting class that
> our agency will sponsor. The agency will have some handout for the
> workshop; for example, teaching about relationships or communication.
> Then I will translate that flyer into Hmong. And when people are asking
> you to help them to apply for something or complete their blue forms
> for insurance, or help them with a court case...I've been able to help
> people.

Almost as soon as they arrived in the United States, Hmong refugees were inserted into a popular narrative that depicted them as a "stone age" people unfamiliar with such commonplace devices as refrigerators, flush toilets, and electric lights. Entering American churches, schools, and workplaces, the Hmong were said to be encountering a strange new universe of signs, symbols, and graphical representations of spoken language—"strange" and "new" because the Hmong were widely assumed to be "preliterate." Yet as we have seen, some of the Hmong arriving as refugees in the United States already had substantial experience with the forms, purposes, and meanings of literacy they would encounter in their new country. Moreover, the contexts in which Hmong refugees in the United States received literacy instruction—the schools, churches, workplaces, and other sites—were not entirely foreign to the Hmong. Nor was the literacy instruction offered in such contexts nearly as exotic to many Hmong as their American teachers and patrons assumed it to be.

So, for example, just as Western missionaries in Laos used literacy as a tool for attracting Hmong converts, so, too, did evangelicals in the United States use language and literacy instruction to advance what I term the *rhetoric of Christian sponsorship,* in which material and symbolic resources were used in tandem to proselytize new arrivals. And just as village schools in Laos taught Hmong schoolchildren to read and write in ways that encouraged them to think of themselves as "Laotians," so, too, did the *rhetoric of public schooling* in the United States offer Hmong students curricula and materials that encouraged them, as one Hmong man expressed it, to "think American" and identify with the values taught in U.S. schools. Finally, just as Hmong scribes in L'Armée Clandestine were offered literacy in the context of an institutional structure that organized reading and writing practices, so, too, were Hmong in American factories, offices, and other workplaces introduced to new forms and meanings of written language through what I call *the rhetoric of workplace writing.* From this perspective, Hmong refugees to the United States, even those with minimal exposure to literacy, were not entering a strange new universe of signs, symbols, and graphical representations of sound. Rather, they were resuming relationships with rhetorics and literacies not unlike those they had experienced in Laos.

As in Laos, the various forms of rhetorically sponsored literacy in the United States offered the Hmong multiple ways to understand themselves and their places in the world. Whether in bible study groups, ninth grade English classes, or on factory floors, Hmong readers and writers received specialized forms of literacy training that invited them to define themselves in ways consistent with the aims and ideologies of the sponsoring institution. In this way did literacy training in the United States serve as a means, as it had in Laos, of preparing human beings to accept a set of roles and positions that had been created for them by more powerful interests.

While each of these rhetorics of literacy can be seen as an attempt to "write" or inscribe the Hmong in ways that were consonant with the interests of those offering literacy instruction, the effects of these rhetorics were neither ineluctable nor determinative. Wherever there is literacy, there is a struggle for meanings, and this proved as true in the United States as it had in Laos. Hmong learning to read and write as Christians, as students, and as workers continually appropriated and re-imagined the literacy skills they had learned, using these to advance their own notions of identity, position, and conceptions of the world. The identity of "refugee," in other words, was complicated by the patterns of literate symbolic interaction and exchange among institutions and individual Hmong readers and writers.

Before turning to these interactions, however, let us consider the institutional processes that brought the Hmong to the United States as refugees.

Known to Unknown: Hmong Diaspora and Resettlement

The withdrawal of U.S. military forces from Southeast Asia in 1975 resulted in one of the great migrations in human history, as citizens from Vietnam, Cambodia, and Laos began to leave their countries for resettlement in the West. Escaping on boats from Vietnam or walking across borders from Cambodia and Laos into Thailand, well over one million people left their homelands for resettlement in third countries. The majority of these people eventually resettled in the United States. The Southeast Asian Resource Action Center reported that from 1976 to 1998, approximately 1.3 million Southeast Asian refugees arrived in the United States.[1] Of these, a small but significant number were the Hmong of Laos. By 2000, according to the U.S. census, approximately 186,000 Hmong Americans were living in the United States.[2]

Upon arriving in the United States, Hmong families were typically greeted by a "sponsor," a person who had agreed to help the refugees obtain basic needs such as food, housing, employment, and language training. Sponsors were recruited by voluntary agencies that had been contracted by the U.S. government to help resettle Southeast Asian refugees under the provisions of the Refugee Act of 1980. For each refugee, the voluntary agencies, or "volags," received a payment of approximately five hundred dollars from the U.S. government, which was to be used to help refugee families survive their first weeks and months in the United States (Hein 1995, 52). Typically, sponsors were members of religious congregations, social workers, or concerned individuals such as relatives, friends, or former business associates (Robinson 1998, 134; Koltyk 1995, 84). As the flow of refugees increased, the volags were under intense pressure to resettle new arrivals and were in some cases unable to screen sponsorship offers, some of which came from unscrupulous individuals and were "little more than requests for indentured servants, bed mates, or cheap labor" (Kelly 1977, 130, in Robinson 1998, 131).

To avoid burdening any single community with more than its "fair share" of refugees, the Immigration and Naturalization Service adopted a policy of dispersing Southeast Asian refugees throughout the country. Hmong and other Southeast Asian refugees frustrated the strategy, however, by relocating so that they might be closer to family and friends, a phenomenon that became known as "secondary migration." The secondary migrations emphasized the importance of family, kinship, and ethnic ties in refugee cultures, as well as the resourcefulness of refugees who recognized the advantages of collective efforts at establishing social and financial stability. By 2000, the majority of Hmong were clustered in five states: California (71,741), Minnesota (45,443), Wisconsin (36,809), North Carolina (7,982), and Michigan (5,998) (Duffy et al. 2004). In these and other states, Hmong people were introduced to literacy in the contexts of U.S. churches, schools, and workplaces.

Material, Spiritual, Textual: The Rhetorics of Christian Sponsorship

As Hmong refugees began arriving in the United States in the late 1970s and early 1980s, members of Christian congregations were among the first to greet them, waiting for the new arrivals at airports with fruit baskets, children's toys, and boxes of winter coats. For many of the Americans who worked with the Hmong and other Southeast Asian refugees in the first few years of their arrival, there was a palpable sense of excitement at greeting the newcomers and helping them begin to integrate into American society. To quote from one newspaper article reporting on a Laotian family arriving in the Wausau area: "The smiles, the hugs and the hand holding said it all. The language barrier didn't matter, because the message of love came across loud and clear" ("Laotian family greeted with warm welcome," *The Wausau Daily Herald,* n.d.).

The excitement was nurtured by the sense felt among many religious groups that welcoming the Hmong and other refugees was consistent with the edicts of the sponsors' Christian faith. "The Scripture says," noted one Lutheran pastor whose Wausau congregation sponsored a family of Hmong, "to welcome the strangers of the world" ("Sponsors felt moral duty to help refugees," *The Wausau Daily Herald*, n.d.). Many Christian groups interpreted their sponsorship activities in such moral and religious terms.[3]

Hmong adults interviewed for this project often spoke warmly of the religious communities that had sponsored them. Blia Vang, for example, recalled that when her family arrived in the United States, their Christian sponsors immediately helped them locate housing and employment. "We were sponsored by the Lutheran church, and their role was to find us a house before we came. And they helped my older brother locate a job before we came because the manager at the R. Company was also a member at the church. So they found my brother a job, and he started to work after three days in the U.S." Similarly, Bee Lor remembered that when his original sponsor failed to provide assistance to Lor's family, the local church stepped in to help: "Our first sponsor didn't come over and help us much, so the church tried to take over in his place. They brought us some food and after that, we felt, Oh, this is just like our parents were. It's like home."

For some Hmong, the generosity of sponsors was a living example of the Christian teachings they were receiving in the religious classes organized by their sponsors. Zer Lee explained,

> I thought that the church had been doing a lot for us, and we saw that
> these people have Jesus Christ in them because they were so generous.
> They will do anything you ask. They will give you anything you wanted.
> And they always taught us to come to Bible studies, and they invited
> neighbors to come, and we all studied together in how Jesus Christ came
> to save our lives, and things like that.

In addition to material assistance, sponsors provided Hmong refugees with valuable opportunities to hear and speak English. Bee Lor remembered that before he learned to read or write English, he improved his speaking skills by conversing with his sponsors at church services.

> I learned how to speak English because they would speak very slowly
> to me, the church members. They would come over and say, "Hi, how
> are you doing? My name is ..." And they spoke very slowly. I learned
> from them. We went to church every Sunday. Every Sunday and
> sometimes Wednesdays because they had classes and teaching on
> Wednesdays. ... And we would talk with American people ... before and
> after church. And that was helpful for practicing English.

Teng Thao remembered being enrolled by his sponsor in a bible class after he and his family arrived in the United States; these classes enhanced his listening and speaking skills in English. Thao explained, "They put us in the confirmation class, my cousins and me. They put us in the confirmation class, the Bible study class, where you read a couple verses and then you tried to have a discussion about them. So in a way it helped a lot because it forced you to share your ideas."

In some cases, congregational sponsors introduced non-Christian Hmong to church services and teachings. Christopher Xiong's family was not Christian upon arriving in the United States but was nevertheless placed in religious classes within weeks of their arrival. Xiong recalled,

> When we were sponsored by the church, without question, they just
> took us to church on Sunday. They just called and said, "Get ready, we'll
> pick you up by 9:00. We'll go to church." So we said, "Okay." And then
> we just did that. And they said, "Okay, well let's put you into confirma-
> tion class." And we said, "Okay." And they just took us to church, to
> Sunday school, and classes for learning the Bible.

Students receiving instruction in religious literacy from their American sponsors were generally taught reading rather than writing skills, as was true of Christian instruction in Laos. Chia Vue, for example, recalled her American sponsor sitting beside her in the pews of the local church and teaching her to read the words of a Lutheran hymn.

> We went to church...I would say every Sunday, since we lived next door
> to the church. We had a Bible, and we went to Sunday school. We sang. I
> don't know how well I read then, but I remember holding a Bible during
> the discussion session. I remember holding the songbook, but I don't
> know how well I read. The songbook was in English. It was from the
> Lutheran Church....The tutor, she would normally sit next to me, side
> by side, and we would read together. I'd do most of the reading and then
> she would do the corrections.

Lee Xiong Lo remembers that the first summer after he arrived in the United States, before he could speak or write in English, his sponsors enrolled him in a Christian summer camp where the primary focus was on bible reading and interpretation. Lo recalled the difficulty he experienced in such classes.

> With my very limited English skills, I could not understand the Bible
> very well and reading the text in the Bible was very difficult for me. It

was a very difficult language and even today, you know, it still is for me. After reading a text, or a page, or a paragraph in the Bible, I couldn't quite understand what the meaning was or what they were trying to express in the Bible. So it was sort of like going along, you know. Acting and going along with the group.

Once students had learned enough English, spoken and written, they were ready to begin the explicit study of Christian doctrine, learning the language, beliefs, values, and teachings of the Christian faith. Bee Lor spoke of the bible classes he took as his English steadily improved. "And they taught us about God, about why he became human, all this. And they also taught you how to become a good person, to believe in God, and how do you believe, and why should you believe."

Such testimonies suggest that the Hmong experience of congregational sponsorship was a complex mixture of the material and spiritual, the pragmatic and the prayerful, the interested and the selfless. Hmong families sponsored by Christian organizations were given assistance finding apartments, employment, education, and other necessities. More, they were welcomed into communities of faith, tolerance, and advocacy. Yet the testimonies also indicate, as we have seen above, that in some instances Christian congregations displayed little regard for the traditions brought by the Hmong from Laos, choosing instead to press religious beliefs upon refugee families and to link material assistance to spiritual conversion.

The testimonies also make clear the importance of Christian sponsorship to Hmong literacy development in the United States. Christian congregations provided Hmong refugees with materials, forms, and opportunities for literacy practice, which were for many Hmong vital in learning to read and write in English. But it is equally apparent that literacy in the Christian context represented more than learning to make sense of graphical marks upon a page. In the rhetoric of Christian sponsorship, literacy practice was a solicitation, an invitation to Hmong readers to identify with Christian values and embrace the rites and rituals observed by the congregations that had welcomed the refugees. So when Chia Vue sat beside her tutor turning the pages of an English-language hymnal, she was not simply learning to decode a collection of decontextualized marks upon a page. Rather, she was participating in relationships of faith, power, and hierarchy.

Chia Vue and other Hmong Christians in the United States did not necessarily renounce their traditional beliefs. Many Southeast Asians who converted to Christianity were comfortable moving between belief systems, bringing two traditions together in synthesis. Nor did it mean that the literacy skills that Chia Vue learned in the pews could not be transported to other settings and assigned other meanings, as we have seen in the preceding chapters. We may say, however, that in sitting beside her tutor and reading the words from the Christian hymnal, Chia Vue was learning a new language through which she might make sense of herself, her culture, and her relationship to a particular version of God. English language literacy was a critical instrument for communicating these relationships and for teaching Hmong readers and writers, as Bee Her put it, "about God, about why he became human, all this."

Yet the contribution of Christian sponsors to the literacy development of the Hmong was not limited to English-language literacy. As was true in Laos, Christianity also played an important role in promoting literacy development in the Hmong language, a literacy that expressed a different set of identities and ways of defining one's place in the world.

Rhetorics of Transformation: Literacy in the Hmong-Language Church

Even as members of Christian congregations were welcoming Hmong refugees into U.S. churches—transporting them to services, enrolling them in bible classes, sitting beside them in pews—Hmong Christians in Wausau were beginning to establish their own religious communities, either within the framework of English-speaking churches or by forming separate congregations. Hmong Methodists, for example, stayed within the existing Methodist church but hired a Hmong pastor. Similarly, Hmong Catholics in Wausau remained under the authority of the local diocese but celebrated Hmong-language masses in one of the local churches. Still other Hmong Christians organized their own churches. Hmong belonging to the Christian and Missionary Alliance, for example, raised funds to build a church on the outskirts of Wausau where parishioners could worship in the Hmong language and teach the RPA, the Hmong writing system, to their children. As a result of these and similar initiatives elsewhere in the city, the Hmong Christian community in Wausau continued to grow.[4]

Hmong-based religious communities offered Hmong Christians the opportunity to express a degree of cultural solidarity that was perhaps not possible in the English language. They also offered ample opportunities for literacy teaching and practice in the RPA. Hmong pastors, for example, composed sermons in the Hmong alphabet, while lay churchgoers published newsletters, kept membership rolls, maintained financial records, communicated with other congregations, and translated "the words of [the] English bible" as Bee Moua put it, into Hmong written language.

Indeed, Hmong churches became an important venue for teaching the RPA, as literacy classes were organized for children and adults. For many Hmong, especially the young, Hmong Christian churches in the United States served as their introduction to the literacy in their first language.

For example, Joua Hang, who later became a public school teacher, recalled that the first Hmong word she learned to read was *Yesu* (yay-zu), or "Jesus." Hang could read and write English, she explained, but had never studied the written form of the Hmong language. She remembers learning Hmong words by reading along with her mother in a Hmong-language hymnal during services at her local Baptist church.

> I remember when my mother read from her hymnal, I could pick it up. I noticed the consonants, because they were written in the Roman type of alphabet. So I'd try to read along, although I wasn't very skillful at it. But I tried, you know, and the one word I always recognized is in the Hmong language was *Yesu*, because that was "Jesus." And so here's my mother reading, and I would say, *"Yesu,"* and my mom would say, "Yeah." And she would read on, and every time I saw that word, I would say, *"Yesu."* So I was very proud to be able to know that word.

May Yang similarly recalled that she first saw the RPA in a hymnal at her local church. Gradually Yang came to make the connection between the words in the songs she sang and the shapes printed in the pages. "I really learned how to read and write Hmong by singing. Singing Hmong in church, seeing the words written down, that got me excited. And then I wanted to learn how to read it."

For Kou Lee, exposure to Hmong literacy also began with hymns, this time at a Catholic church in the Midwest. But for Lee, proficiency in the RPA really developed when she began attending a class taught by one of the Hmong Catholic parishioners.

> My earliest memory of reading Hmong is reading the passages that were in the hymnbook at the Catholic church. And afterwards someone in the church offered some Hmong classes at his home. So a couple of us, maybe eight of us or so, including my sister, we went to these classes. We would take the classes after school, maybe for an hour or two. We'd start out with the basics. I remember him teaching us the sound of each letter.

Teaching methods and curricula varied, as teachers combined lessons in Hmong phonics, scripture readings, and the singing of hymns. While some classes made the bible central to literacy instruction, others eschewed religious content altogether, preferring to concentrate on teaching sound-symbol correspondences. In classes at one Methodist church, for example, the focus was on phonics, with little if any overt religious content. Christopher Xiong explained, "We have Sunday schools for teaching the Hmong language.... Kids memorize the consonants and memorize the tones, how you put the consonants and tones together to make words. And the teachers read stories to the kids. Or sometimes they have the kids read stories, or read short sentences or words, things like that. The stories were not religious; they were just for teaching." In the minister Pao Lee's classroom in the Hmong Missionary Alliance Church, in contrast, the emphasis was on reading and understanding scripture. "I wrote stories that would help explain the Bible, things like that. These were in Hmong. I wrote in Hmong. Each Sunday I would write a lesson or a story and then talk to the children about the story."

Whether oriented toward religious instruction or not, one of the salient differences in the literacy practices of the English- and Hmong-language churches was the opportunity the latter offered to practice writing in addition to reading. While English-language congregations in the United States focused their educational efforts largely on the reading of bible passages, prayer books, and other religious materials, Hmong-language congregations provided pastors and laypersons with ample opportunities to author their own texts, thus extending the possibilities and potentials of their literacy practices. For Pastor Lor Tong Cha, who drafted all of his sermons in the RPA before delivering them, writing was part of the process through which he interpreted the meaning of the biblical teachings he shared with his parishioners. "First, I have to read from the Bible, then I will write according to the passages of the Bible for that period in the calendar. So I read first, then interpret the main ideas of the reading, then write. After I write it, then I type it and take it to the church."

The management of church affairs also called for a good deal of writing, most of it administrative or financial. Vang Lee Xiong recalled that his position as the secretary for his congregation required various forms of writing and record keeping.

> When I came to Wausau I became involved with the...church. I served on the board of directors, acted as secretary, and this year I'm the editor of the church newsletter and the financial auditor. I was the church secretary for four years. Mostly I jotted down notes on church discussions, what people were talking about at meetings, and what solutions were proposed. I would present these minutes to the board of directors

and the different committees, for example the men's committee, the women's committee, the youth committee.

Teng Thao had similar duties as an officer with the Methodist church. Thao explained that communication with other members of the congregation required that he use his Hmong-language literacy skills. "I would write a monthly financial report to the congregation. I wrote in Hmong because the majority of adult churchgoers in our church do not read English very well. So it's better for communication purposes to write in Hmong instead of English."

Church newsletters were still another venue in which to write. Typically, newsletters produced in local Hmong churches were a mixture of religious teachings and information, perhaps combining stories from scripture with information about schedules, fund-raising, and news from other Hmong parishes across the country. Hmong parishioners could contribute to these newsletters if they wished, contributing letters or religiously oriented stories. Joua Hang remembered that her father wrote bible stories that were published in his church newsletter. "He was kind of like the elder for the church, so that's where he did most of his writing.... He did a lot of reading the Bible passages, and then would make up his own examples illustrating the scripture. So he would write those."

Hmong churches affiliated with national organizations might also receive newsletters and magazines published by their parent organizations. These publications would circulate among the Hmong parishioners, giving them additional texts to read in the Hmong language, and more opportunities to develop their Hmong-language literacy skills. And while such newsletters fostered reading over writing skills, they did provide opportunities for at least some readers to publish their writing in national or even international forums. For example, the French-trained catechist Chang Lo wrote in response to a letter published in an international Catholic publication on the role of the shaman in the Hmong Catholic church.

A couple of years ago, there was a guy who wrote that Hmong Catholics were going against the teachings of Catholicism because they still practiced shamanism. He asked why, if you are a Catholic, do you still call the shaman to your house, and call the spirits, and do those kind of things? He said it's not right. So I tried to answer that. I wrote to say, "No, Hmong Catholics do not do that. You may know someone who does, but that person is probably not a strong Catholic. And that person may do those things, but I don't think most Catholics are going to do that."

These accounts reveal something of the nature of the Christian contribution to Hmong-language literacy. Hmong churches provided a site and a rationale for learning the written language, and they supplied many of the material necessities for the teaching of Hmong literacy: teachers, books, and classroom space. More, individual pastors organized Hmong-language literacy classes, encouraged parishioners to enroll their children, and often served as teachers. At stake in learning the new language was something beyond literacy, and perhaps even something beyond Christianity. For some, the RPA served as an emblem of ethnic identity. Not to learn the language was to lose something intrinsic to being a Hmong person, some conception of self and the world that, for older Hmong at least, could not be expressed in English. For Teng Thao, who taught himself to read and write in the RPA, Hmong-language literacy was essential to preserving his understanding of the language and, beyond that, his sense of being a whole person: "As I got older I realized how important the Hmong language is. And, I said, well, is there anything I can do about the Hmong language? And if I don't learn how to read it or write it, this part of me will always be gone."

For Christopher Xiong, Hmong literacy was also part of a larger project of preserving cultural memory and identity. "I think that if you don't have the written language, eventually you'll lose the language as a whole and you'll lose the culture right along with it. The written language is what's going to keep people from not losing the culture.... We may lose something and eventually we may lose everything, but I think maintaining the reading and writing is very important for maintaining the culture."

Once the RPA was learned by significant numbers of American Hmong, it was applied to a variety of purposes that had little or nothing to do with Christian teachings. Hmong readers and writers variously used their native language literacy skills to write memoirs, sell real estate, promote political candidates, and compose poetry. In Wausau, the printed Hmong language could be found in citizenship and health primers published by local agencies, in signage hung in Hmong food markets, and in advertisements published in Hmong publications, such as these that appeared in the newsletter published by the local Hmong Association.

M & I TSEV CIA NYIAJ MUAJ PEEV
XWM PAB TAU KOJ HUAJ VAN THIAB

[M & I BANKING OPTIONS CAN HELP YOU SUCCEED]

Tsoom Phooj Ywg Hmov Tshua:
Nej puas txhawj txog tus nqe thiab qhov zoo/phem ntawm lub tsheb uas

nej yuav npaj siab yuav? Rosemurgy Toyota to taub nej kev txhawj xeeb
thiab mob siab pab cuam cov neeg tuaj yuav tsheb ntawm nws.

[Dear Friends:
Are you concerned about the quality and the price of the car you are
going to purchase? Rosemurgy Toyota shares your concern and cares a
lot about its customers.]

TUB ROG
KOJ XAV UA YAM TWG LOS
KOJ YEEJ UA TAU XWB

[ARMY. BE ALL THAT YOU CAN BE.]

The experience of Hmong-language literacy in the United States demonstrates how an alphabet originally designed to encourage a particular
identity can become a means through which readers and writers may invent
multiple identities and assert their own places and ways of living in the
world. Hmong-language literacy practices in the United States encouraged
Hmong Christians to deepen their faith, participate in church-based communities, and pass along religious tradtitions to their children. But the transformations of the alphabet meant that it also became, for many Hmong—and
in some cases for non-Hmong—an instrument for remembering, entertain-
ing, politicking, selling, and recruiting. The alphabetic characters of the RPA
retained their basic sound-symbol correspondences, but the meanings to
which these correspondences were applied had been opened for re-inter-
pretation, transformation, and re-imagination by readers and writers. Literacy, the Hmong experiences and testimonies suggest, is mechanical, an
exercise in coding and encoding. Meanings, in contrast, are rhetorical.

"The New Mentality": Rhetorics of
the Public School, 1975–1985

If the literacy offered in Protestant and Catholic churches sponsoring Hmong
refugees in the United States was meant primarily to offer a Christian identity and a conception of the world, then literacy instruction in U.S. public
schools was meant to suggest, to a far greater number of Hmong and in a
far more systematic fashion, a way of understanding themselves and their
place within a larger social hierarchy. In the public schools, Hmong students learned to read and write in ways that taught them to think of themselves as "Americans" and identify with the beliefs, values, and practices

of the dominant majority culture. This meant that Hmong students learning to read and write in U.S. schools in the late 1970s through the middle 1980s were taught more than decoding skills, thesis statements, outlining models, and grammatical accuracy. They were also taught what one Hmong man called "the new mentality," or the ways of thinking, speaking, writing, and acting practiced by members of the majority culture. Moreover, since few, if any, public schools made an effort to integrate the "old mentality" with the new, literacy training in U.S. schools also had the practical effect of diminishing Hmong-language practices of the home and supplanting these with the "ways with words" privileged in school.

Such experiences were not unique to the Hmong, of course. Previous generations of immigrants and refugees had also seen their languages and cultures subjected to the thresher of American schools, which have historically functioned, as Sucheng Chan (1994) has written, as "major agents of assimilation and builders of national unity" (56). Educational "reformers" of the late eighteenth and early nineteenth centuries grasped the potential of schooling and literacy as a means for maintaining social control. In their view, education was a means through which to instill discipline and prepare the working class, including immigrant populations, for their places in an increasingly urban, industrial society. Literacy and education were offered not for their own sake, as a means for promoting intellectual and personal growth, but were intended to instill secular moral values and faith in commercial and industrial capitalism (Graff 1995). In this way might education, wrote a nineteenth-century New York City school principal, "solve every problem of our national life, even that of assimilating our foreign element" (in Higham 1973, 235).

The literacy training of the Hmong in the United States of the late twentieth century in some ways reflected these earlier values. Education and literacy training in public schools served to introduce Hmong students to the values of the majority culture, preparing them, in essence, to "think American" by adopting the discursive practices of the majority culture. However, this was not the only purpose or effect of schooling. Hmong students in U.S. schools were also introduced to academic resources and skills that enabled them to study, read, and write in ways that had never before been available to the majority of Hmong. While many Hmong students, as we shall see, felt pressured to learn "the new mentality," others spoke of being encouraged by their teachers to write research papers, short stories, and newspaper editorials that explored dimensions of Hmong history, language, and culture. The experience of schooling, then, was not monolithic but offered multiple forms of literacy practice and expression, multiple identities and conceptions of the world.

Nightmares and Shining Lights: The Social Contexts of Schooling

For many of the Hmong interviewed for this book, memories of learning to read and write in U.S. public schools involved not only books, teachers, and computers, but also memories of loneliness, racism, and physical abuse. While Hmong refugees sponsored by Christian churches were typically greeted with warmth and friendship, conditions that supported both the teaching of literacy and the dissemination of the Christian message, many Hmong recalled their public school classrooms as confusing, even hostile, places for students who did not speak English proficiently and had little experience of the majority culture. For these students, school could be a "nightmare"—a word used in several testimonies—as stories of becoming literate in America became enmeshed with narratives of isolation and harassment. May Yang, now a social worker and mother, recalled her first days as a kindergarten student in Minnesota in the late 1980s.

> I was very scared. All the kids, it's like they have their eyes on you. You know, it seemed like they had never seen someone like you before.
> At that time the population of Hmong was very small when I came to kindergarten.... And so I guess there was a lot of prejudice and racism going on, and they didn't accept who you were. Like, if you had a hot lunch, they took all your food away, and you didn't have anything to eat. And I got scared, and so every time we'd come back to the classroom, I was always crying and I hid under the teacher's table. And I didn't want anybody—I thought they were going to beat me up, or hit me, or something.

Yia Yang, today a government worker and mother of three, recalled similar emotions. She spoke of attending middle school as a student in Minnesota in the late 1970s. "I was very afraid. I didn't want to go to school. I thought I was the stupidest one in the class, and I felt embarrassed. But there was nothing I could do. I had to go to school. I cried all the way through it. It was very hard, just like a nightmare.... The other kids treated you badly. They came near you and—oh yeah—it seemed like you were junk, or garbage. I didn't go near them."

While some Hmong spoke of emotional stress, others remembered enduring physical abuse in school. Song Thao, now a public health worker, recalled her first months in a Minnesota elementary school in the 1980s. "It was a nightmare. I hid because the kids were so mean. They would pull on my hair. My hair was long and they would come and pull on it. I thought they were so mean, so when I was in a class, I would hide from them because I was afraid of them."

For some, such encounters distanced them from the majority culture, resulting in a sense of difference and alienation. Lee Xiong Lo explained how it was for him: "I felt lonely, isolated, uncomfortable. Yes, in school I felt that way. You know, whether I'm going to the classroom, or lining up for lunch, or working out in the gym, I guess I always felt like I'm different than the other people. And maybe that set me apart, you know that made me feel like I'm different."

Not all Hmong accepted such treatment. Some resisted, fighting back and using the bullying they experienced as a motivation to excel in school. Joua Hang, at the time a teenage mother, remembered that the taunting she encountered in school shocked her but also strengthened her. She recalled an incident in high school that marked what she called a "turning point" in her life.

> And then these boys pushed me. Here I am, a ninth grader, a mother of a two-year-old son, feeling really strong about myself, having the biggest pride about what I've accomplished in my lifetime. You know, throughout school I've always been a straight-A student and...I've tried to be a leader for other Hmong students...to be role model for them. Well, these two students come up and pushed me. And I was just totally freaked out. I didn't know what to do. I was like, "Oh! Two boys are pushing me!" So what could I do? What could I do? I turned back around, and they were walking away. So I ran after them, and I gave both of them the biggest push of my life, and they fell to the ground. And I ran. I ran away.

Not all testimonies recalled emotional or physical abuse. Other Hmong remembered teachers who supported and encouraged them, playing a vital role in helping the students adjust to their new lives in the United States. The testimonies are populated with recollections of educators who tutored after school, visited students' homes, studied the Hmong language, and generally encouraged students to believe they could succeed in American society. Song Thao, for instance, remembered, "Mrs. S. was my history teacher. She introduced me to history. And when I think about how far I have gotten to this day, I think about her. She encouraged me to reach beyond my reach, to go after what I knew. She was the one that shone the light for me in the dark."

Social contexts of schooling, of course, determine to a great extent whether students feel welcome and accepted in school surroundings.

Beyond this, however, the treatment of a racial or ethnic minority may play a role in the academic success or failure of students from that group. John Ogbu (1983) argued that the success or failure of minority students in U.S. schools ultimately has less to do with students' linguistic or cultural backgrounds than with the social and economic histories of the cultures to which the students belong. The disproportionately high failure rate of students belonging to what Ogbu called "subordinate cultures," by which he meant African Americans, Chicanos, and Native Americans, is explained not by differences in communication patterns or learning styles, but by the "historical and structural context" in U.S. society that has marginalized certain minority peoples and denied them meaningful economic opportunities. While the privileged classes in U.S. society have learned to use literacy as a means to economic mobility, those Ogbu called "subordinate" groups have come to see that literacy does not necessarily lead to economic gains and may therefore be suspicious of the claims of schools and educators. The meaning and potential of written language for a particular culture, in other words, are part of the broader social ecology.

As newcomers to the United States, the Hmong did not share the legacies of violence and attempted identity eradication suffered by some minority peoples in the United States. However, as nonwhite, non-English speaking Asian people, the Hmong were subjected to the anti-immigrant, anti-Asian sentiment directed at previous Asian immigrants, including Chinese, Japanese, and Filipinos (Chan 1991; Takaki 1989, 1993). Nineteenth-century Chinese migrants, for example, were viewed as threats to "white racial purity." They were the target of anti-miscegenation laws and excluded from public schools (Takaki 1989, 99–112). Chinese, Japanese, and Filipino immigrants were brought to Hawai'i in the nineteenth century to harvest the sugarcane fields and were subjected to degrading living conditions and other forms of exploitation (Takaki 1993, 246–276). Nor are such attitudes entirely consigned to the past. Violence against Asian Americans has persisted in the United States to the extent that the U.S. Civil Rights Commission issued a report in 1986, when Southeast Asian refugees were arriving in large numbers, concluding "that the issue of violence against Asian Americans is national in scope" (in Chan 1991, 175).

So while the Hmong themselves have endured no legacy of discrimination in the United States, they occupy an ethnic and economic position—Asian American immigrants—that has been historically subjected to economic discrimination, racism, and violence. The harassment of Hmong students in U.S. classrooms, the slights in the lunchroom, the shoves in the schoolyard may be seen as efforts to connect the Hmong to that historical legacy of discrimination and abuse, to position the Hmong within it. The resistance of Hmong to those efforts may be interpreted as an effort to create an alternative legacy, a counter-narrative, in which Hmong people have adjusted to their new environment, are successful in school, and have become economically independent.[5]

We cannot, however, understand the Hmong experience of public schooling by looking only through the lens of social context. To better understand how Hmong students were taught to read and write in U.S. public schools and the identities and positions these teachings offered, we must look also to the interactions of students and teachers in the classroom, to the acts of teaching and learning that defined Hmong literacy education in U.S. classrooms.

"Dreaming American": Learning to Write in Public School

The classroom experiences of Hmong students in U.S. public schools were by no means uniform. The literacy instruction that students received varied significantly, depending on students' ages, their prior experiences of English, the availability of English as a second language (ESL) instruction, the presence or absence of Hmong-language aides in the classroom, and the experience of the school district with nonnative speakers of English generally and Hmong learners specifically. Yet the testimonies collected here do suggest, in general, that the literacy instruction of Hmong students in U.S. schools stressed conventions before communication, grammar before content, and form before meaning. In this respect, their education was consistent with the majority of their white American peers. However, the testimonies also suggest that the further Hmong students advanced in school, the greater the pressure they felt to adapt themselves to what one Hmong man called "the new mentality," or the identification with American values.

In the early stages of their education, however, Hmong students were focused by their teachers on the mechanics and conventions of school writing. When Yia Yang arrived in the United States, for example, she had little experience of written English beyond having learned to write her name. She remembered that her schooling in English began in her ninth grade classroom, where she was taught to copy and memorize lists of spelling words. She described the process as follows.

> We did a lot of spelling. For example, the teacher would teach us five
> words in class—words like desk, chair, apple, orange, things like that.

And then we would study those at night and spell them in the classroom the next day. So I would practice spelling. I would write orange, orange, orange, orange, orange. First, I would copy the word, then cover it up, then try to spell it myself. . . . First we'd have five words, then we had eight, then we had ten, and so on.

Eventually, Yang recalled, she was taught to write narratives that stressed simple grammatical patterns. "We started writing short stories. For example, Why do you like Minnesota? And I would say I liked Minnesota because my family lived there, or because I liked the snow, or because a lot of Hmong lived there, something like that. . . . Sometimes, the teacher would tell us, 'I want a story written in the future tense.' So we would write those, too."

As students progressed in English, they were taught the formal conventions of academic literacy, learning such skills as outlining, paragraphing, and summarizing. Zer Lee recalled the writing instruction she received in her high school ESL class.

They taught you how you write your outline first. And then, they taught you how to jot down all your main ideas. They taught you how to write by placing all your points, all your good points, in your body. Then they taught you how to write the introduction and how to summarize in your last paragraph.

They taught you to try and stick with three paragraphs if you're writing a letter. And if you're going to write a term paper, you have to write your outline first. And if you start with your outline, then you should know how each point is going to fit into your body, which one's going to go into the introduction, or the summary, and things like that.

Christopher Xiong recalled that in his high school English classes he learned the conventions for writing and formatting a research paper. "Yes, the teacher taught us how to do the bibliography, you know, how you develop and find your source, how you do the bibliography, or the crib note, how you quote something in your paper, and a few things like that. They taught you how you write a story: you have the introduction, the body, and the conclusions, and those things."

These testimonies recall elements of what is known as "current-traditional" rhetoric, the system of beliefs about language that has until recently dominated writing instruction in the United States. In this approach, as James Berlin (1984) has written, students were taught to "select the subject, narrow it to a thesis, make an outline of the essay, and edit it for correctness" (74). Current-traditional rhetoric emphasized the written product over the writing process, the analysis of words and paragraph patterns rather than complete discourses, and the avoidance of error over virtually all else in the production of written language. All of this, according to Berlin (1984, 1987), was for decades characteristic of the writing instruction offered to U.S. students in public schools, and it was consistent with the Hmong experience of writing instruction as it was recalled in the testimonies.

As the complexity of school writing assignments increased, however, so did the pressure upon Hmong students to identify with the existing social order. Yang Thao remembered that learning to read and write in school called for more than the knowledge of sounds, symbols, and letter combinations. Beyond these, literacy in his high school ESL class involved a shift toward what Thao called "the new mentality."

> [I took] an introductory writing class, where you were writing a lot, and you wrote in your journal a lot, and the teacher would read a story from a literature book, things like that. In that class, I guess I was still thinking in Hmong most of the time... but I started to feel like I was switching from my mentality at the time, and trying to adjust to the new mentality, the new thinking, the new way of reading and understanding the new language.

The movement from the "old" to the "new" mentality was not without its costs. Historically, immigrants and refugees in the United States have found that learning to speak, read, and write English does not mean adding a language so much as exchanging one for another (Takaki 1993). For some Hmong students, this meant crossing a bridge that seemingly disappeared behind them. For Thao Lue, the shift from Hmong to English—from the "old" to the "new" mentalities—introduced difficulties that he had yet to sort out as an adult. He said,

> My teacher in the writing class, he taught me one thing. He said, "Lue, you must start thinking like an American before you understand my class." And then he asked, "Have you ever dreamed an American dream?" And I said, "No, I still dream in Hmong. I still keep dreaming Hmong dreams." So he said, "You must change that. If you don't change that, you're going to have a difficult time learning the English language. Think American," he said.
>
> Up to now, every day, I've never forgotten the idea that I should think American. Right now, this is the one thing that I remember the

best in terms of my whole lifetime of school up to now in the U.S. Think American. I still remember it's still fresh in my mind. And, I still don't know how to think American, and I'm still kind of struggling even now.

Yet there were teachers and students for whom the "new mentality" did not mean excluding the old. Joua Hang, for example, said that as a fifth-grader she was encouraged by her teachers to enter an essay-writing contest sponsored by a local chapter of the Daughters of the American Revolution. The contest called for essays on the meaning of being an American, and Hang chose to examine this topic through the perspective of her own family's history.

> I wrote about my father's ancestry, where we came from, dating it all the way back to our ancestors who came from China. . . . I interviewed my father. He was very strong about preserving our history, where we came from. As much as he tried to Americanize us, he always tried to make sure that we knew our roots. . . . He told me everything that he never had a chance to tell my brothers and sisters, my siblings.

Bee Lor remembered writing a paper for his high school history class that explored the experience of the Hmong in China and Laos. Like Joua Hang, Lor interviewed a Hmong elder to learn what could not be found in his textbooks.

> I wrote a paper about Hmong history, from China to United States. I interviewed an elder who was born in China. I asked him where he was from in China, and how he dealt with the war in Laos before he got to the United States. He explained a lot. He explained exactly what is a Blue Hmong, what's a White Hmong, and what the differences were. Why [did some become] Blue Hmong? Why [did some become] White Hmong? And he explained about the struggle when moving from China to Laos. And why General Vang Pao became a general. And why we had to lose our country to come here. He knew so much.

Hmong students who went on to college had additional opportunities to examine aspects of their history and culture. Ndrua Thao, the young man who studied French and Chinese in Ban Vinai, earned a master's degree by writing a thesis on Hmong ethnomusicology, tracing the history and characteristics of the Hmong *qeej* (keng), a musical instrument central to Hmong cultural events. Thao's project involved interviewing elders from the Hmong community and reproducing their knowledge in written form.

"I got interested into the study of ethnic music. Specifically Hmong music, and more specifically the *qeej*....I basically interviewed the elders, [in particular] my father....I asked him why the *qeej* had come to exist in the Hmong culture. When? What for? And how did it get constructed? And what had changed since then?" Thao would later design a Web site on which he would post his papers, poetry, and religious writings.

In sum, for Joua Hang, learning to write in English meant addressing the topics of nationhood and patriotism through the memories of her Chinese ancestors. For Bee Her, learning to write involved moving between the language and his tenth grade history class and the language of a Hmong elder recalling life in China and Laos. Ndrua Thao's college writing offered him the opportunity to contribute to the academic literature on Western music by writing down his father's stories of the Hmong *qeej* and posting these on his Web site. The different rhetorics of American schooling, then, were "populated," in Bakhtin's (1981) apt phrase, "with the intentions of others." In these examples, Hmong learners populated the language and literacy of the majority with their own intentions, using their newly acquired literacy skills to examine aspects of Hmong history and culture.

Franklin Ng (1993) has argued that the writing of Hmong students in school, specifically the writing of students studying Hmong history in U.S. colleges, represents a "first generation Hmong history in written form" (63). Hmong student writers, Ng argues, are using the writing and analytical skills they have learned to amplify, dispute, clarify, or correct published accounts of Hmong history and culture, most of these offered by Western scholars. While the three accounts we have heard above diverge in terms of age, educational level, and topic, they share certain commonalties that may speak to the "first generation Hmong history in written form." For one thing, they are written about topics that have been largely ignored by U.S. school curricula and thus reflect the writers' perceptions of what counts as significant historical knowledge. Moreover, they all draw deeply upon oral accounts, suggesting the continued importance of Hmong oral traditions in the United States, even as the majority of the Hmong learn to read and write.

So while many Hmong in public schools experienced pressure, implicitly or explicitly, to "dream American," others found in their classes opportunities to examine aspects of Hmong cultural and historical life. For these students, learning to write was not entirely an agent of assimilation but also a means through which the students might articulate new knowledge and insist upon the place of the Hmong in the broader narrative of the immigrant experience in U.S. public schools.

Working Stories: Rhetorics of the Workplace

Of the many challenges facing Hmong refugees in the United States in the 1980s, perhaps none was as daunting as finding employment. Language differences, low literacy levels, large families, and a dearth of marketable vocational skills all served as obstacles to full employment for most Hmong adults. Compounding the problem was the economic recession of the early 1980s, which according to economist Simon Fass (1991) "created more joblessness than any time since the 1930s and forced Hmong newcomers to compete with long-time U.S. residents and other refugee populations for entry-level jobs" (14). Given such conditions, it is perhaps not surprising that the unemployment rate for Hmong arriving in the United States in 1980 and 1981 hovered between 80 and 85 percent, more than quadruple the unemployment rate of Hmong who had arrived just two or three years earlier (Fass 1991, 14). As a result, many Hmong were forced to accept public assistance to support themselves and their families, a discouraging situation for a people who had historically prized independence from government institutions. As late as 1988, some 73 percent of Hmong families in Wisconsin were receiving some form of public assistance, compared to 7 percent of Americans nationally. In Wausau, the figure was 71 percent (Fass 1991, 19).

However, by the early 1990s, the employment situation began to improve for the Hmong. Most important, the recession had ended, with the effect that competition for jobs was not quite as fierce as it had been in the early 1980s. Many Hmong, too, had by this time received some schooling—ESL, vocational, and other forms—which made them better prospects in the eyes of employers. Added to this, local innovations in government assistance programs in Wisconsin had allowed the state to meet the needs of refugee families more efficiently. The result was that Hmong receiving public assistance in Wausau declined 18 percent between 1988 and 1990 and fell from 73 percent to 54 percent statewide in the same period. Hmong in the 1990s, Fass concluded, could not as a whole be called economically "successful" but had made encouraging progress nonetheless.

The transition from public assistance to full or partial employment brought the Hmong to yet another collection of literacy practices, those of the U.S. workplace. In factories, offices, schools, and other settings, Hmong employees were taught to read and write in ways that allowed them to perform their jobs successfully and further the goals of the company or institution. Hmong factory workers, for example, might learn to read directions on how to operate a lathe, measure a square of plywood, or read a receipt. Neng Vang remembered that in his first year in the United States he was placed by a local employment agency in a factory that produced car radiators. His position required that he read job orders and parts catalogs. "For every job, you had to look through the catalog. When they ordered a radiator for the car, when you saw the number there, then you had to open the book, and then read... what size [radiator], how big, and whatever it said there."

Vue Lee similarly remembered that his job as a machine operator called upon him to read customer order forms. "I read the procedures regarding the material I needed to make, and I read the orders of the customers each day. There was no writing. Just read and do my job, operating the saw, cutting things." For Pao Lee, literacy in the workplace meant reading a ruler to measure and cut materials and then recording the measurements in a company ledger. "And then I got a job where I had to read a ruler. I had to read the ruler and write whatever numbers I cut for the night. . . . I wrote the measurements down on a certain kind of paper they had for that job."

For Hmong who were more proficient in English, different types of employment were available, many of which called for more complex forms of literacy. Bilingual Hmong were especially valued and found work in government, medical, educational, business, and other settings. The primary role of the bilingual professional was to provide translation services, oral and written, in such settings as job interviews, doctor-patient consultations, teacher-parent meetings, police proceedings, lawyer-client conferences, and in other situations at which Hmong and English might be spoken. Bilingual employees were also called upon to translate the numerous documents produced by institutions that sought in various ways to assist, inform, service, regulate, or transform the Hmong population, whether in the course of providing public assistance, job training, medical care, religious guidance, or English-language instruction.

Gia Nhia Thao, for example, worked in a county employment office, where he helped find jobs for Hmong adults in local factories and businesses. In this position, he interpreted at job interviews, helped fill out employment applications, and translated company documents such as personnel policies into the Hmong language. "I help people fill out their applications, that's one of my key responsibilities. I go over the employer's policies with the clients. . . . I help translate the personnel policies of different companies into Hmong—the safety policies, things like that. Sometimes I translate the policies verbally, but if they want me to translate the policy into writing, then I have to write it down."

As a part-time customer service representative at her local bank, Zong Her's duties involved helping Hmong customers negotiate the language and literacy of loan applications, translating these from English to Hmong. "For the last three or four years, I have been working in customer service for the bank. A part-time job, after school...I help Hmong parents apply for loans and fill out applications. I'm an interpreter. I translate brochures and other banking material."

Yang Thao, in turn, worked as a bilingual aide in the public schools. His job involved assisting the classroom teacher during the school day, but also translating school announcements, policies, and regulations into Hmong. "In my job right now I do a lot of letter writing....I write letters to...the Hmong parents. I tell them about the events sponsored by the school, the places and times....I also translate the new policies that the school puts in place, and the school adds the translations to the parent/student handbook."

To the extent that they acted as conduits for the majority culture, translating its directives in oral and written form, bilingual professionals were not unlike the scribes of the Hmong military, performing specialized literacy functions at the behest of an institution that sought to direct the rank-and-file toward a particular goal or outcome. Moreover, just as the literacy skills of the military scribes offered them a distinctive identity and status, so, too, did the language and literacy skills of the bilingual professionals elevate them to a position they might not have otherwise achieved. Bilingual professionals gained a measure of stature among whites and other non-Hmong as presumed leaders of and spokespersons for the Hmong population, and they were often the people to whom white politicians, police, and educators turned when they wanted information about the Hmong. They were also granted access to majority venues where they might represent the Hmong community to majority audiences. There were, for example, invitations to speak and write on issues relating to Hmong culture, politics, history, and gender. We explore some of these writings in chapter 6.

The position of the bilingual professionals also affected their status in the Hmong community, which had traditionally reserved leadership positions for male elders. Many of the bilingual professionals were women, and their positions offered them a standing within the Hmong community they might not otherwise have been granted. Zer Lee, for example, was a Hmong woman who had graduated from high school in the United States. Hired as a social worker, she soon became known in the Hmong community as an authority on such issues as government housing programs, public assistance regulations, and medical insurance. With this knowledge, Lee helped newly arrived Hmong negotiate the bureaucratic labyrinths to which they were obligated, including the seemingly endless rounds of paperwork required of immigrants receiving public assistance. As a result, she became a figure of some prominence in her community. She reflected,

> To my close relatives, my clan, I'm a woman but I'm not just a woman to look at. The men also value me as a person that can help them. And then sometimes they will ask for my opinions for other things too. And I see that other people who do not have skills or do not know how to read and write—they don't get that respect. When you know the community resources well...when people talk to you about a problem...and when they are asking you to help them to apply for something, or complete their blue forms for insurance, or talk about their court hearing, and you're familiar with it, and you say, "This is how it's done." Well, it's a big part of getting the respect from your community.[6]

That Wider Field of Force

The testimonies we have considered in this chapter indicate that the Hmong who came to the United States were not, as was commonly supposed, entering a strange new universe of signs and symbols. Rather, Hmong readers and writers in the United States were re-encountering some of the same rhetorics and literacies they had encountered in Laos and Thailand. In Laos, Thailand, and the United States, Hmong people were introduced to literacy in the contexts of schools, Christian missions, and work-related settings, and they were invited to define themselves as citizens, as believers, as functionaries within larger institutional entities. This suggests that the rhetorics of literacy shaping Hmong reading and writing practices were transnational and transglobal, operating across the boundaries of states, faiths, and economies and through the continuing upheavals of warfare, displacement, and exile.

For literacy scholars, the Hmong experience suggests, if not a revision, then at least a reconsideration of accepted orthodoxies. For decades now, one of the truisms of literacy studies has been the *situated* and *local* nature of literacy development, its adherence to particular settings and moments in time. In seeking to explain how people come to read and write, scholars have emphasized these situated and local contexts to the degree that they have come to distrust, as Cushman et al. (2001) say in their important sourcebook, "comprehensive historical narratives [of literacy development], even the most magisterial ones" (7). Instead, literacy scholars have focused upon the immediate, the contextualized, the nuanced, the particular.

Nothing in the Hmong experience reverses that orthodoxy. Indeed, the uniqueness of the Hmong experience underscores the contextualized character of literacy and the ways in which reading and writing practices may be understood as a response to specific settings and local circumstances. What the Hmong experience does reflect, however, is the continuing potency of certain "grand narratives," such as colonialism, Christianity, and capitalism, in shaping the lives of human beings and, in the process, their experiences of literacy. While it is not possible to understand Hmong literacy development without understanding the role of local schools, churches, and employment conditions, neither is it possible to account for the Hmong experience of literacy, in its extraordinary scope and sweep, without viewing these local scenes through a wider historical lens. A Hmong woman recalling how as a child she learned to read and write from a hymnal while sitting beside her American sponsor in a Midwestern church provides a vivid illustration of how literacy is nurtured in local contexts. Yet our understanding of the image remains incomplete and insufficient if we do not also understand the historical forces that led that child to that church, in that city, reading those words. Literacy development is local, situated, and specific, but it is also global, transnational, and profoundly historical.

To say this is not to dismiss the particularity of literacy development but rather to recall Eric Wolf's (1982) appeal that we consider the interrelated and undeniable totality of forces—what he called "that wider field of force"—that influence the ways in which human beings make sense of who they are and where they belong in the world. The wider field of force is, of course, articulated and redefined by individuals in local contexts and situations, as the testimonies make clear. Yet what the testimonies also suggest is that literacy scholars may learn as much about their subject by occasionally stepping away from the object of study, expanding their focus, and looking at the broad forces that shaped the situated and particular literacy practices they are scrutinizing. Rather than discounting the influence of "grand narratives," we may look to the ways they mediate the ethnographic contexts that are the subject of so much literacy scholarship.

CHAPTER 6

Hmong Americans Rewriting

Testimony, Gender, and Civic Life

> One's own discourse and one's own voice, although born of another and
> dynamically stimulated by another, will sooner or later begin to liberate
> themselves from the authority of the other's discourse.
> —M. Bakhtin, *The Dialogic Imagination*

Literacy, as we have seen, is often institutional, a means through which
national, religious, educational, and other organizations seek to impose
their intentions upon others and assert powerful conceptions of reality.
This is done, I have argued, largely by means of symbolic activity, through
the assertion of what I have called "rhetorics" or the use of language and
other symbols to fashion understandings of the world and invite human
beings to take up identities and positions within existing social hierarchies
and arrangements. Literacy is the written representation of such rhetorics,
a technology for communicating, disseminating, or imposing them. In this
way can literacy serve as a shaping instrument, a means for inviting readers and writers to understand themselves, whether as citizens, Christians,
soldiers, refugees, or members of some other group.

But individual readers and writers do not always accept such invitations. Instead, they may work apart from institutional rhetorics, or around
them, or even, in some cases, in collaboration with them to reconceive
and "rewrite" the identities they have been offered. Outside of the schools,
churches, and workplaces where literacy is taught, reading and writing
may be largely self-directed, a response to the needs of particular groups
of people at specific moments in history. Such writings may be as diverse
as poetry, prayers, petitions, and letters to the editor. Equally varied are the
functions of such literacies, which can include remembering, dissenting,
or revealing. Outside of institutional contexts, moreover, readers and writers create their own settings for literacy practice, whether in the home, at
community meeting places, or elsewhere. Whatever their form, functions,
and scenes, such self-directed literacies are rhetorical in that they express
the identification of the reader or writer with other language users and
suggest identities and positions in the world.

This chapter examines some of the self-directed writings of Hmong refugees in Wausau, Wisconsin, and the rhetorical identities constructed through these writings.[1] One of the most powerful of these identities is that of the participant in history, in which the writer is both witness and actor, observer and agent. In what I call the *rhetoric of testimony,* Hmong writers used the literacy skills they had learned in schools and elsewhere to author first-person accounts, mostly unpublished, of their life histories. In such narratives, writers rejected the identities, so frequently offered to them in writings about the Hmong, of bystanders and victims, helplessly swept along by the ineluctable forces of historical events. Rather, writers "rewrote" themselves as resourceful, capable individuals who had survived the violence of the war, endured the dislocation of the refugee camps, and overcome the estrangements of resettlement in the United States. In their role as diarists and historians of the Hmong experience they recalled those events for their children and for posterity.

While most of the testimonies that I collected in the course of this project were written by men, Hmong women in the community also used their literacy skills to define and redefine themselves. A deeply patriarchal culture, the Hmong have long assigned women to subordinate status in both the public and the domestic spheres (Donnelly 1994). Literacy and education in the United States, however, represented for many Hmong women a means through which to challenge that status. In what I call the *rhetoric of new gender relations,* Hmong women wrote from the perspectives of mothers, wives, and daughters, but also from the perspectives of students, professional women, and community activists. Publishing their writings in the local newspaper, in Hmong newsletters, and in Hmong women's publications, these writers used their literacy skills to critique traditional gender relations and put forward alternative ways of thinking about the standing of Hmong women in the United States. In this way did the rhetoric of their writings invite new identities and social positions for Hmong women in the city.

Hmong writers also wrote, finally, to engage members of the majority culture. In what I have termed the *rhetoric of the Fair City,* so named after a letter published in the local newspaper that decried the presence of Hmong refugees and lamented the decline of "our fair city," Hmong writers published a series of letters and editorials responding to attacks upon refugees and explaining to members of the majority culture something of Hmong history, culture, and values. In these texts, the writers appropriated the rhetoric of the anti-immigrant letters—their topics, genre, tropes, and audience—to author a civic identity for themselves as tolerant and fair-minded people and to invite city residents to reconsider the nature of the "other" in an American city. More, the writers expanded, in the course of this dialogue, their repertoire of literacy practices to include forms of public and civic writing that represented an innovation in the history of local Hmong literacy practices.

Each of these rhetorics—those of testimony, new gender relations, and the Fair City—can be understood as marking a particular moment in the history of Hmong literacy development, a moment when a select number of Hmong people called upon written language to express something of what it meant to be a Hmong person in one central Wisconsin community at the end of the twentieth century. Beyond this, the Hmong writings are important for the ways in which they articulate the cultural work that literacy performs in minority communities in the United States, especially those communities in which reading and writing practices, whether in English or the first language, are still developing. The Hmong writings demonstrate the ways in which the members of such minority communities may claim the possibilities of literacy for themselves, using it, in essence, to "rewrite" their identities and positions in the majority culture. Let us consider these writings, beginning with what I have called the rhetorics of testimony.

"The Path Here Now": Rhetorics of Testimony

The year was 1978. The celebration of that New Year had just come to a close. Life for the new year had begun. Then something happened. It marked the beginning of a journey that changed my life forever. One beautiful January morning we were awakened to the sound of roaring thunder. No, it was not the sound of thunder in the monsoon season nor the sound of thunderstorm. It was the sound of rocket grenades exploding in destruction in the heart of our mountain village. The roaring sound echoed across mountains and valleys, disappearing through the edge of the morning sky.
—Shu Blong Her, "A Journey to Freedom" (unpublished essay)

Nao Shoua Xiong[2] was getting ready for his shift at a local window-manufacturing plant when his daughter came home from school confused and upset. Her public school teacher, Xiong recalled, had said that many white residents of the community believed that the Hmong had no right to live in the United States. The teacher said there had been several letters published in the local newspaper stating that the Hmong came to the United States to collect welfare benefits, were unwilling to learn English, and were having too many children. What's more, the teacher said, some letters claimed that the Hmong were illegal aliens and would soon be sent back to Laos. "My daughter asked me," Xiong said, 'Why, Dad, can't we stay in the United States in the future? My teacher said we may not be able to stay in this country legally.' "

Like many Hmong, Nao Shoua Xiong learned to read and write in one of the village schools in Laos, studying Lao language, history, and culture. At age fourteen, he enlisted in the Hmong military, where he learned the RPA, which he used to write letters to family and friends. After the collapse of the Royal Laotian Government in 1975, Xiong fled Laos for the Ban Vinai refugee camp, where he learned to read and write Thai and hired a private tutor to teach him the English alphabet.

Upon arriving in the United States, Xiong was placed in a vocational English as second language (VESL) class meant to prepare him for entry-level work. For three years he practiced the circumscribed language of following directions, filling out job applications, and making small talk with coworkers. But he also used his growing knowledge of English to pursue his interest in Hmong history. He began visiting his local library and reading English-language accounts of the Vietnam War, especially those addressing the Hmong involvement with the CIA. He created a photo album of his wartime experiences, writing English-language captions for pictures taken in Laos and Thailand. And he became an avid reader of the local newspaper, particularly articles concerning the Hmong community.

At the same time, Xiong continued to practice his Hmong and Lao literacy skills. He taught the RPA to his children and wrote occasional articles for a Hmong-language newsletter. A former officer in the Secret Army, he took an active role in a national Hmong veteran's organization, writing letters for the organization in the Hmong, Laotian, and English languages. And as a clan leader, he helped create a credit union for members of his clan by writing the organization's bylaws in the Lao script.

So when Xiong sat down to draft a response to his daughter's teacher, a response that would eventually become his life history and a history of the Hmong people, he was able to draw upon multiple languages, literacies, and rhetorics. He had available to him all the concepts, vocabularies, metaphors, and ways of knowing that had been asserted in rhetorics of literacy he had learned previously. Writing in the Hmong language, using Lao vocabulary words he had learned in village schools, and editing the English of the essay after it had been translated by a cousin, Xiong recounted the history of the Hmong people in the context of his own life story, beginning with his memories of the war.

During the time my father and I joined the military to take the lead in organizing and fighting against the communists, many crucial family members were killed. Only myself and a few others were left after the killing, and were able to come to the United States. In fact, prior to the beginning of the war and the joining into the military, my whole clan—immediate relatives—consisted of 300 families with 5,400 people living in Laos. But many things affected my clan during the war...war casualty, people dispersed, and scattered because of the war. We never found everyone again and were not able to collectively gather everyone like we once had. Many of us lost contact and didn't know who lived where, or who survived and who were deceased.

Replying to the charge that the Hmong had been eager to come to the United States to collect welfare benefits, Xiong described his twelve-year stay in Thai refugee camps and the wrenching decision to relocate his family to the United States.

Life in the refugee camps in Thailand was not easy. I was first sent to Nong Khai Refugee Camp and had lived there for two years, and then to Vinai Refugee Camp for ten years. While there, I was not thinking about coming to the United States....I was hoping that Laos will one day turn around and become a democratic country and have elections....When such things [took] place I [would] then return to Laos. I spent 12 years in Thailand for that dream....[By] 1989...no changes [had taken] place in Laos, which led me to...resettle in the United States.

When leaving for this country, I came with a lot of griefs. I cried for having to leave many loved ones behind in Laos or Thailand, and at the same time coming to a country in which I have no skills to transfer to rebuilding my life. I thought of my family members, about all the people, the living, and...the dead ones.

To the assertion that the Hmong did not want to learn English and support themselves economically, Xiong recounted his experiences as an ESL student looking for work as an adult refugee: "Upon arrival in the United States I started learning A, B, Cs...in school like a little child who was in kindergarten....After a couple of years, I started to understand little by little because English is a very hard language to learn, especially for the older Hmongs."

———

In popular accounts of the Hmong role in the Vietnam War, the Hmong have typically been cast as primitive mercenaries who served as foils to colorful Western diplomats, generals, and CIA operatives (Parker 1995; Robbins 1987; Warner 1995). In such writings the Hmong are typically rendered as a loyal, backward, somewhat childlike tribal people, "brutal and stoic," as Roger Warner (1995) describes them, who incidentally have a great capacity for warfare. Even histories that purport to study the war from the Hmong perspective tend to focus on the exploits of Hmong leaders such as Vang Pao or Touby LyFoung, often portraying these individuals in accounts that border on hagiography (e.g., Hamilton-Merritt 1993; Quincy 1988), a stance that inevitably diminishes the experiences of ordinary Hmong.

For many of the Hmong interviewed for this project, however, the meaning of the Hmong involvement in the Laotian civil war was not to be found in the writings of Western academics and journalists, but in their own experiences as ordinary people who lived the extraordinary events of recent Hmong history. For these individuals, the war was neither picaresque adventure nor geopolitical abstraction nor spectacle in which a handful of their leaders played a starring role. Rather, the war was a profoundly difficult experience that changed the lives of those who lived it and suffered its effects.

Literacy, for some, was a means to testify about their experiences in the war, to write about and remember them. Many of the Hmong interviewed for this project spoke of using the literacy skills they had learned in school, church, or even at work to compose autobiographical accounts of their wartime experiences. For example, Nao Shoua Xiong's memoir described an operation in which he and other Hmong were ordered to rescue one of the CIA pilots shot down over Laos.

> One day a jet plane fighter was shot down by the enemy and the pilot
> maneuvered the plane back into the sanctuary where we occupied. We
> heard the unusual sound of the plane, witnessed the smoke and fire on
> the airplane. The pilot bailed out on parachute. We, as ground troops,
> were instructed by General Vang Pao over the two-way radio transmitter,
> bellowing to order our troops to be deployed and surged toward the
> direction of the downed pilot to rescue him before the enemies were
> to capture him. Sixty soldiers were dispatched out and were led by a
> commander. During the rescue mission we were heavily ambushed
> by the enemies. We returned with 24 soldiers. The rest were killed or
> captured. Among the returnees many were also wounded. We had no
> choice but to do our best in the ground in order to save the life of the
> most precious CIA pilot as we had been ordered by the General. His
> order was clear and specific that we should sacrifice our lives for the

pilot, no matter how heavy the casualty might be. We sacrificed our lives for many pilots, and we had saved many of them.

Similarly, Shu Blong Her's memoir recalls the catastrophic events that took place as his family attempted to leave Laos for Thailand.

> On the third day, we came across an enemy trail, a trail between two villages. Cautiously, the people crossed the trail one by one. All of a sudden, a round of shots were fired. It was enemy fire. One man yelled out. And his voice sent the marchers scattered in all directions, while a 6-year-old boy was shot and died on the crossing point.... Unfortunately, the boy who was shot was one of my clan members. At the request of the boy's father, three men and I sneaked back to take the boy's body. We carried him up the mountain and buried his body under a pile of tree leaves.

Memoirs were typically written in the home, often on word processors purchased to help children with their schoolwork, and were carefully stored on disks or in notebooks kept out of the reach of children.[3] Writing was often done after work or on weekends, meaning that memoirs could take months or years to complete. Essays could be as short as two pages or as long as a hundred. The choice of language in which to write reflected the writer's age and educational background. Older Hmong generally wrote in the Hmong language, using the RPA or, occasionally, Laotian script. Hmong writers educated primarily in the United States typically wrote in English, rendering their experiences in the vocabulary, syntax, grammar, and written conventions of their new language.

The intended audiences for these accounts were in most cases the writers' children. Writers composed their memoirs, they told me, because they wanted their children to know something of their parents' lives and the events that had forced them to leave Laos. Gia Nhia Thao explained,

> I write for my children. As I get older, I write to remember, but the main thing is for my children to read what I have been through and what Grandmom and Grandpop have been through, things like that.... If I don't write, they're not going to know most of the things that I have been through.... And I keep telling them what my country was like, what the mountains were like... how you feel when you stand on the mountain and the clouds are all behind you... things like that.

Similarly, Vue Lee, the former military scribe, spoke of writing so that his children might understand something of their family history and of the circumstances that had caused the family to leave Laos and to take what he called "the path here now."

> I just write to remember the past.... Put it in my computer for my kids to read it and remember.... Yeah, mostly for my children, so they can read about my brother, my grandfather and my fathers, and...the war going on, and the path here now.... And I just want my kids to read and understand what it was like when we were in our country, and how our life was like over there.... Yeah, I show it to them now so they will understand my past.

One function of the memoirs, then, was to remember. Literacy was seen as an aid to memory, a means by which writers could remember lost family, friends, rituals, places, and times. The memoirs function in this sense as a kind of archive preserving stories, beliefs, and rituals that might otherwise disappear. As Gia Nhia Thao explained, "My grandparents, my great-grandparents, they told stories for me when I was young. But if I don't write that down now, then when I am gone nobody is going to hear that story anymore. Because when my great-grandparents, my grandparent, my parents, when they're gone, then my children won't know those stories. So I want to keep the story alive."

As Gia Nhia Thao's testimony suggests, the memoirs were also a way to pass along cultural traditions, especially Hmong-language literacy traditions. Chang Yang explained that he wrote his narrative in Hmong as a way to demonstrate to his children the importance of learning the Hmong language, as well as how to read and write in Hmong.

> It's really important for children to know their language. And if they see me write in Hmong, they are going think that, Oh, that's my dad. My dad knows how to write Hmong. And that's how we can teach our children. And I want to keep...our writing, our language, and our characters. For my children, generation to generation, I don't want them to lose our culture. Writing in Hmong is very important because you can sit down and write about your culture: put everything into a story.

In this sense, the Hmong memoirs were more than just remembrances, and literacy more than simply a technology of memory. Beyond this, the Hmong memoirs were meant to have a didactic function: to teach Hmong children, many of whom had been born in Thailand or the United States, about their history; who the Hmong were, where they came from, and how they had come to live in such a distant land. As Joua Hang explained,

You know, for those who will grow up not knowing much about their family history, about why we are here, our participation in the war, and our love for our country and our people, and why we did what we did, I want them to know all of this. I want them to know how much we had to suffer and how much we've lost in the process of doing all this. Because it's important that they know. . . . Young people, especially the students today, they think that, you know, life is great and all that. But it's also important for them to know that their parents' experiences were harsh in Laos. . . . For the future generation, they should know that they weren't here on a free ride . . . that they had to remember what was lost.

The Hmong memoirs were in this sense Janus-like, looking forward as well as backward. They preserved memories and served as a family archive, recalling parents, brothers, and sisters who may have been killed. Yet they also taught children something of morals, behavior, and ways of knowing that would be expected from them in the years to come. The memoirs were thus a way of communicating to children the obligations incumbent upon them: their responsibilities to their families, language, and culture.

The other audience for the Hmong memoirs was whites, or members of the majority culture. Writers spoke of publishing their stories for the benefit of readers in the majority culture who were ignorant of the Hmong or even hostile to them. Joua Hang, for example, described Western accounts of Hmong history as "unreal" and saw her writings as a way to offer a deeper understanding of the Hmong to Western readers. "Because, you know, some of the stories and some of the books I've read about Hmong . . . they seem . . . well, because the Hmong are illiterate, so they have American interviewees who write the literature and all that stuff, so it seems really unreal. And I want for the first time for people to look at this from a personal side—something that's real."

The Hmong memoirs also tell us something about the interconnected and tangled processes through which literacy develops, the ways in which writing can result from multiple sources, motivations, sponsors, and desires. While the Hmong memoirs represent examples of non-institutional literacy practices, they could in some cases result from writers' involvement with U.S. institutions such as schools or the workplace. Vue Lee Mai, for example, had begun writing his family history while living as a refugee in Thailand. After arriving in the United States, he resumed the work as part of an assignment for his ESL class in Wisconsin.

I had a woman when I was studying at ESL, a woman teacher who wanted to know my life. She wanted me to tell my life story, and about my mother and father, and so I wrote. I wrote about how our country fell into despair, about how poor my dad's life was, how poor my life was, about how the war caused our relatives to die and become poor. I had a woman teacher, and she said that I should write my stories down, so that when I am no longer alive my children can read them.

Vang Her, known as a local shaman and herbalist, began writing his memoirs as part of a unique arrangement with the state welfare office, the local Hmong association, and the area vocational-technical college. To satisfy the requirement that Her do community service in exchange for receiving public assistance, the county office mandated, with Her's assent, that he begin writing a history of the Hmong people and culture, which he did in the form of a personal narrative. He explained,

> I wrote about the ways of shamanism, ways of getting and giving herbal medicines, about the marriage ceremony and the death ceremony, Hmong music, the Hmong pipes, the important things like these that we try to preserve. I wrote it into a book. . . . The Job Service gave me the equipment. They gave me paper and support, and the local technical school gave me two computers. . . . I think we had a tape recorder also. And I wrote.

Such testimonies speak to the complexities of literacy production, the ways in which it can be tangled up in competing interests, languages, sponsors, and rhetorics. One might write a memoir in one's native language, but also use the language of the dominant majority. One might write for one's children, but also for a wider reading public. And one might write as an individual, in the solitary Western model, but also at the behest of a larger network of institutions such as schools, government agencies, and community organizations. All of these competing languages, processes, and rationales of literacy were realized in the memoirs, which offered the Hmong writers another genre in which to represent themselves. The genre was not new to the Hmong—they have been telling their stories for thousands of years—but the modality of written language was, for most, a relatively new medium in which to perform their narrative accounts. In these accounts, Hmong people were not reduced to the caricatures of "primitives," "warriors," and "fierce anti-communists," as in many Western writings. Neither were they simply "refugees" "victims," or childlike strangers bereft in a new land. Rather, the writers constituted themselves as actors in history—witnesses, interpreters, and scholars whose extraordinary life experiences obligated the writers to preserve their stories for themselves and their families, but also for members of the majority community who were mostly ignorant of Hmong history and culture.

Toward a "Different World": Rhetorics of New Gender Relations

Today I still remember most of my childhood wishes. There I was. I was a girl, not a boy. I was disappointed and angry. I wanted to be a boy rather than a girl because I wanted to have all the attention that boys have and girls do not have. I wanted to have the ability to go to school. I didn't want to work with my mother or help her. I wanted to play outside and hang around with all of my friends. I said to myself that I wanted to be a boy and I did act like one. I kept my hair short; also I dressed as a boy all the time. I kept telling people that I was a boy.
    —Ma Moua Vang, "Childhood Dream," *Wausau Hmong-American News, Wausau Xov Xwm Hmoob-Asmesliskas* 10(2) (April 1997): 11

Nancy D. Donnelly (1994) has written that "the most immediately striking aspect of gender roles in Hmong society, described again and again by researchers, is the apparent hierarchical relationship between men and women" (30). In patriarchal Hmong society, Donnelly argues, both men and women believed that "men's words were more important than women's, that men's decisions carried more weight than women's, and that a woman took on the social standing of her husband, never the other way around" (114). Everyday cultural practices reflected such inequalities between men and women in Laos. Marriages were arranged by men, the practice of "bride capture" was common, and polygamy was an accepted practice. One Hmong woman, quoted in Mattison, Scarseth, and Lo (1994), described her everyday life in Laos.

Chong Houa and I lived a life of subsistence farming. We raised chickens and pigs, and killed some for the children to eat. We had fields of rice, of poppies, of corn; we planted squash and cucumbers. Our life was very hard, but I also liked to grow sugar cane and many bananas to please the children. I would go out to the fields, tote this, carry that. Sometimes I would combine the two baskets into one. It was so heavy I would have to drag it through the dirt to get it to the house. As I think of it now, I knew a life of complete drudgery. For my next life, I would like to be as a bird so as to have a better life. (137)

Such recollections may explain Donnelly's comment, "No Hmong woman [living in the United States] has ever told me she wanted to live in Laos again" (75).

Hmong women who resettled in the United States discovered new possibilities and opportunities for education, work, and self-expression. Young Hmong women enrolled in public schools, while older women developed their literacy skills through adult education classes, employment, or participation in community organizations in which they might write, publish, and network with other women. Women who did become educated used their skills as a means for personal advancement to benefit their families economically, but also as a cultural tool, a means through which they might examine and challenge existing cultural paradigms, especially those concerning gender. All of these, we shall see, led to new ways of expressing what it meant to be a Hmong woman in the twentieth century.

Hunger to Learn: Literacy, Gender, and Desire

Song Thao remembered that even as a young girl she felt an intense desire to learn how to read and write. Thao recalled watching her father and brothers read letters the family occasionally received, and she remembered her father writing letters in return. Instinctively, Thao linked these practices to power and began to experience what she described as a "hunger to learn."

> I would see people read and write, and I wanted very much also to read and write. It's just like if you saw somebody eating ice cream and it looked like, it looked like it tasted so good. And I had that urge to say that I wanted to read and write too. But at that time—and you have to understand Hmong culture regarding boys and girls—my dad sent his sons to school, then he didn't have enough money to send his daughters to school. But [I wanted to learn] because I saw someone read, and I saw someone write. And it was just like, my gosh, that's powerful. I want to do that too.

While individual motivations for learning to read and write were of course varied, the common themes offered in the interviews for pursuing education were economic, personal, and cultural. That is, women interviewed for this project viewed literacy as a means of attaining economic independence, enhancing their self-worth, and serving the wider Hmong community. Beyond this, the women interviewed for this project spoke of the ways in which their education enabled them to reconsider and in some cases challenge traditional Hmong conceptions of gender. Song Thao's testimony is representative. She viewed education as a means of making a statement about herself to the men in her family, especially her father. When Thao arrived in the United States, she spoke no English and could not read beyond the ABCs. Despite this, she persisted in her studies, graduating from high school and then from college. At the time of the interview, Thao was working for a local social service agency and studying for admittance to law school. Thao was motivated to continue her educational and professional development, she said, by the prevailing attitudes toward women in Hmong society, as expressed by her father and brothers.

> I think one of the—and I don't want to talk down about my dad and my brother—but I think one of the powers motivating me to want to learn so much is that my dad and brother were saying that even if I had an education, I still am a woman, a girl, and I am not as good as a boy. I think that one of my strengths was that I was trying to prove to them that I am—that I can learn, I could have an education, even though I'm a woman....I wanted to prove to my father and my brother that I could do it.

May Yang, who became a mother as a teenager and yet managed to graduate from high school, also connected literacy, gender, and self-worth. For Yang, learning to read and write was a way of demonstrating to her father that Hmong women were equal to men.

> And the other thing is that my dad always wanted a son. At that time we had only two brothers, and there were lots of sisters. And my dad, and my uncle, they said that girls are nothing, you know. They go and get married and that's it, you know. The son is more important. And when I was young, I think that really broke my heart, and I wanted to be able to learn how to read, learn how to write—to do as much possible to prove to my parents that they were wrong; you know, to prove that girls can do as much as boys....And so I took every course possible [in school] to help me achieve, help me be better, help to prove to my family and to the world that, you know, a girl is not just a "girl." ...A girl could be born with leadership, could be born with the power to be as strong as a boy.

Beyond issues of personal validation, the economic imperative for literacy was ever present. Women spoke of wanting to learn to read and write so that they could find a job, help their families, and, importantly, reduce their dependence upon men. A woman who could support herself and her children was less reliant upon a man and would be in a better position to cope if the man were to suddenly leave the family. In Zer Lee's words, "And if the father leaves, the woman is not handicapped. She can still pay her bills, can still take care of her kids."

Whatever their motivations, the testimonies of the women spoke both to the obstacles they encountered in pursuing their educations and the support they received from family members. Resistance to women's education often came from male members of the family—husbands, brothers, and fathers who either did not see the value of education for women, or doubted women's abilities, or believed the proper place for a woman was in the home. The situation was especially difficult for married women with children. May Yang, for example, dropped out of high school at age sixteen to marry. After delivering her second child, she decided that she wanted to return to school and finish her education.

> After I had [my baby], I told my husband, I'm going back to school. He didn't approve of it. We had a lot of arguments. I said, "Trust me. . . . And I will show you I can do it." Because my GPA in high school when I married him was 4.0. And he said, "You will never do it. You will never get good grades. Why are you so interested in going to high school again? You won't succeed because you're married, you have your child, and there will be a lot of responsibility."

Since the family was experiencing financial problems and would have difficulty paying for child care, Yang proposed to her husband that she take a job as a waitress to support herself while she was enrolled in school.

> So I asked my husband if I could go to work. And he said, "No." And I said, "Well, you're only getting paid seven dollars an hour, and it's not going to be enough. It's not going to be enough for the children and for us. . . . It's not going to cover us." And so I worked as a waitress. I got up at seven o'clock, went to school until three o'clock, went home, then worked as a waitress from five o'clock to one o'clock in the morning, then did my homework until three o'clock. Then I would get up at five o'clock, cook for my in-laws, and go to school. It went on like that for one whole year.

Yang's schedule was exhausting but not unique. Hmong women wishing to continue or resume their education had the burden of fulfilling traditional gender roles while at the same time trying to meet the expectations placed upon them in high school or college. Even women who had supportive family members were often called upon to continue their domestic duties and in some cases hold down jobs while pursuing their educational aspirations. Yia Yang's husband, for example, helped with cooking, cleaning, and child rearing when Yang decided, after having three children, that she wanted to obtain a college degree. Yet the burden was still on Yang to perform in the manner traditionally expected of a Hmong wife, even as she took college classes. She recalled,

> During the day, I went to school, and my children were with the babysitter. And each night, I came home, I worked, and they went to bed early so I could study. And early in the morning, when they were still sleeping, I got up to study. . . . People said, "How can you cook?" I said, in the morning, I bake. And while I'm baking, I'm studying, and the family is sleeping. And I have my microwave, so I could cook a lot of food and then put it in [the] refrigerator, and then warm it up later to eat. It wasn't fresh but some things you can survive. And people laughed at me, but I told them, "This is not forever. This is a thing that is only temporary. Few months, few years, I will be done with it."

Hmong women pursuing education often seemed to live in multiple worlds. Not only would they be students and part-time workers—waitresses, cashiers, clerks—but they would also be expected to fulfill their roles as wives, mothers, or daughters. Zong Her, a mother of three, a teller at a local bank, and a part-time college student, explained it this way: "I think being a woman and having a family is very hard because you try to be a good a role model for your children, and try to be a good wife for your husband, and try to be a good daughter-in-law for your family, and a good worker for your employers. It's very hard. I try the best I can. How can I . . . wear so many hats?"

Yet if there were obstacles to education, there could also be family support. Fathers who may once have expected their daughters to follow the conventional paths of early marriage and child rearing began to see the economic limitations of such choices and to encourage their daughters to explore alternative possibilities. Nhia Lo recalled,

> Initially I don't think I really felt [my father's] support. . . . But I think that as I got older, he began to learn more about society and the importance of education for not only men but women. I started to sense that he was really there, probably when I was in seventh grade, eighth grade. He

started saying, "I know a lot of people your age are getting married. But I don't want you to get married because you see how hard it is for your sisters.... One of your sisters got married and had two kids before she graduated from high school, and that's just really hard. So I want you to go to school."

Yia Yang described a similar shift in her father's thinking.

In Thailand and Laos, my father would say, "No, you don't go to school. You stay home and help your mother."...I think when we first came to America my dad thought that way, too. He said you finish high school and you get married. You don't go any further—you're too old. Nobody will marry you. But right now my dad, he doesn't say that anymore. I think he's changing. Now he says, "Finish high school, get your degree, then you can marry." So my father is changing.... And when I finished college, he was happy for me. He said, "See, you can do it." I told him, "If you supported me back then, I would have been done before I got married."

The opportunities for education were not the same for all Hmong women in the United States, and the literacy experiences varied from city to city, clan to clan, and family to family. Some women were discouraged from pursuing education in the United States by husbands or fathers, while other women spoke of the generous support they received from men in their family, who encouraged them to return to school and assisted with domestic work. What is perhaps most striking about the testimonies, however, are the sacrifices women made—the long hours, multiple responsibilities, and rigorous discipline to which they subjected themselves—to pursue an education, regardless of whether they were encouraged or censured by Hmong men.

Institutional Collaborations: The HOPE Women's Committee

Beyond school and family, literacy development for Hmong women in Wausau was promoted by a mixture of institutional and non-institutional sponsors, including churches, state refugee organizations, and Hmong community associations. One such local association was the Women's Committee of the Hmong Organization for the Promise of Enrichment (HOPE), which offered a small number of Hmong women new opportunities for literacy practice and which provides a window through which to see the influence of women's community organizations upon Hmong women's literacy development.

Founded by Hmong in Wausau in the early 1990s, HOPE was a community organization created to address long-range political, cultural, and intellectual issues facing Hmong in the United States. Shortly after HOPE was established, women members of the organization established the HOPE Women's Committee, which addressed issues specific to Hmong women, including women's opportunities for higher education. The HOPE Women's Committee was made up largely of Hmong professionals—teachers, social workers, counselors, and nurses—although it also included non-Hmong professional women from Wausau. The committee viewed its role as providing practical resources to Hmong women in the city—for example, information on going to college—and as providing a model for younger Hmong women seeking to balance family and professional responsibilities.

For women serving on the HOPE Women's Committee, there were numerous opportunities to develop their reading and writing skills: committee members collaborated with locally born women to write mission statements, grant applications, summaries of meetings, and community announcements. Other committee members kept written records of enrollments, meeting agendas, budgets, and other records. Beyond opportunities for its members, the HOPE Women's Committee also sponsored projects designed to promote literacy and education, especially higher education, for younger Hmong women. For example, the committee sponsored a scholarship fund for Hmong women applying to college. To apply for the scholarship, students had to write an essay on a question posed by the committee. The committee's panel of outside readers, which included Hmong and non-Hmong readers, evaluated the essays and awarded cash prizes of one hundred to two hundred dollars. Xy Moua, a founding member of the committee, explained, "As part as their scholarship, the applicants are asked to answer the essay questions. And we would evaluate them according to the essays and according to the criteria. We have a separate committee that does the evaluation.... This year we're giving out five awards. Last year we gave out four, and we had fifteen applicants."

The Women's Committee also worked with state refugee organizations to organize workshops and conferences that addressed issues affecting Hmong women in the community. These conferences were important venues where women might meet with others, exchange ideas, and network with peers who had successfully balanced the competing claims of Hmong and American traditions. Yi Yang explained, "I told my husband, I thought

I was well educated. But when I went there, I met a lot of Hmong women who were more educated than I am. And they're amazing. They stand up for themselves. I'm still kind of shy, and pull back, but they are anxious to go and promote themselves. I told my husband after I went to that conference that I want to go for more school."

For Pang Moua, a Hmong women's conference she attended was an occasion to reflect upon the progress that Hmong women have made in the United States.

> Hmong women, right now, we have more leadership and more education. It's very amazing. . . . In October, I went to a conference, and I saw many Hmong women who are very successful and very good English speakers. They are good role models compared to what I saw ten years or eight years ago. In the past, I never saw this. So we have become very successful. We still have long way to go, but we're improving now.

Women also had the option of writing for the *HOPE Quarterly,* a newsletter devoted to Hmong news, culture, politics, and the arts. Several women interviewed for this project published essays in which they challenged traditional conceptions of Hmong gender roles. For example, Blia Xiong wrote,

> Throughout history, Hmong girls have been brought up to respect their husbands and families and have been given few opportunities to decide what to do with their lives. During the Chinese Hmong war, young Hmong women were even traded for food. Many times, these acts were done without the consent of the women.
>
> As children, girls were taught the skills needed to serve their future husbands and children whereas their brothers were taught to read and write and were encouraged to follow their dreams. Women also had few rights. For example, if she married outside her husband's clan after he has died, a widow frequently lost her children and the property she formerly shared with her deceased husband. . . .
>
> By becoming well educated, girls can begin to understand the laws of the country which will help them if an unrighteous act should occur. They will also be able to understand the Hmong community better, and once they know the community better, they can begin to see what actions would be effective in changing old beliefs that may prevent their own daughters from obtaining independence. ("Encourage Men and Women Equally in the Pursuit of Higher Education and Independence," *HOPE Quarterly* 1 (4) (1992): 6)

In these and other writings, Hmong women used literacy as a medium through which they might critique the historically subordinate status of women in Hmong culture. Several women interviewed for this project spoke frankly of themselves as agents of change, meaning that they wished to reform what they considered inequitable gender roles in Hmong culture and to propose new roles for themselves and other Hmong in the future. These women used their newly developed literacy skills to further these projects and, not incidentally, to fashion rhetorical identities for themselves that stressed a historical and critical consciousness. Literacy was a means, for these writers, to articulate what I have called a rhetoric of new gender relations, a rhetoric in which Hmong women posited new positions for themselves relative to Hmong men and Hmong culture generally, as well as to members of the wider majority culture.

Letters from The Fair City: Rhetorics of Public Voice

In July 1989, a letter appeared in *The Wausau Daily Herald* that ignited a bitter controversy in the city. The letter accused the Hmong refugee population of defrauding the welfare system, having too many children, and eating local dogs. The writer went on to say that she had moved away from Wausau to avoid contact with Hmong people, and she advised other Wausau residents to do the same. The letter concluded, "I sure am glad I moved away from Hmongville. But something should be done to clean them out of Wausau, so us folks can pick up a few scraps. . . . A big shakeup in Wausau is long overdue" ("No friend of Wausau Hmong," *The Wausau Daily Herald,* July 4, 1989).

Local reaction to the "No friend" letter was pronounced. Several city residents wrote to defend the refugees, reminding readers of the Hmong role in the Vietnam War and praising Hmong attitudes toward children and elders. Others wrote to call for compassion toward refugees and other minorities. However, letters critical of the Hmong continued to appear in the local paper. Published under such captions as "Send refugees back to Asia," "Reader resents aid to immigrants," and "The refugee program must go," these letters assailed refugees for accepting public assistance, speaking their native language in public, damaging rental properties in which they lived, and eating ducks from a local park. Still other letters criticized the churches and volunteer organizations that sponsored the Hmong, as in the following: "That old excuse, English is what they need. I'm sick of that. Why didn't the churches tell them that before they bring [sic] here? They are to blame and they should pay for the teaching of these people. Not the taxpayer. I'm surprised more people don't stop giving to the church after the mess they put on the people of Wausau" ("Welfare, churches to blame," *The Wausau Daily Herald,* July 6, 1989).

One way to read such letters is to place them in the broader context of U.S. immigration history and its discontents. The sentiments expressed in anti-Hmong letters recall the rhetoric of earlier American nativist groups that associated immigrants with joblessness, degeneracy, and the specter of racial corruption (Archdeacon 1983). In the local version of this rhetoric, which I call the *rhetoric of the Fair City,* Southeast Asian refugees in Wausau, and particularly the Hmong, were the newest in a long line of what immigration historian David Reimers (1998) called "unwelcome strangers," an alien people whose presence signals the decline of the idealized community.

There is, however, another way of reading the exchange of letters, one that has implications for understanding the literacy development of the Hmong specifically and for understanding literacy learning and practice generally. In this reading, the rhetoric of the Fair City is a generative force, one that motivated and shaped the writing of a group of Hmong writers in one Midwestern city. In responding to the rhetoric of angry whites, as some Hmong eventually did, the writers appropriated the constituents of their rhetoric—its topics, genre, language, and intended audience—using these both to rebut the charges made against them and to author their own counter-narratives of culture and experience. In so doing, these Hmong writers expanded their repertoire of literacy practices to include previously unfamiliar forms of "public writing," or what Susan Wells (1996, 326) defined as the work of constructing a public sphere through discursive practices to advance social and civic arguments.

To read the exchange of letters this way is to think of writing beyond private acts of mind or the boundaries of supposedly coherent cultures, the familiar dichotomies. Instead, it is to think of writing as compelled by other writings, words enmeshed with other words, and symbols derived from opposing symbols. In this reading, the Hmong-authored letters are a response to conflicting local discourses, to what Bakhtin (1981) called "the battle between points of view, value judgments, and emphases" (315). To think of literacy this way is to think of it as a response to rhetoric and the rhetorical struggles of competing peoples, cultures, and institutions seeking to impose meanings and establish authority in contexts of everyday life.

I do not mean by this that the Hmong writers learned to read and write as a result of the rhetoric directed against them, or that these writers had no language of their own prior to reading the anti-immigrant letters, or that public writing of any kind was unknown to the Hmong. My argument, rather, is that the rhetoric of the anti-immigrant letters suggested to a group of immigrant writers a particular kind of literacy, one the writers had not practiced previously. In this sense, the literacy practices of the Hmong writers were a response to the rhetorical worlds in which they lived and in which they sought to intervene.

To see literacy development as a response to rhetorical struggles in community settings is to offer a sharp contrast to standard treatments of literacy acquisition by immigrants, refugees, and adults generally, which are often framed in terms of life-skill competencies (Seufert 1999), vocational training (Grognet 1997), and citizenship (Nixon and Keenan 1997). Such treatments typically view literacy as instrumental, a means for assimilation into the dominant culture, political institutions, and economy of the United States. In a rhetorical perspective, literacy practice is framed more dynamically, located within arguments about such topics as race, language, history, and the place of the "other" in contemporary American life. Such arguments were played out, as we shall see, in the letters-to-the-editor section of the local newspaper, which served as a site of struggle between Hmong and white Americans writers and as a starting point for new forms of Hmong writing in the local community, as writers drew upon the content, form, language, and imagined audience of the anti-refugee letters to author their own narratives of identity, history, and position within the majority community.[4]

Strangers at the Gate: The Roots of Anti-Immigrant Rhetoric

Perhaps the high point in public discourse about the Hmong in Wausau was reached in April 1984, when a group of city residents traveled to Baltimore, Maryland, to represent Wausau in an "All-America City" competition. While her fellow delegates extolled Wausau's business climate and such amenities as a new whitewater-rafting course, a Hmong woman named Youa Her made an emotional speech about the city's efforts to resettle Southeast Asian refugees. "In Wausau, Wisconsin," she said, "we are given the freedom and necessary support to build a better life. And that is all the Hmong people have ever really wanted." When Youa Her finished her speech, one delegate later wrote, "some of the people in the audience were crying" (*The Wausau Daily Herald,* April 9, 1984). Wausau won the competition, and Youa Her's speech received front-page coverage in Wausau's daily newspaper.

This public triumph notwithstanding, the increased numbers of refugees arriving in Wausau began to engender, perhaps inevitably, a backlash against the Hmong. By 1984, the same year Youa Her made her speech at the All-America City competition, Hmong in Wausau were reporting incidents of intimidation and harassment. The Marathon County Human Rights Committee heard testimony that Hmong students were being verbally and physically abused in school (*The Wausau Daily Herald,* February 15, 1984), while Hmong adults reported being the victims of random acts of violence (*The Wausau Daily Herald,* August 29, 1984). A business forum on race relations resulted in participants—none of whom were Hmong— creating a document cataloging "positive" and "negative" traits of refugees. The "positive" traits included well-behaved children, intolerance of delinquency, and strong family bonds. The "negative" traits, of which there were nearly twice as many, included the following.

- They always seem to drive nice cars, when other people that are on welfare can't even afford to buy a $200 beater.
- They have too many children per family.
- The adults always seem to speak Hmong instead of English. I think they should all learn to speak English when they move here.
- They kill and eat dogs. ("Positive comments about our Hmong neighbors/Negative comments!" N.d.)

Such sentiments were not unique to white residents of Wausau, but echoed anti-immigrant rhetoric of the past and present. Immigration scholar Joe R. Feagin (1997) has written that American nativist rhetorics of the eighteenth and nineteenth centuries stressed the racial inferiority of immigrants, their inability to assimilate into American culture, and their desire to "take" American jobs (13–14). To these complaints were added objections about the criminal behaviors, ill health, immorality, allegiance to foreign religious powers, and "radical alien ideas" said to characterize immigrants (Reimers 1998, 16). And we have discussed previously the racism directed at Asian-American peoples. Contemporary versions of nativist rhetoric, David Reimers has noted, eschew for the most part overtly racist themes in favor of economic, cultural, and environmental arguments—that is, that large immigrant families lead to overpopulation (1998, 40–41). This was also true in Wausau, as seen in the complaints that Hmong families had too many children.

As practiced in Wausau, anti-immigrant rhetoric was oral and written, spoken in the city's bars, businesses, and social clubs and published in the letters section of the daily newspaper. The letters published through the

1980s and 1990s leveled increasingly vitriolic attacks upon Hmong refugees, accusing them of welfare fraud, contempt for American values, and criminal activity, among other transgressions. The unifying theme of these letters, however, was the alleged abuse of public assistance, an allegation that became a prism through which to interpret Hmong culture, history, and values. A letter published in 1993, for example, declares, "Our American society...can no longer support a segment of the population that is under-educated, unskilled and ultimately nonproductive" ("New citizens, adopt our values to be Americans," *The Wausau Daily Herald,* February 19, 1993). More, the receipt of public assistance by the Hmong was perceived as a form of discrimination against working-class whites. "My children envy the 'treasures' that Hmong children have," wrote one woman, "the nice bikes, roller blades, brand name high top shoes and jacket, memberships in the YMCA.... What a slap in the face to White Americans who can't afford these luxuries ("Hmong plight doesn't make sense," *The Wausau Daily Herald,* June 23, 1993).[5] The Hmong were portrayed as shiftless and deceitful, manipulating the system to collect welfare benefits and avoid working. Another letter writer asserted, "EDITOR: Perhaps they were hard working farmers in the years gone by but I certainly don't perceive them as hard workers at all in the United States. Why should they? I see many of them always dressed up with built up shoes, gold chains around their necks, driving new cars and vans with six or 10 children, on food stamps....We the taxpayers cannot absorb all the extra taxes" ("Hmong should pay back elderly," *The Wausau Daily Herald,* January 16, 1993).

In the same way, Hmong language and history were reinterpreted through the distorting construct of alleged welfare fraud. "With the opportunities to learn English available to them," one writer asked, "why aren't they attending English classes, so they can get employment?" ("Don't go to casinos, learn English," *The Wausau Daily Herald,* April 4, 1994). Other letters discounted the Hmong role in the Vietnam War and deemed U.S. obligations to the Hmong nonexistent or already repaid. "EDITOR: That old talk, they helped us in the war, really is silly. Most of the [Hmong] people here were too young to even fight in a war when the U.S. was there. The ones that were are paid back already with all those free programs" ("Wausau in for a rough time ahead," *The Wausau Daily Herald,* n.d.). "The war is over for 20 years," another letter writer concluded, "[so] let's quit rewarding people who can't support themselves."

Hmong youth were portrayed as dangerous criminals who had introduced gang violence into a formerly tranquil community. Letters called for "little punks and hoods to be taken off the streets" and for police to "throw the book at them." "What is going on around here!" demanded one writer. "I used to feel pride living in Wausau with very little crime and certainly, no 'drive-by shootings.' . . . If this is what 'All-American City' means maybe we should go back to the way it was!" ("Let's nip crime in the bud," *The Wausau Daily Herald,* May 5, 1993). "What has happened," lamented one letter writer, "to our fair city?"

In these ways did the rhetoric of the Fair City offer both white and Hmong residents a collection of identities and positions. White residents were constituted as victims besieged by unwanted aliens, while the Hmong and other refugees were framed as deceitful and dangerous outsiders. This rhetoric, however, did not silence Hmong residents of the city but spurred a literate response as some Hmong writers took up the themes and forms of the rhetoric to present alternative conceptions of themselves and their place in the city. In doing so, they illustrated the role of public and civic rhetorics upon their evolving literacy practices.

Rewriting the Fair City: Relationships of Rhetoric and Literacy

Hmong literacy practices in Wausau did not begin, of course, as a response to the rhetoric of the Fair City. By the 1980s, when the resentful letters began appearing in the local paper, Hmong refugees had been living in the city for nearly a decade, and we have seen in this chapter and in chapter 5 the numerous examples of writings by Hmong authors, composed for a range of purposes. Nor were the Hmong historically unfamiliar with public writing. In Laos, a small group of French-educated Hmong had for a short time published letters on issues relating to Hmong culture and language. Tou Meng Vang, a Hmong social worker, explained,

> In Laos we also wrote some articles like this too, you know, to provide information to people. We wrote in Hmong and Laotian. . . . Now we write in Hmong and English. . . . The information is not just for Hmong people but for our friends, the American people too. They, and us, we are living in the same city, in the same area, and the same places, and we need to know about the good and the bad things together.

Although there is no sense in which the anti-immigrant letters spurred the Hmong of Wausau to become literate, or even introduced them for the first time to public writing, the letters did promote a distinctly new type of literacy practice in a particular context at a given moment in the history of Hmong literacy. More, they illustrated, as previously mentioned, how public and civic arguments influence literacy practice by offering a set of topics, a genre, a language, and an audience that writers can appropriate and use in their own acts of public writing. Let us consider these elements and how they were appropriated and used by a select group of Hmong writers in an attempt to "rewrite" the idea of the Fair City posited in the anti-immigrant rhetoric, thereby offering both white and Hmong readers alternative conceptions of identity and social position.[6]

"Fighting on Paper": Topics of Literacy

I think the reason I decided to write that article is because I was, you know, people wrote to the editor accusing the Hmong for doing certain things that I felt wasn't very appropriate and was not true. Also I went and talked to groups of students, clubs in the community and the same questions always come up. Which were not true, were just rumors. So I felt that we should not continue with that on the back burner. You know, we should be open and talk about the facts. So that's why I decided to write the article to clarify any misunderstanding that people may have.

—Christopher Xiong, on why he had chosen to write a letter to the editor
to *The Wausau Daily Herald*

With every anti-immigrant letter that was published in the local paper, critics of Southeast Asians offered Hmong writers another topic on which to write, as the writers sought to rebut criticisms of the Hmong. The Hmong letters to the editor were in this sense rejoinders in a dialogue, writings linked to other writings, words addressed to prior words in a continuing exchange about culture, history, and the nature of community life. The source of these writings was the language of the interlocutor, or the rhetoric that was used to transcribe and position Southeast Asians in the city. This rhetoric provided Hmong writers both with a rationale for writing and a specific subject matter for their texts. So, for example, a letter criticizing the Hmong for speaking their own language in public resulted in the following exchange.

EDITOR: When I hear you people talk I hear you speaking your native tongue. Are you Americans now or are you Laotian? You people expect us to adapt, adapt to us...USA." ("Asians shouldn't speak native tongue, but adapt," *The Wausau Daily Herald,* August 17, 1993)

EDITOR: I also would like to respond to the article called "Asians shouldn't speak native tongue, adapt!" There are many people like myself who have been here in the U.S. for about 14 years and still want to, and can, speak Hmong. I am glad to be a bilingual. I took French and Chinese in school so I could communicate in other languages. The more I know, the better for me. ("Don't blame Hmong, but work to solve problems," *The Wausau Daily Herald,* September 11, 1993)

In the same way, a letter accusing the Hmong of eating dogs became the subject of a tart response: "We also do not eat dogs. Now Mr. Miller is trying to tell everyone that we ate all the ducks at Duck Island. I wonder what's next, humans?" ("If Wausau's worse, blame racists," *The Wausau Daily Herald,* August 11, 1992).

And a letter accusing the Hmong of gang activity prompted this reply from a Hmong man: "EDITOR: I am writing this letter in response to Marsha Imhoff on her letter to the Editor on Nov. 2, 1991.... She stabbed the Hmong community in the back and put a red tag on us as bad guys, putting every Hmong's life in danger ("Not every Oriental person in Wausau is Hmong," *The Wausau Daily Herald,* February 19, 1992).

But the Hmong writings were more than simply responses to criticisms. Hmong writers also used the accusations made against them as an opportunity to question the values and ideals of the larger community. The following letter responding to allegations of gang violence by Southeast Asians recounts the writer's own experience of racial violence, effectively shifting the subject from violence by Hmong to violence against them and to the racism expressed against Southeast Asians. "One day after Marsha's letter was published, I was viciously attacked by a white man when I stopped at Kwik Trip on Campus Drive. I have to believe this man was acting on behalf of Marsha or he is responding to Marsha's... story."

Similarly, letters disparaging the Hmong role in the Vietnam War became, for one writer, both an occasion to reply to anti-immigrant rhetoric and an opportunity to make a proposal concerning the teaching of history in American public schools. "I've gone through my fair share of history textbooks and not one even spends a paragraph to help explain the Hmong/American alliance during the Vietnam War. So why not develop a short curriculum on the Hmong and integrate it into already existing American history courses" ("History classes should include Hmong role in War," *The Wausau Daily Herald,* June 8, 1993).

Another writer responded to the spate of critical letters by questioning the American ideal of "freedom of speech" as it applies to linguistic minorities such as the Hmong. His editorial equated the notion of free speech with an act of violence against non-English-speaking minorities and a means to silence "those of us who cannot write and speak English."

> Unfortunately, a few people have in recent months turned the Opinion Page of the *Wausau Daily Herald* into a fighting ground. I've spent my adult life and received my education in the United States, believing in freedom of speech.... However, after reading many of the articles, I have changed my belief to some extent—that freedom of speech only benefits those can write and speak, and those who can use it....
>
> I came from a country where war was a daily activity. But at the battleground in Laos, both sides were having an equal chance of life and death. Fighting on paper, however, the Hmong-Americans don't have the same chance of being able to articulate our points or the facts, because of the language and other barriers....
>
> Communism in Eastern Europe has collapsed, the Berlin Wall was torn down and the relationship between the United States and Vietnam has improved; I believe that cultural diversity in the Wausau area will continue to improve. Together, we can make the area a better and safe place to live and raise our children. ("Free speech doesn't benefit all," *The Wausau Daily Herald,* December 8, 1992)

In this response, the writer blends diverse rhetorics and rhetorical traditions, invoking the anti-immigrant rhetoric so that he can repudiate it by means of a personal narrative that combines elements of Hmong history, world events, and the values of tolerance and reconciliation. In this way does the writer attempt to create for himself what Sandra Stostky (1990) called a "civic identity," or a sense of membership in the wider community (72). In his essay, the writer projects his commitment to American values of progress and improvement and his dedication to the wider public good by making the city "a better and safe place to live and raise our children." Beyond this, however, the writer attempts to create a civic identity for his readers, who are invited to reflect upon their own values and their conception of the city. Are they aligned with the forces of historical progress, acknowledging, for example, that "communism in Eastern Europe has collapsed, the Berlin Wall was torn down and the relationship between the United States and Vietnam has improved" and that racial relations between Hmong and whites will also, inevitably, improve? Or do they align themselves with those who practice intolerance by perverting the values of free speech by silencing minority voices? What kind of people are the readers, and what are the values of the city in which they live? In this way does the essay challenge readers to examine the place of refugees in civic life and to define for themselves the nature of the "Fair City." The essay also affords the writer an occasion to begin to liberate himself, as Bakhtin (1981) would have it, "from the authority of the other's discourse" (348).

"I am writing this letter...": Genre as Shared Space

Well, I would say that I usually look at the people who are good writers, I usually read the people who are good writers, their papers and, you know, their words to try to imitate them, learn from them.
　—Ger Lue, explaining how he learned to write in English

The rhetoric of the Fair City offered Hmong writers more than a set of topics for their acts of public literacy. The rhetoric also suggested a genre in which to write: the letter to the editor and the related form of the op-ed ("opposite the editorial") essay. The genre requirements of the two forms are straightforward. Letters are expected to be brief, timely, and limited to one or two main ideas presented early in the text. Paragraphs should be short and their language unadorned. In Robert Jensen's (2003) book on publishing unpopular ideas in the mainstream media, he advises writers to "avoid flowery language, write in a clear and concise fashion, keep paragraphs to no more than one or two sentences" (37). Letters and essays are expected to include an introduction, evidence to support the claim, and a conclusion that suggests some constructive action, such as contacting a congressional representative or attending a meeting. Guidelines on writing letters and op-ed essays also typically remind writers to adopt a civil tone and avoid personal attacks.[7]

If the anti-immigrant letters violated some of these precepts, especially those concerning civility and the avoidance of personal attacks, Hmong writers displayed a surer grasp of the genre. In general, their letters and editorials were topical, concise, and clearly written. More, they adhered to the conventional architecture of introduction, evidence, and conclusions. The Hmong-authored letters frequently contain, for example, introductory sentences or paragraphs that establish at once the question at issue.

EDITOR: I'm writing this letter concerning "gangs" in Wausau. ("Ex-member says police cause Wausau gangs," *The Wausau Daily Herald,* May 19, 1993)

EDITOR: The Hmong community supports partner schools. ("Partner schools best for children's futures," *The Wausau Daily Herald,* December 12, 1993)

Most of the Hmong-authored letters and op-ed essays, moreover, contain evidence to support the claims made in the text. Typically, this evidence takes the form of a personal narrative, experiences from the writer's life in Laos or the United States. So, for instance, in an editorial on the difficulty facing Hmong women trying to negotiate two cultures and the need for the Hmong community to support such women, the writer draws upon personal experience as a form of proof.

> Have you ever felt like you were torn between two worlds? I feel that way most of the time. Being bilingual and bicultural is not easy, especially for women.
> I came to the United States when I was 12. At this age, I had already learned and knew the traditional culture well. The traditional role for women, in Laos, included having children and taking care of them, cooking, feeding animals, sewing clothing and working in the fields....
> [Now] I'm employed full time and attend school. I can't always do everything like I used to, but I'm trying very hard to keep my traditional culture and yet work toward success. Women like me need understanding and support from the Hmong community, not criticism. ("Women are in between two cultures," *The Wausau Daily Herald,* July 14, 1992)

The use of personal narrative in such letters is significant. Walter Fisher (1989) has written that narrative arguments are essentially universal, a part of human nature and the socialization process. In Fisher's view, narrative arguments are also fundamentally democratic, a form of reasoning that relies not upon specialized or technical knowledge but rather upon the proofs of character, sequence, and morality that resonate across the borders of language, ethnicity, class, and race. In the Hmong "Fair City" writings, stories are a primary form of evidence and a means to appeal to the shared values of writers and readers. When a Hmong writer addressed the charge that the Southeast Asians are defrauding the welfare system, for example, he grounded his argument not in statistical proofs or other forms of documentary evidence, but in a personal narrative that recalls for readers, in language that is nostalgic, almost lyrical, a typical day in the life of a Hmong family in Laos.

> While my parents did their chores, my wife and I got water buckets and walked about a quarter of a mile to the stream. My parents' village did

not have running water. While my father fed the pig, my sister helped by making sure that no other pigs came to steal the food.... At 5 o'clock that morning we had our breakfast. Soon after the breakfast, we walked out to work in the dry rice field. We started about 7 in the morning and worked until noon, weeding the field....

Each of us worked until about 11 or 12 o'clock before we could go to bed that night. It was the end of a long day, and we needed our rest for tomorrow. Almost every family worked this way. Those days are far away now, but I remember them well. Many of the Hmong adults in Wausau still think about and remember the "good, old-hard-working days" as I do. We miss those days, even now. ("A day in the life: Hmong in Laos," *The Wausau Daily Herald,* August 11, 1992)

The narrative communicates more than the writer's yearning for his homeland. In a social climate in which the Hmong were continually accused of being lazy and unwilling to work, the story illustrates for readers the grueling physical labor that defined Hmong life in Laos and the willingness of Hmong people to sacrifice for their families. The evidence used to refute charges of welfare fraud, then, is narrative, taking the forms of a story that, in Fisher's conception, can be meaningful "across communities as well as cultures, across time and place" (1989, 65–66).

Finally, the Hmong writings contained, in most cases, conclusions grounded in a call for action—activities that readers might take in connection with the topic. In many cases, these were appeals for tolerance and understanding that not only offered a perspective on race relations in the city, but also established a "civic identity" of writers as responsible members of the community, concerned with the welfare of both white and Hmong city residents.

Instead of questioning and blaming the Hmong in the paper, please sit down and discuss our concerns and differences. ("Free speech doesn't benefit all!" *The Wausau Daily Herald,* December 8, 1992)

I don't mean that everyone has to do this, but it would be a good idea and we will live peacefully if we can reach out to our neighbors for friendship today. ("Build bridges of friendship with neighbors," *The Wausau Daily Herald,* November 16, 1993)

The appropriation of these forms, the letter and the op-ed essay, gave the Hmong writers a scaffolding on which to build their arguments and challenge the rhetoric of the Fair City. More, it afforded them an entrée into the shared space—the "public commons"—of the local newspaper so that they might speak beyond the circle of their families, friends, and acquaintances to the broader audience of the white community. In entering this space and addressing a larger audience, the Hmong writers publicly contested the representation of themselves as undesirable aliens by positing an ethos grounded in principles of moderation, tolerance, and values shared with other city residents. In the language of Burke, these forms allowed the writers to forge a sense of consubstantiality with fair-minded readers, white and Hmong. More, the use of the letter and op-ed essay illustrated how those rhetorical forms shape the literacy practices of writers seeking to participate in arguments of public and civic life.

Dogs, Ducks, and "$80,000 Houses": The Struggle for Tropes

They see all these Hmong people driving $20,000 cars and buying $80,000 houses with cash....I have read that in a letter, and I just want to clarify.
—Xiong Lue, explaining why he decided to respond to a letter alleging that Hmong people receiving food stamps were buying "$80,000 houses"

Beyond its suggestion of topics and genre, the rhetoric of the Fair City also suggested to Hmong writers a language, a collection of words and phrases, that they might use in writing their letters and editorials. In the rhetoric of the Fair City, complaints against the Hmong were in many cases expressed in the form of tropes, or patterns of words that involve, as Edward Corbett (1990) put it, "a deviation from the ordinary and principal signification of the word"(426). In the context of the anti-immigrant letters, selected words and phrases were freighted with meanings that went beyond their "principal signification" to suggest identities for members of the refugee population and undermine their status and legitimate presence in the city. Hmong writers, in response, borrowed these same figurative words and phrases and animated them with opposing meanings. Consider the following example: "EDITOR: Everyone in Wausau needs some answers... [about] how Asians can afford to buy new cars and *$80,000 houses*. What kind of unjust system do we have? Well just the other day I saw a family member that just bought that *$80,000 house* buying food at a grocery store with...you got it! Food stamps!" [emphasis added] ("You just don't get it, writer says," *The Wausau Daily Herald,* July 26, 1992).

In this letter, the phrase "$80,000 houses" is a trope: a code, or a form of shorthand meant to communicate a larger set of attitudes and beliefs.

Michael Calvin McGee (1995) has argued that human beings are conditioned by external forces to recognize and respond to a "vocabulary of concepts" that do not in themselves explain the meanings and nuances of social phenomena, but function instead as "guides, warrants, reasons or excuses for behavior and belief" (445). Such terms, McGee writes, serve as "one term sums of an orientation" and can be used to symbolize an entire line of argument. These terms—McGee calls them "ideographs"—are the "building blocks of ideology" and signify, beyond their conventional lexical meanings, a "unique ideological commitment" to a set of ideas or beliefs (445). The "$80,000 house" represents one such commitment. It serves as a proposition more than a phrase, encapsulating a certain set of beliefs about refugees, the "system," and the city itself. The meaning of the term, in this reading, is both literal and figurative, a concrete referent to a real object, but also an emblem of Hmong duplicity and a marker of identity. Thus does the phrase exceed, in Corbett's language, the "ordinary and principal signification" of the words contained within it.

For some Hmong writers, however, such terms invited revisions and re-interpretations. Responding to the letter above, a Hmong community leader wrote the following.

> EDITOR: What about the Hmong man who buys an *$80,000 house* when he has been here only a couple of years, when there are so many people who were born in this country who cannot afford a $30,000 home? Before getting mad at this person, maybe we can all learn something from him and try to live our lives as he did. Obviously, if he bought an *$80,000 house,* he is not on welfare. . . . I can almost guarantee that he neither smokes, nor drinks, nor goes out to eat regularly, nor drives a $20,000 car. ("Expand the clan; we're all one Wausau family," *The Wausau Daily Herald,* n.d.)

In this reply, the trope of the "$80,000 house" is transformed. No longer an emblem of duplicity, it symbolizes the inherent rationality of Hmong economic priorities. Not only are Hmong homeowners represented as financially prudent, but they are also depicted as free of the vices—smoking, drinking, and spending money unwisely—that presumably make it impossible for some white residents of the city to afford houses of their own. Indeed, the Hmong are constituted in the letter as models to be emulated. "Before getting mad at this person," the writer suggests, "maybe we can all learn something from him and try to live our lives as he did." In his response, the writer is contesting a point of fact: people on welfare do not buy "$80,000 houses." Beyond this, however, he is also implicitly chastising those who have not exercised the same fiscal discipline as the Hmong and who, as a result, may not be able to afford "$80,000 houses" of their own. As a linguistic artifact, the trope acts as a pivot between the letters, a shared territory on which to map opposing meanings. The trope has become "populated—overpopulated with the intentions of others" (Bakhtin, 1981, 294) and functions to express competing visions of community life.

A similar transformation is effected in the persistent accusation that Hmong in the city ate dogs and ducks from local parks. This charge circulated both orally, as in the business forum cited earlier, and in writing, as in the following letters.

> EDITOR: Also good people of Wausau, if you have a *dog* you love, keep him on a good leash. The Hmong people tried three times to have mine for lunch.... Lots of *ducks* missing on Oak Island too. [emphasis added] ("No friend of Wausau Hmong," *The Wausau Daily Herald,* July 4, 1989)

> EDITOR: *What happened to all the ducks on Duck Island?* We've been there twice and saw one duck. [emphasis added] ("Hmong children should teach," *The Wausau Daily Herald,* July 28, 1989)

> EDITOR: [I plan to run for office] to stop this outrageous discrimination against Whites.... P.S. *Where is my dog?* [emphasis added] ("Man with complaints says he'll run," *The Wausau Daily Herald,* n.d.)

Rhetorical questions, Corbett reminds us, are asked "not for the purpose of eliciting an answer but for the purpose of asserting or denying something obliquely" (1990, 453). In the rhetoric of the Fair City, "Where is my dog?" was not a literal question but a symbolic one, intended to assert the frightening otherness of Southeast Asians and their incompatibility with American life. Readers were expected to answer by affirming the alien character of the Hmong and rejecting their place in the life of the city. In this sense, the question functioned as an enthymeme, or "rhetorical syllogism," in which a key premise of an argument is left unexpressed. In the enthymeme, listeners are invited to supply the missing premises themselves and so to participate in the process of their own persuasion (Bitzer 1959). The rhetorical questions considered here work in a similar fashion, insinuating rather than declaring and inviting readers to invoke for themselves the lexicon of the anti-immigrant prejudice.

As with the "$80,000 houses," however, the "dog eater" trope became a starting point from which to examine issues of race relations and community life. In the op-ed essay "Heard a Hmong rumor? Check it out!" (*The Wausau Daily Herald,* June 9, 1992), a Hmong writer begins,

> Have you heard? *Hmong people eat dogs and ducks from Duck Island* [emphasis added]. Hmong don't pay taxes for seven years. The government buys them new cars and houses when they arrive in America.
>
> Have you heard these rumors? I have. I'm a Hmong man living in Wausau, and I hear these kinds of things frequently. These statements are wrong, but that hardly seems to matter. Rumors about the Hmong continue to exist in our community. These rumors are a source of racial tension that divides us all.

Rather than simply dismissing the allegations made against the Hmong, this writer seizes on them as an opportune moment to address the ignorance of readers. "Are we in Wausau really so isolated from one another that some of us don't know anything at all about the others?" Beyond this, the construct of the Hmong as "dog eaters," like the trope of the "$80,000 house," is an occasion for recalling the tumultuous history that has brought the Hmong to Wausau.

> The Hmong...came to America and to Wausau because they lost their homeland. They were allies of the U.S. and fought side by side with American soldiers during the Vietnam War. Thousands of Hmong died during the war, and many thousands were brutally punished or killed after the communist North Vietnamese and the Pathet Lao took over Laos. The Hmong had no choice but to leave their country.

The writer even borrows the device of the rhetorical question—"Have you heard these rumors?"—featured in the anti-immigrant letters as a means of addressing non-Hmong readers in the community. The essay illustrates that while the rhetoric of the Fair City presented a catalog of tropes to denigrate Southeast Asians, these could not, once introduced, be contained or controlled. Hmong writers seized upon them as vehicles for broader, potentially transformative discussions of race, history, and the place of the "other" in the American city. In doing so, they challenged the meanings assigned to the tropes in the anti-immigrant rhetoric and offered examples of how rhetorics and rhetorical struggles shaped the language of their literacy practices.

"Our Community" and "You People": Constituting Audience in the Rhetoric of the Fair City

> "Welcome Home to Wausau"
> —sign posted on city limits

While Hmong writers appropriated the topics, genre, and tropes of the anti-immigrant rhetoric, they were also competing for its readers and their conception of the city. Susan Wells (1996) has written that public writing involves more than simply persuading a preexisting public to accept or refuse the appeals of writers and speakers. Instead, Wells argues, writers and speakers "must work to build a public" to which persuasion might be addressed. The public is not a given, but is "a performance in time, located at specific historical junctures, temporary and unstable" (326). The rhetorical construction of the audience, in this view, occurs prior to its persuasion, a point made in Maurice Charland's (1993) revisionary treatment of Aristotle's conception of audience: "If it is easier to praise Athens before Athenians than before Laecedemonians, we should ask how those in Athens came to experience themselves as Athenians" (214).

For Hmong writers, this meant offering readers an alternative conception not only of Southeast Asian refugees, but also of themselves as residents of the city. Hmong writers had to posit another kind of public life, one in which readers came to see themselves as members of a polity committed to principles of justice, tolerance, and fair play. To recall the language of Burke, Hmong writers had to constitute an audience that would reject anti-immigrant rhetoric and experience a sense of identification with the writers and with Hmong refugees generally. In the anti-refugee rhetoric and the Hmong responses to it, the struggle to constitute an audience can be tracked in the conflicting values assigned to pronouns and in the markedly different meanings each set of writings invested in the proper noun "Wausau."

In the Fair City rhetoric, pronouns are used as barriers between the Hmong and the majority community. The use of pronouns in the anti-immigrant rhetoric is exclusionary, underscoring the breach between the first-person plural "we" of the victimized majority and the othering third-person plurals "they" and "them" of the victimizing strangers. Pronouns in the Fair City rhetoric have a spatial dimension, with "we," "our," and "us" indicating nearness, immediacy, and identification, while the demonstrative pronoun phrases "these people," "those people," and the related "you people" indicate distance, strangeness, and disassociation. For example,

We took the Hmong people in. *We* gave *them* homes. *We* paid for *their* clothes. *We* fed *them*. [emphasis added] ("Hmong, don't sue, be grateful," *The Wausau Daily Herald*, February 10. 1994)

Until I can learn to live with *these people* without my blood boiling... [emphasis added] ("Hmong 'plight' doesn't make sense," *The Wausau Daily Herald*, June 23, 1993)

You people came here to enhance *our* community. Not destroy it. [emphasis added] ("Asians shouldn't speak native tongue, but adapt," *The Wausau Daily Herald*, August 17, 1993)

In their responses to the Fair City rhetoric, Hmong writers invoked these same lexical items, but inverted and used them toward radically different ends. If pronouns are a means of division in the rhetoric of the Fair City, they are, in the Hmong writings, enticements to become, in Burke's (1969) phrase, "substantially one" with a minority people. In the Hmong public writings, "we" and "our" do not restrict, but rather invite connections, expansions, and relationships. In their letters and editorials, the Hmong writers use the pronouns to portray their issues as community issues, their interests as identical to majority interests, and their values as universal values of decency and compassion. "Early this year, one of my neighbors passed away. When *she* passed away, it hurt *me* and my family. *They* are white and *we* are yellow, but *we* shared the same sorrow with *her* family. If *we* love one another, *our* relationship makes *us* feel like a blood relation" [emphases added] ("Build bridges of friendship with neighbors," *The Wausau Daily Herald*, November 16, 1993).

In the above essay, the writer joins Hmong and whites upon the common ground of "we," "our," and "us," inviting readers to experience themselves as members of a single family brought together by the shared grief over the death of a neighbor. Rather than dividing Hmong and whites, pronouns become intimately condensed spaces in which the two groups can meet and declare their common human values. Identification and consubstantiality replace division and exclusion.

In the same way, the name "Wausau" represents a ground of struggle, a proper noun in which to contest conflicting visions of identity and position. In the anti-refugee writings, "Wausau" is a call to arms.

Come on *Wausau*, stand up. Let's show them what America really is, you work for what you want. [emphasis added] ("Treat Hmong like everyone else," *The Wausau Daily Herald*, n.d.)

I suggest a change of name, from Wausau to Hmongville. [emphasis added] ("No friend of Wausau Hmong," *The Wausau Daily Herald,* July 4, 1989)

In the Hmong writings, the same proper noun suggests a different set of truths and possibilities. Hmong writers invoke the term as a way of offering white readers the opportunity to identify themselves with a set of principles that transcend racial and cultural divisions. While the tensions inherent in the name "Wausau" are never far from the surface in the Hmong writings—"*Wausau,* a town full of natural beauty...has a subtle racist community [emphasis added]," writes one Hmong woman—there is a larger sense in which the city's name is meant to invoke connectedness and extended family: "How about expanding the family? Do not say Yang's family, Vang's family, or Xiong's family? Instead say *Wausau's* family" [emphasis added] ("Expand the clan; we're all one *Wausau* family," *The Wausau Daily Herald,* n.d.).

In the Hmong writings and the Fair City rhetoric, then, pronouns and the proper noun "Wausau" are used to profoundly different understandings—both of Hmong refugees and of readers' own identities. Both sets of writings illustrate, further, how pronouns and proper nouns can be used to constitute an audience prior to its persuasion, to induce "Wausau residents to experience themselves as Wausau residents," to paraphrase Charland (1993). The role of literacy in these transactions is to express the values of both sides and to work as a modality for expressing competing rhetorical conceptions of social and economic life. In this way may we say that literacy—its purposes, motives, and form—is shaped by the rhetorical worlds in which writers live and in which they seek, through public writings, to intervene and change.

The letters written by Hmong writers represent a singular moment in the history of Hmong literacy. From their beginnings in the United States as a primarily non-English-speaking people, many of whom did not read or write in any language, the Hmong began in the late 1980s and early 1990s to use English-language literacy to respond to social and political questions concerning Hmong refugees. In this sense, the letters mark a stage of literacy development in which Hmong writing moves from the domains of school, church, work, and family to more public and civic contexts. Literacy becomes a means to sound a public voice.

The Hmong letters also speak to the intersections of rhetoric and literacy in multicultural, multilingual, and multiliterate nations such as the United States. As the forces of globalism and the so-called "new economy" continue to result in population shifts around the world—a phenomenon that is actually centuries old—capitalist nations in North America and Europe continue to experience large-scale immigration. The Hmong letters offer an example, in one context, of how a minority people new to the language traditions of the majority can borrow, inflect, and transform these traditions in contexts of public argumentation. In doing so, the Hmong letters offer an example of how a minority people—even one formerly thought to be "preliterate"—can use writing to advocate for themselves and their ideals.

Conclusion

This chapter has suggested some functions literacy can serve when people to whom it has been denied begin to learn and use it for themselves. Literacy functioned for Hmong in one Midwestern city as an instrument for remembering and teaching, as in the family memoirs; as a tool for challenging cultural norms, as in Hmong women's writing; and as a means through which to address issues of public life, as in the Hmong editorials and letters to the editor. In each case literacy was a response to specific social and historical contexts. Hmong writers in Wausau learned to write letters and editorials because they needed a forum and set of literate conventions with which to respond to criticism of their culture. Hmong women learned to write grant proposals and public essays in support of a nascent women's movement. And Hmong of different ages, educational backgrounds, and genders learned to write memoirs because these were necessary for recording the past. And while the literacy practices of the Hmong were diverse—different groups writing in different genres for different ends—what was constant in Hmong literacy practices in the city was the role of rhetoric, the use of symbols for the purpose of shaping reality, in influencing literacy practice. In the writings we have considered here, however, the rhetorics of literacy were not imposed or preordained by an institutional power, whether the state, the church, or the school. Rather, the rhetorics guiding the literacy practices considered here were generated by the writers who sought, through their writings, to articulate their understandings of themselves, their histories, and their place in Hmong and majority cultures.

Conclusion
The Rhetorics of Literacy

I saw the Pa Chai [soldiers]. They were crazy, and they were fighting
in that war. I saw their writings also. Those writings, they were Hmong
writings.... And when they had finished writing, they explained in detail
from the beginning when the world was flooded with water, to explaining
about the Hmong king, to explaining everything. They explained all those
things in their writings.

> —Lue Vang Pao, recalling the day when forces of the messianic Hmong leader
> Pa Chai Vue brought a writing system to his village in Laos, circa 1920

The first time that I remember it was my dad, he was in the battlefield, and
he wrote a letter back to my mom to say that he was okay. And my mom had
one of the soldiers that delivered the letter read it to her. And that's how I
remember reading.

> —Blia Thao, recalling her first encounter with literacy in Laos, late 1960s

We were in Illinois. And I wasn't in school yet. My dad was in school every
day, and so my mom and I, and my sister and brother, we were at home
every day, and there was nothing to do, and the only show we watched was
Sesame Street. And then from the TV show we learned how to sing A-B-C. I
learned how to count 1-2-3. And I just watched exactly what they did on TV,
and I just kind of learned from that. And then ... when I started in school, it
was like, "Oh, yeah, I saw this somewhere. It was on, you know, on *Sesame
Street*." So it really started ... on the TV.

> —May Yang, remembering her introduction to literacy in Illinois, 1980s

On the one hand, the Hmong literacy narrative is one of singular, even
inimitable, particulars. It is a story of reading and writing set in contexts of
mythical alphabets, centuries of warfare, religious conversions, and exile
to Western nations. Its cast of characters includes missionary linguists, CIA
operatives, and messianic revolutionaries, as well as American evangelists,
public schoolteachers, and ordinary Hmong people learning to read and
write. It is a narrative, moreover, enmeshed in what was a global struggle

190

among Cold War superpowers that resulted in the Vietnam War, the scope and carnage of which had devastating consequences for the Hmong in Laos and which forever changed Hmong rationales, forms, practices, and interpretations of literacy.

And while there are parts of the Hmong story that parallel the literacy experiences of other cultures in other historical settings—Western missionaries introducing literacy in the South Pacific to spread Christian doctrine (Besnier 1995; Clammer 1976); public school teachers using literacy in American classrooms to promote assimilation (Graff 1979); and readers and writers everywhere turning literacy to their own ends, cultural, political, and mystical (Street 1995)—there may not be another narrative that contains all these diverse elements, all experienced within a relatively compressed historical period. In this respect, the Hmong may have a history of literacy unique among the cultures of the world.

But what does this singular narrative offer, if anything, beyond the boundaries of the tumultuous Hmong experience? How does the Hmong story help us understand literacy development in other settings? Among other peoples? What can be shared? Generalized? Extended? What can we learn from the Hmong story about the following questions that prompted this book?

- How do individuals learn to read and write? How does literacy take hold in cultures in which reading and writing have not been widely practiced? How is literacy learned across borders, by immigrants and refugees, and through the political, economic, religious, military, and migratory upheavals that we call "globalization"?
- What are the effects of literacy? What purposes does it serve for those who disseminate it, and what does it offer those who learn it? How does it act upon readers and writers, and how does it work for them? How is literacy implicated in relationships of identity, power, and the construction of reality?
- Finally, what do these questions and their possible answers mean for literacy teaching? What does the Hmong narrative suggest for those who teach and study literacy in other contexts?

In exploring these questions, we do not look for "universal truths" about literacy development, for some chimerical essence or unchanging nature. Such a search would certainly fail, since, as contemporary scholarship has made clear, literacy is always marked by the particular, the specific, and the situated. Indeed, much of the project of New Literacy Studies has been to demonstrate the culturally contextualized character of literacy and the legitimacy of reading and writing practices long regarded as outside the mainstream. This insight is, at least in my view, indispensable. What accounts for literacy in one setting will not account for it in another, and the outcomes of literacy will change from generation to generation (Brandt 2001; de Castell and Luke 1983). Shaped by the contexts in which it is learned, literacy does not lend itself to summative pronouncements or undisputed truths. Rather, there are, as Harvey J. Graff (1995) has noted, "multiple paths of literacy learning" (329), multiple ways in which human beings learn, use, and value literacy.

For the Hmong, the pathways have been numerous, individuated, and seemingly exceptional. And yet the Hmong experience does offer, I believe, ways of understanding the wider patterns, lines of inquiry, and common language of literacy development. The Hmong story in this sense may help us—teachers, researchers, and other literacy workers—understand the literacy development of other learners, in other settings, at other moments in history. What follows, then, is a kind of coda, a concluding reflection, an effort to follow the multiple pathways of the Hmong to see what their literate journeys might tell us about the processes and meanings of reading and writing generally.

Recalling Reading and Recalling Writing: Literacy Is Personal

Ask different people to tell you about their earliest memories of literacy and you are likely to hear about a time in childhood, located at home or at school, often warmly remembered. This was the question I asked at the beginning of each of my interviews with the Hmong people I spoke with, asking them to tell me about their first memories of written language, their earliest memories of learning to read, or copying letters, or simply seeing written language on a page. And while there are certainly differences in the way people remember learning to read and learning to write (Brandt 1994), the people I spoke with were usually able to recall both in careful detail, remembering the settings, the materials, and the subjects of literacy.

For example, Lue Vang Pao's first memories of literacy, cited at the start of this chapter, brought him back to his village, to childhood, to a time when he was, in his words, "too young to wear my pants." For Blia Thao, also quoted above, the earliest memory of literacy resided in the letters sent home by her father from the battlefield, letters that were an important source of emotional support to the family. May Yang, who was just an infant when she was brought by her parents to the United States and whose testimony recalls her first exposure to written text, remembers that literacy began with a television program viewed in a rented house in Illinois, during a quiet moment with her family.

Read individually, these and similar narratives speak to the diverse circumstances under which literacy can be learned and its adhesion in learners' memories to the particulars of time, place, and events. The details of these stories also suggest the unusually intimate nature of reading and writing and how it may be connected to familiar recollections of childhood, family, and home. As I listened to the accounts I had solicited, I sometimes felt I was intruding on some intensely private meditation, some cloistered set of memories that had been left quiet for many years. To remember how one learned to read and write, it seemed, is to revisit a time of beginnings, of starting out, and then to reflect upon where the journey led. Given the unusual density of events crowded into the lives of many Hmong, such reflections were complex, sometimes emotional, often marked by ambiguities.

To read the Hmong narratives as individual stories, then, is to emphasize the personal dimension of literacy development, or the ways in which individual readers and writers direct their own learning to their own ends. As the testimonies throughout this book make clear, individual readers and writers play a critical role in their own literacy development, deciding what they will learn, at what times of life, and for what purposes. Whether driven by the need to understand a mystical alphabet, to read a letter from a distant parent, or to comprehend text on a TV screen, people learn to read and write for reasons of their own. The personal perspective, as I shall call it, has of late been neglected in literacy studies. In recent years, the trend in scholarship has been to move away from the focus upon individual readers and writers in favor of examining the broader cultural and material contexts of literacy learning. This trend has come at least partially in response to earlier scholarship, which, as Brandt (2001) observed, "theorized, researched, critiqued, debated, and sometimes even managed to enhance the literacy potentials of ordinary citizens," while attending less confidently to the "larger contexts of profit making and competition" (18–19). More recent scholarship, in contrast, reflects what has become known in the humanities as "the social turn," or research that looks beyond the individual "to the social, cultural, and political contexts in which people lead their lives" (Cushman et al. 2001, 3).

Given these socially and structurally oriented trends in literacy studies, it may appear counterintuitive to begin this review by looking first to the experiences and perspectives of individual readers and writers. But I would argue that it is a mistake to formulate theories of literacy development without accounting for individual motives, behaviors, and aspirations. People often undertake and direct their literacy experiences to satisfy some personal objective, agenda, or desire, whether to read a messianic alphabet, or comprehend a letter from a family member, or understand the ABCs of *Sesame Street*. And these personal objectives and desires drive and motivate literacy learning in ways, sometimes deeply and even passionately felt, that exist apart from the social and structural forces organizing literacy learning. This was made clear to me as I sat in the kitchens and workplaces of adult Hmong men and women, listening to them explain what was at stake in becoming literate, what measures they took to attain literacy, and why it was, for at least some of them, a matter of such urgency. Literacy, the Hmong stories compel us to acknowledge is a profoundly personal undertaking, a response to individually felt needs and desires. Let us take this as our starting point, the first pathway: literacy development is *personal*.

Where the Story Connects: Literacy Is Cultural

Stories of learning to read and write, as we have seen, often recall scenes of life that are vividly remembered and perhaps deeply felt. Literacy, we conclude from this, is a deeply personal affair. Yet those same memories, read another way, make clear that literacy is more than personal and transcends the private.

Lue Vang Pao's memories of the revolutionary soldiers entering his village, for example, recall a moment from childhood, one that remains vivid and perhaps cherished in his mental archive of family and village remembrances. Yet his testimony also invokes, beyond the personal, the cultural narratives of a lost Hmong alphabet that would be restored to the Hmong by God, heralding the return of the *Huab Thai* and the revivification of the Hmong people. Pao's narrative intersects here with the older Hmong narratives of the lost book, the one eaten by the horses, or fallen into the river, or eaten by the Hmong themselves when they were starving. Pao's memories, in other words, take us to the place where the story connects—where the personal becomes the cultural, where individual conceptions of reading and writing meet and are intermingled with long-held cultural beliefs, aspirations, and values. Lue Vang Pao's personal story underscores the cultural dimensions of literacy development, or the ways in which literacy development may be understood as an expression of the wider cultural context.

The relationship of culture to literacy development is by now a truism in Literacy Studies, having dominated discussions of theory and research since the publication in 1983 of Shirley Brice Heath's indispensable work, *Ways with Words,* which demonstrated the myriad ways in which literacy is responsive to cultural practices. Heath showed how learning to read and write, once thought to be the sole province of classroom and school, was in fact deeply and inevitably influenced by the language and values of home and community. Following Heath's study, scholars employing ethnographic research methodologies fanned out across out across the world, quite literally, to study the intersections of literacy and culture in such venues as a Papua New Guinean village (Kulick and Stroud 1993), a Polynesian atoll (Besnier 1995), an Alaskan fishing village (Reder and Wikelund 1993), and elsewhere. The unifying theme of much of this research was that literacy must be understood as an element of a larger set of social and cultural practices, embedded in the events and interactions of everyday life.

The Hmong story enriches and complicates this perspective. What we learn from the Hmong narrative is that a cultural "context" or "perspective" is not a single, inherently coherent framework but instead a number of multiple perspectives, social alignments, and processes in motion, experienced across time and distance, each with its own ways of learning, practicing, and understanding literacy. The experience of revolutionary soldiers teaching a sacred alphabet, or that of a young girl hearing her father's letters read aloud, or that of a refugee family watching *Sesame Street* in a rented house are representative of profoundly different episodes in the history of the Hmong. Yet each articulates an aspect of the Hmong cultural experience, and each offers a unique context for literacy practice. The "cultural perspective" so often discussed in literacy research, the Hmong experience suggests, is perhaps better represented as a kaleidoscope of perspectives, shifting and variable.

With this as our understanding of culture, we may elaborate our conceptions of literacy development. The Hmong narratives teach us that literacy is *personal,* but it is also *cultural.* People learn to read and write for their own reasons, but they do so in contexts of cultural intersections, movements, and change. Recalling the metaphor from Graff, we may say the pathway to literacy is a *personal* pathway but also a *cultural* one and that the cultural pathway is not one road but many different branching ones.

Never for Its Own Sake: Literacy Is Institutional

So we have expanded our understanding of literacy development to account for the personal and the cultural. Yet the Hmong story compels us to go further. Expansive as personal and cultural explanations may appear, there is a sense in which they can also limit understandings. Exclusively personal approaches to literacy, as noted, may miss the wider forces that structure the reading and writing practices of the individual. Cultural interpretations of literacy development, in turn, may in some cases represent cultures and their literacy practices as atomized, a product of the unique characteristics of particular groups of people rather than an outcome of historical and violent contacts between peoples of unequal power. The Hmong testimonies make clear that the literacy development results from connections of individuals and cultures, but also, crucially, through contacts with the institutions that influence the lives of individuals and cultures. This is our third pathway: the institutional path to literacy development.

The testimonies cited at the start of this chapter speak implicitly to the influence of institutions upon literacy development. As we have seen, the writing system introduced by Pa Chai's revolutionary soldiers in Lue Vang Pao's village was an expression of Hmong cultural yearnings for literacy, a technology that some Hmong believed would mark them as equals to more powerful peoples. Yet we enrich this reading by locating within it the role of institutions in motivating and shaping Hmong attitudes toward literacy. In this understanding, the desire for literacy was an element of a broader political and cultural response to Hmong oppression at the hands of French colonial authorities, whose bureaucracies used written language to maintain their dominance over the native populations of Laos. The colonial institutions that oppressed the Hmong and that used literacy as an instrument of this oppression stimulated a long-standing desire among Hmong people to have this same technology for themselves. The desire for literacy, in this reading, was expressive of cultural values, but these values were animated, in French colonial Laos, by the role of literacy in consolidating their status as a politically subordinate people.

There were, of course, more explicit Hmong encounters with institutional literacies. In Laos, the primary institutions disseminating literacy, as we have seen, were three: the Laotian state, which organized the village classrooms; missionary Christianity, whose agents, in the words of Gia Nhia Thao, "came to our town to talk about religion, and they also taught you how to read and write in Hmong"; and, finally, the Hmong military, which offered soldiers the opportunities to learn and practice new literacy skills essential to the prosecution of modern warfare. In the United States, the institutional sources of literacy for Hmong refugees looked much the same: the public schools, where Hmong children such as Thao Lue learned to "dream an American dream"; the evangelical churches, where friendship, literacy, and proselytization freely commingled; and the different workplaces that required specialized forms of literacy such as those learned by Zong Her, whose work at a local bank involved "helping Hmong customers negotiate the language and literacy of loan applications, translating these from English to Hmong." Collectively, all of these illustrated the ways in which Hmong literacy development was directed by powerful institutions.

Examining such influences, we relearn an enduring lesson: that literacy is rarely, if ever, taught for its own sake. It is a means to an end, an instrument for furthering the agenda of the institution purveying it. "Reading...was not just reading," Soltow and Stevens (1981) observed in their study of the rise of the American common school; "it was the reading of something." Whether to administer colonies, fight wars, convert souls, or transform individual consciousness, institutional literacies are rarely, if ever, innocent of motive. They have been a means, instead, to advance a strategy, manage a population, empower one group at the expense of another. This does not mean that institutional literacies are by definition oppressive, inevitably used by powerful interests to dominate others. Rather, they are inherently pragmatic, a means to an end, an instrument of policy. Nor are learners powerless to divert the intentions of institutional literacy, as the Hmong stories make clear. But if ends, means, and responses are variable, what is invariable is the role of institutions, when they are present, in furthering literacy development. Literacy, the Hmong testimonies tell us, is *personal* and *cultural,* but it is equally *institutional.*

Enduring Narratives: Literacy Is Transnational and Historical

As we have seen, many Hmong arrived in the United States with some knowledge of reading and writing, whether acquired in village schools, bible classes, or L'Armée Clandestine. As refugees, they came into contact with U.S. institutions offering literacy instruction—public schools, evangelical churches, and workplaces. But the forms of literacy offered in these sites were not, for many Hmong, an altogether unfamiliar and mysterious technology, as was commonly assumed in much scholarly and popular literature about the Hmong. Rather, Hmong refugees learning to read and write in the United States were in some cases resuming relationships with written language that had begun decades earlier in Laos. The forms, functions, and meanings of literacy in the United States were, for some Hmong, familiar to those that had been previously encountered. In this sense, the Hmong were re-entering worlds of symbols and signs that were, in some cases, known to them—even when they could not decode or encode these symbols and signs. Hmong literacy development, in other words, was not confined to local contexts, whether personal, cultural, or institutional. Instead, the sources, forms, and meanings of literacy had been transported across the boundaries of states, cultures, languages, and generations. And this indicates the next pathway: literacy is transnational and historical.

By this I mean that immigrants and refugees from cultures in which literacy is not practiced may not be encountering, as is commonly supposed, entirely new modalities of communication when they arrive in Western countries. Instead, they may bring with them a history saturated by contacts with colonial, socialist, and capitalist powers. Similarly, the forms of literacy practiced in the West may be anything but novel to refugees and immigrants, even those presumed to be "preliterate." Instead, twenty-first century migrants may have had extensive contact with the emissaries of European and American expansion—the teachers, administrators, missionaries, military commanders, and other bearers of the written word. Refugees and immigrants who do not read and write and whose cultures have a scant history of reading and writing may in fact arrive in the their host nations with long and freighted histories of literacy.

For literacy scholars, these facts may demand a reconsideration of current orthodoxy, specifically the idea that literacy is primarily or even exclusively a response to local and specific effects. The Hmong experience illustrates that while literacy is indeed responsive to local conditions, the languages, symbols, and rhetorics observed in these local settings are global and historical, transported by readers and writers through time and space. The Hmong experience with French administrators, itinerant priests, and CIA agents, each with their own uses for written language, suggests that literacy development may be as much a product of the enduring "grand narratives," colonialism, Christianity, capitalism, and others as it is an expression of the cultural perspectives articulated in local contexts. To say this is not to dismiss the local and the situated nature of literacy, its adhesion to the particulars of time and place, but rather to press for accounts of literacy that elaborate the links between the local and the global, the immediate and the historical. It is to urge consideration in discussions of literacy of "that wider field of force," or the totality of historical events, contacts, and connections that influence the ways in which human beings make sense of who they are, where they belong in the world, and the role of written language in mediating these.

Such considerations have practical implications for literacy educators. In conventional approaches to the teaching of literacy to refugees, immigrants, and other adults, the presumption has largely been one of deficits, as educators have sought to supply what is assumed to be absent from learners' experiences: basic English, everyday life skills, job training, and citizenship education. While such learners do arrive with certain basic needs, the Hmong experience makes clear that refugees and immigrants may also come to the United States with long histories and deeply held values regarding literacy. These histories and values can inform classroom instruction in the form of syllabi and teaching methods, as teachers explore the literacy histories and experiences of learners instead of focusing primarily upon their presumed deficits. The specific methods for exploring such histories will depend largely upon local contexts. Teachers may collect oral histories, publish student writings, create video archives, or work with students to find other ways to integrate students' experiences of literacy with the institutional curriculum. In teaching literacy, in other words, teachers may enrich their classes by acknowledging the *transnational* and *historical* pathways of literacy.

The Connecting Pathway: Literacy Is Rhetorical

Learning to read and write, I have argued, is *personal, cultural, institutional, transnational,* and *historical.* When we ask how people learn to read and write in the present day, when we ask more specifically about the literacy development of immigrants and refugees from cultures in which literacy was not widespread, our answers must address, to some degree, these multiple dimensions and possibilities. This means we can no longer limit ourselves to the familiar binaries: "cognitive" versus "social," "literate" versus "oral," and others. Such categories have the effect of reducing the rich and complicated experiences of human beings to a set of simplistic, dichotomous, and ultimately misleading labels. Rather than informing, they act, recalling Burke (1966), as "terministic screens," or selections of reality that deflect alternative understandings of reality. What is deflected in dichotomous notions of literacy are what Harvey Graff (1987) termed its "continuities and contradictions," or the ways in which literacy is expressive of both elements in the binary, the cognitive and social, the oral and written, the local and the global, the contemporary and the historical.

Still, the identification of literacy's multiple dimensions is but a beginning. Cataloging these tells us something of literacy's diversity, but it does little to explain how they may be related and what is common among them. We learn, in other words, something of the diverse pathways of literacy development, but not what connects these pathways in different settings for different learners at different moments in history. What is shared, for example, in the experiences of learning to read and write in a Lao village classroom, in a bible class in Thailand, in an English class in a Wisconsin high school? What is general, going beyond the Hmong experience, in the literacy lessons offered at an elite university, in a special education class in an inner city high school, in a reading club at the local bookstore? How are these scenes of literacy related? What is common to all? What are the "general tendencies," as James Collins and Richard K. Blot (2003) put it, "that hold across diverse case studies" (5)? Writing of the recent proliferation of finely observed ethnographic studies of literacy, Cushman et al. (2001) have challenged literacy researchers to "find the best ways to compile these specific studies into a larger theoretical understanding of literacy" (11). How do we connect the many contexts of literacy to that larger theoretical understanding?

The answer I have offered in this book is what I have called the *rhetorical perspective,* or the view that literacy development is a response to the symbolic activities of institutions, cultures, groups, or individuals. This is the connecting pathway. Rhetorics are the symbolic means—the shapes, pictures, forms, gestures, sounds, words, and texts—through which conceptions of reality are communicated. Rhetorics offer the languages through which human beings come to understand a sense of the world and their place within it. Literacy, I have suggested, is a constituent of rhetoric, a communicative modality, a technical contrivance for disseminating the version of reality preferred by a given institution, culture, group, or individual. How literacy is learned, what it looks like, and ultimately what it means to learners are products of the shaping rhetoric, the symbolic environment in which literacy is learned and practiced. While the activities of reading and writing are always more or less the same, involving decoding and encoding symbols—whether pictographic, syllabic, alphabetic; whether proceeding from top to bottom or left to right—the rhetorics that give meaning to these activities may be fundamentally different and assert radically divergent conceptions of reality. Literacy is a means for disseminating the rhetorical motive.

What is general in contexts of literacy development, therefore, and what connects the different pathways is the shaping rhetoric. More accurately, what is general in contexts of literacy development are the different and contending rhetorics of institutions, cultures, and individuals competing to express conceptions of the world. And this, I think, is the significance of the rhetorical perspective for teachers and scholars of literacy. In the understanding I have outlined in this book, teaching literacy is always a rhetorical act, a way of offering, asserting, or imposing a "sheer identity of the symbolic." "Every pedagogy," to quote James Berlin (1997), "is imbricated in ideology, in a set of tacit assumptions about what is real, what is good, what is possible, and how power ought to be distributed" (697). To learn to read and write in, say, a high school classroom that stresses the measurement of literacy through standardized tests is to participate in a rhetoric that offers a specific identity and social position to students and teachers. To read and write, in contrast, in a high school classroom that stresses critical thinking and independent research skills is to be offered a quite different identity and set of assumptions about one's place in the world. Implicit in any literacy lesson, therefore, is a set of questions: What is this reading or writing activity asking students and teachers to become? What are the implications of accepting or refusing that identity? What positions and ways of living—social, political, and economic—does this reading and writing activity offer the reader or the writer? How might learners revise those positions and ways of living?

A rhetorical perspective, finally, is focused not on the best methods of teaching, measuring, or even describing literacy, whatever these might be. Rather, a rhetorical approach to literacy is an attempt to understand more clearly the effects of reading and writing upon human beings. To say it another way, a rhetorical approach to literacy considers the "ways with words" that are used in literacy instruction, especially the imposed and inherited words that shape the ways in which students and teachers think, talk, and write. In these imposed and inherited words do learners and their teachers find the catalog of institutional identities awaiting them, whether "preliterates," "remedial," "disabled," "drop-outs," or any of the other rhetorically constituted identities offered to human beings. Literacy is both a means for imposing these rhetorical identities, but also for resisting and reimagining them in ways that may open new political, social, and economic possibilities in the world beyond the classroom. This is what the Hmong story teaches about literacy development and why their story matters for us all.

Appendixes

A: Numerical Profile of Hmong Interview Subjects

 I. Total Number of Interview Subjects: 41
 II. Distribution by Gender
     Men: 25
     Women: 16
 III. Distribution by Age
     20–30 years old: 12
     31–40 years old: 14
     41–50 years old: 6
     51 years and older: 9
 IV. Distribution by Date of Arrival in U.S.
     Arrived 1976–1980:   26
     Arrived 1981–1985:   3
     Arrived 1986–1990:   11
     Arrived 1991–1996:   1
 V. Employed/Unemployed
     Employed: 33
     Unemployed: 8
 VI. Languages
     Fluent English speaker
       (interview conducted entirely in English):   30
     Intermediate English speaker
       (interview conducted in both English and Hmong):   7
     Non-English speaker
       (interview conducted in Hmong with interpreter):   4
 VII. Literacy
     Literate in English: 34
     Literate in Hmong: 34
     Literate in Laotian: 23
     Not Literate: 4

VIII. Level of Education
        1–6 years of schooling: 9
        Graduated high school: 9
        Some college/technical: 3
        Graduated college: 15
        Postgraduate: 1
        No formal education: 4

B: Interview Questions

Biography

Where were you born?
When were you born?
When did you leave Laos?
Why did you have to leave your country?
When did you arrive in the U.S.?
When did you arrive in Wausau?
Why did you come to Wausau?
Now, can you tell me your earliest memories of reading and writing—
the first time you saw printed materials, or read yourself, or wrote
anything?

Laos
SCHOOL
Did you attend school[s] in Laos? If yes:
Where was the school?
How old were you when you attended?
What did you study in this school?
What language[s] was [were] taught?
Where did you study? Was there a classroom?
Who was the teacher? What language did he/she speak?
Do you remember any books you read?
Do you remember writing anything?

RELIGIOUS INSTRUCTION
Were you or your family Christians?
Did you receive religious training? If yes:
What was the training—did you receive tutoring, or were there classes?

Where did you study? Was there a classroom?

Who ran these classes?

What language were they in?

Where were they held?

Who were the teachers/pastors?

What languages did they speak?

Did the church give you any reading materials? Pamphlets, hymnals, bibles?

Do you remember any of these? Can you describe them?

Did you write anything? Records, lists of people, newsletters, prayers, sermons?

What language did you read in?

What language did you write in?

MILITARY

Were you in the military? If yes:

Did you join or were you drafted?

What years were you in? Where did you serve?

What was your job?

Who was your supervisor?

What language did this person speak?

Did you have to read anything for this job? Signs, books, directions, manuals?

What language did you read in?

Did you have to write anything? Record keeping, lists, reports, payrolls?

What language did you write in?

Where would you do this writing? Did you have a room or office for this job?

WORK EXPERIENCE

Did you have other work experience in Laos? If yes:

What was your job? What did you do?

What years did you do this?

Who was your supervisor?

What language did this person speak?

Did you have to read anything for this job? Signs, books, directions, manuals?

What language did you read in?

Did you have to write anything? Record keeping, lists, reports, payrolls, etc.?

What language did you write in?

Where would you do this writing? Did you have a room or office for this
   job?
Did you study any other languages in these years? English?
Did you do any other reading or writing? For example, did you keep
   family records, or a diary?

Thailand

SCHOOL

Did you attend any schools in the refugee camps? If yes:
Where was the school?
How old were you when you attended?
What did you study in this school?
What language[s] was [were] taught?
Where did you study? Was there a schoolroom?
Who was the teacher? What language did he/she speak?
Do you remember any books you read?
Do you remember writing anything?
What languages did you study in?

RELIGIOUS INSTRUCTION

Did you receive religious training in the camps, or continue your religious
   life there? If yes:
What was the training—did you receive tutoring, or were there classes?
Where did you study? Was there a classroom?
Who ran these classes?
What language were they in?
Where were they held?
Who were the teachers/pastors?
What languages did they speak?
Did the church give you any reading materials? Pamphlets, hymnals,
   bibles?
Did you write anything? Records, lists of people, newsletters, prayers,
   sermons?
What language did you read in?
What language did you write in?

WORK EXPERIENCE

Did you work in the camps? Relief agencies, food distribution, medical
   assistance, etc.? If yes:
What was your job? What did you do?
Who was your supervisor?

What language did this person speak?

Did you have to read anything for this job? Signs, books, directions, manuals?

What language did you read in?

Did you have to write anything? Record keeping, lists, reports, medical records, etc.?

What language did you write in?

Where would you do this writing? Did you have a room or office for this job?

HMONG LITERACY

Did you study Hmong in the camps? If yes:

How did you learn it? Who was your teacher?

Where would you study? In what place?

What materials did you use to study with? For example, did you have books?

What things would you read? Can you describe them?

What things would you write? Do you remember writing anything?

Why did you want to learn Hmong?

Did anyone read and write Hmong in your family?

Did you use it while you were in the camp?

ENGLISH

Did you study English speaking and reading/writing there? If yes:

How did you learn it? Who was your teacher?

Where would you study? In what place?

Who ran the classes?

What would you study in the class? What would the teacher do?

Do you recall materials, books, pamphlets that you used?

Do you remember writing anything? What was it?

How much English do you feel you learned there?

Did you do any other reading or writing in the camps? Newspapers, camp documents, letters from relatives?

Did you do any other writing? Letters to relatives, lists, journals?

In what languages did you read or write?

Do you remember others reading/writing? What would they have been reading/writing?

The United States/Wausau

SCHOOL

Have you attended school in the U.S.?

[If elementary]

Where did you go to school?

What languages did you speak when you started school?

What languages did you read and write?

Do you remember anything you read in this school—stories, poems, books?

Do you remember writing anything—stories, paper, homework assignments?

Do you remember anyone teaching you how to write in school? What did they do?

Did anyone else speak Hmong in your school?

Did you use Hmong very much in school?

Did your parents speak English at this time? Could they help you with schooling? If yes:

What would parents say? How would they encourage? How often did they talk with you? Involve themselves? How about clearing space and time for studies? What would they do to help you?

Did any of your siblings help you?

Were there materials for writing—paper, pencils, etc.—in your house for writing?

Was there a place to do your homework?

How did you learn English in school?

How did you learn to read and write in English? What did you do? Did you study a lot? Did you practice with people? Did you get extra tutoring, etc.?

[If high school]

Where did you go to school?

What languages did you speak when you started school?

What languages did you read and write?

Do you remember anything you read in this school—stories, poems, books?

Do you remember writing anything—stories, paper, homework assignments?

Were you in any clubs, organizations? Did you have to read or write in these clubs? For example, did they keep records, lists, publish a newsletter?

Do you take courses in English composition? What did you do in these courses? Did they help you learn to write?

Did anyone else speak Hmong in your school?

Did you use Hmong very much in school?

Did you ever write Hmong during this period?

Did your parents speak English at this time? Could they help you with schooling? If yes:

What would parents say? How would they encourage? How often did they talk with you? Involve themselves? How about clearing space and time for studies? What would they do to help you?

Did any of your siblings help you?

Were there materials for writing—paper, pencils, etc.—in your house for writing?

Was there a place to do your homework?

How did you learn English in school?

How did you learn to read and write in English? What did you do? Did you study a lot? Did you practice with people? Did you get extra tutoring, etc.?

[If college]

Where did you go to college? What years?

What languages did you speak when you started school?

What languages did you read and write?

Do you remember anything you read in this school—papers, articles, books?

Do you remember writing anything—papers, reports, assignments?

Were you in any clubs, organizations? Did you have to read or write in these clubs? For example, did they keep records, lists, publish a newsletter?

Do you take courses in English composition? What did you do in these courses? Did they help you learn to write?

Did anyone speak Hmong in your school?

Did you use Hmong very much in school?

Did you ever write Hmong during this period?

Did your parents speak English at this time? Could they help you with schooling? If yes:

What would parents say? How would they encourage? How often did they talk with you? Involve themselves? How about clearing space and time for studies? What would they do to help you?

Did any of your siblings help you?

How did you learn the English you needed for college?

How did you learn to read and write for college? What did you do? Did you study a lot? Did you practice with people? Did you get extra tutoring, etc.

[If ESL]

Where did you study adult ESL? What years?

Why did you study ESL? Was it your choice or were you required to study?

What languages did you speak when you started ESL?

What languages did you read and write?

Do you remember anything you read in classes—papers, articles, books?

Do you remember anyone teaching you how to write in school? What did they do?

Do you remember writing anything—papers, reports, assignments?

Were you in any clubs, organizations? Did you have to read or write in these clubs? For example, did they keep records, lists, publish a newsletter?

Did anyone speak Hmong in your classes?

Did you use Hmong very much in school?

Did you ever write Hmong during this period?

Do you feel ESL helped you learn to speak/read/write English?

In what ways has it helped you?

How did you learn English?

How did you learn to read and write in English? What did you do? Did you study a lot? Did you practice with people? Did you get extra tutoring, etc.?

WORK EXPERIENCE

Have you worked in the U.S., or are you working now? If yes:

What is your job? What do you do?

How long have you done this?

Do you have to read anything for this job? Signs, books, directions, manuals?

Do you have to write anything? Record keeping, lists, reports, payrolls, etc.?

Who reads this writing?

Do you have to do translations, written or spoken, for other Hmong speakers?

RELIGIOUS INSTRUCTION

Here in Wausau, do you attend religious services? Do you study or teach classes as part of your church work? If yes:

What church do you belong to?

Do you have any responsibilities as a member of the church? For example, are you a church officer, teacher, lay assistant?

As a member of the church, what church materials do you normally read? For example, bible, hymnals, church bulletins?

What languages are these written in?

Who publishes them? For example, are they produced in Wausau, or do they come from outside the community?

Do you do any writing in connection with the church? For example, records, lists of people, newsletters, prayers, sermons?

What language do you write in? Who is the audience for this writing?

CLAN/COMMUNITY WORK

Do you have any obligations as a clan member or member of the Wausau Hmong community? If yes:

Would you please describe these?

Do you do any writing in this capacity? For example, records, lists of people, newsletters, articles?

What language do you write in?

Who is the audience for this writing?

HMONG WOMEN

Has your role as a woman affected your educational opportunities?

In what ways?

Were you encouraged to attend school?

Were you encouraged to read and write?

What is the traditional view of education for Hmong women?

Is this changing? In what ways?

If things are changing, can you say why they are?

Do you belong to any organizations, groups, communities just for women?

Do these groups publish or collect anything that you read?

Do you write anything in connection with these groups?

Who reads this writing?

PARENTING

Do you have children? If yes:

Are they in school now?

What languages do they speak/read/write?

Do you work with them on their reading and writing?

What do you do?

Do you think that they are interested in learning to read/write Hmong?

Why/Why not?

Do you think that they should? Why/why not?

How might they be able to do this? Where would they study the
   language?

OTHER READING AND WRITING
What kind of reading have you done/do you do today?
For example, do you read anything about the Hmong people? What have
   you read? Where did you get this? Who wrote/published/printed?
Do you read writing from outside the community, such as the *California
   Hmong Times,* or anything from St. Paul? What languages are these
   materials written in?
Do you remember reading any articles or books that were particularly
   interesting? Why did you think so?
Are there other materials that you read?
Do you read *The Wausau Daily Herald*?
Are there other things that you write? For example, lists, notes, letters?
   Who would you write these to? In what language?
Other writing? How about autobiographies, letters to the editor,
   newspaper articles?
Why did you choose to write this [these]?
Who was your audience?
What language did you write in?
How did you write it? Did you talk about it with other people? Show it to
   other people?
What did you do with this after you'd written it?
Did you receive any reaction to this writing?
What are the main reasons that you write?
What do you think is the most important purpose or reason for writing?

WRITING AS RESPONSE
[If this has not otherwise come up]
Do you remember reading anything about the Hmong after you arrived in
   the U.S., for example, in the local newspaper?
How about TV—have you seen reports on the Hmong on TV?
What do you remember about these? What were they saying?
Did you respond in any way to this writing? Did you talk about it with
   others? Did you write anything?
What did you write? For what audience?
Why did you decide to write?
Did you receive any reaction to this writing?
Do you write in English, Hmong, or both?

How do you choose? What helps you decide whether to whether to write in English or Hmong?

Finally, can you say how writing and reading has affected your life? Have writing and reading been important to you? In what ways?

And can you speculate on how writing and reading has affected Hmong culture? How has writing changed/ not changed the culture? What difference, if any, has writing made to the Hmong people in America?

Are there positive effects? What are they?

Are there negative effects? What are they?

Finally, can you think of any other Hmong people I should talk with about these topics? Who would you recommend?

Appendix C

Number 1
Early Miao/Hmong Writing Systems in China and Laos

Name of Script	Type of Literacy	Location	Source/Dates of Origin	Distribution	Functions
n/a	Literacy narratives	China/Laos/Thailand	Ethnographic accounts (19th/20th centuries)	Widespread	To explain loss of writing; explain Hmong political status
n/a	Mnemotechnic (notched sticks, knots, feather letters, grass strings, etc.)	China/Laos/Thailand	Chinese accounts, Western missionaries (19th/20th centuries)	Widespread	Record keeping; rebellion
n/a	Ideographic(?); related to Chinese(?)	South China	Lu Ciyun (1683)	Unknown	Recording songs; other(?)
Chengbu Stele Writing[1]	Related to Chinese(?)	Hunan	*Baoqing fuzhi* (1740/1989)	Unknown	Record keeping; rebellion(?)
Leigongshan Stele Writing	Ideographic/syllabic(?)	Guizhou	Wen You Discovered 1951	Unknown	Adminstrative(?); shamanistic(?); historical; rebellion(?)
n/a	Chinese	South Sichaun	d'Ollone (1906–1909)	Unknown	Shaman writing(?)

1. Enwall (1994, 65–66) discusses three possible versions of this writing.

Number 2
Missionary Scripts for the Miao/Hmong

Name of Script	Type of Literacy	Location	Source/Dates of Origin	Distribution	Functions
n/a	Pictographic	Yunnan	Paul Vial (early 20th century)	Unknown	Missionary: Catholic
n/a	Romanized	Guizhou, Sichuan	Samuel Adams ca. 1900	6,000 (approx.)[1]	Missionary: Methodist

Name of Script	Type of Literacy	Location	Source/Dates of Origin	Distribution	Functions
Pollard Script	Phonetic	Yunnan	Samuel Pollard ca. 1904	34,500[2]	Missionary: Protestant
Pollard Script	Phonetic	Sichuan	Samuel Pollard ca. 1904	1,000	Missionary: Protestant
Savina Romanized Alphabet	Romanized	Laos/China	F. M. Savina	Limited	Missionary: Catholic
Trung Alphabet	Thai based	Thailand	C. K. Trung 1932	None known	Missionary
Homer-Dixon Romanized Alphabet	Romanized	Vietnam 1939	Homer-Dixon	Limited	Missionary
Romanized Popular Alphabet (RPA)	Romanized	Laos	William S. Smalley, G. Linwood Barney, Yves Bertrais 1951–1953	Worldwide	Missionary: Protestant Catholic
The Whitelock Thai-based/ Lao-based Alphabets	Lao/Thai-based	Laos/ Thailand	Doris Whitelock 1960s–1970s	Limited	Missionary: Protestant

1. This figure is based upon the number of converts given in Enwall 1994, 100.
2. Enwall 1994, 216.

Number 3
National Writing Systems for the Miao/Hmong

Name of Script	Type of Literacy	Location	Source/Dates of Origin	Distribution	Functions
Vietnamese Romanized Alphabet	Romanized	North Vietnam	Vietnamese linguists 1956–1957	Unknown	Unknown
Pathet Lao Alphabet	Lao based	Laos	Pathet Lao 1960s	Unknown	National literacy
Chinese Romanized Alphabet	Chinese based, Pinyin	China	People's Republic of China 1957–1958	Limited	National literacy

Number 4

Hmong Spiritual Writing Systems

Name of Script	Type of Literacy	Location	Source/Dates of Origin	Distribution	Functions
Pa Chai's Alphabet(?)	Unknown	Vietnam/Laos	Pa Chai 1919–1921	Unknown	Spiritual/ Political
Phaj Hauj	Phonetic	Vietnam/Laos	Shong Lue Yang 1959–1971	7,635	Spiritual/ Political
Xyooj Zeb Script	Unknown	Laos	Xyooj Zeb 1960s–1970s	Unknown	Spiritual/ Political
Xauv Yeeb Script	Unknown	Ban Vinai Refugee Camp, Thailand	Xauv Yeeb 1976	Unknown	
Sayaboury Script	Syllabic	Chiang Kham Refugee Camp, Thailand	Ga Va Her Reported 1983	Unknown	Spiritual/ Political
Yaaj Xub Script	Unknown	Phou Bia Mountain, Laos	Yaaj Xub 1980s(?)	Unknown	Spiritual/ Political
Embroidery Script 1	Unknown	Ban Vinai Refugee Camp, Thailand	Hmong Education Foundation 1990	Unknown	Spiritual/ Political
Embroidery Script 2	Unknown	Fresno, CA	Yiengyouav Whachor	Unknown early 1990s(?)	Unknown

Notes

Epigraphs

The epigraphs for this book are drawn from Tapp 1989, 126; Reder 1985a; and the author's interview with Thao Lue in Wausau, Wisconsin.

Introduction

1. The phrase "the welfare system" refers here to the various forms of public assistance formerly available to low-income families prior to the passage of the Welfare Reform Act of 1994, signed into law by President Bill Clinton.

2. Wausau's population also included African Americans, Native Americans, Pacific Islanders, and Asian people who were not Hmong, such as Chinese, Japanese, and Filipinos. However, the majority of the Wausau community has historically been the descendants of Northern European immigrants.

3. The Southeast Asian refugee population in Wausau also included Vietnamese, ethnic Laotian, and Cambodian refugees. However, the overwhelming majority of Southeast Asians in Wausau were Hmong.

4. See appendix A for a profile of Hmong participants in this project.

5. See appendix B for the complete script.

6. See "Notes on Language, Orthography, and Transcription" for transcription guidelines.

7. Data were organized initially in terms of places—e.g., writing and reading in Laos, writing and reading in refugee camps, writing and reading in the United States. I then divided these into categories describing the various functions of literacy: writing for bible classes, writing for newspapers, writing for family, etc. Finally, I grouped these into conceptual categories: writing as spirituality, as disruption, as identification, and others.

8. The use of an interpreter was problematic. I relied upon the interpreter to communicate not only the main ideas of the discussion, but also the asides, uncertainties, jokes, and unexpected turns in the conversation. Moreover, as Joanne Koltyk (1995) has pointed out, differences in gender, age, and religious background may affect dynamics of the communication between the speaker and the interpreter (430–435). While I never perceived such problems, it is of course possible that I missed the cues.

9. For good discussions of Burke's relationship to contemporary theorizing about the relationship of rhetoric to subjectivity and agency, see Wess 1996 and Clark 2004.

Chapter 1: Lost Books and Broken Promises

Epigraph. Tapp 1989, 126.

1. Southeast Asian scholars distinguish between two wars that involved Southeast Asian nations and Western powers. "The First Indochina War" refers to the war fought principally between Ho Chi Minh's Viet Minh and the French from 1946 to 1954. "The Second Indochina War" refers to the war between North Vietnam and the United States. The latter conflict, although it was fought in Laos and Cambodia as well as Vietnam, is popularly known in U.S. culture as the "Vietnam War." In this book I use the designation "Vietnam War," as this is the term recognized by most Americans.

2. For perspectives on Hmong cultural life, see, among many, Chan 1994; Koltyk 1995; Lee 1996; Mattison, Scarseth, and Lo 1994.

3. Much of the political history of the Hmong has been written in the context of histories of the Vietnam War and of French colonialism. Sources include Branfman 1972; Dommen 1964; Gunn 1990; Lee 1990, 1982; McCoy 1972, 1970; and Yang 1985.

4. For discussions of the origins of the Hmong, see Bernatzik 1970, 6–42; Geddes 1976, 3–34; Mottin 1980; Quincy 1988; Tapp 2004, 1989. For accounts of Hmong origins from the perspective of Hmong traditional narratives, see Johnson 1992, 1–22, 113–120, 343–352.

5. While the term "Miao" is broadly applied to non-Chinese minorities, the Chinese have also created categories meant to describe distinctive Miao groups. Geddes (1976, 16–21) cites the "weirdly exotic list" of classifications of the Miao in China: the Western Miao, the Eastern Miao, the Steep Slope Miao, the Trumpet Miao, the Robe-Wearing Miao, the Pot Ring Miao, the Iron-Making Miao, the Tooth-Knocking Miao, the Dog-Ear Miao, the Horse-Saddle-Flap Miao, the Crow-Sparrow Miao, and the Magpie Miao.

6. Tensions between the competing clans were exacerbated when the daughter of Lobliayao, the leader of the Lo clan, committed suicide by eating a fatal dose of opium as a result of mistreatment by her husband, a leader of the Ly clan. In anger, Lobliayao severed relations between the two clans.

7. Buell was a colorful figure from Stueben County, Indiana, who, at the age of forty-seven, traveled to Laos as a volunteer with the International Voluntary Services. A biography of Buell authored by *Saturday Evening Post* reporter Don Schanche portrays Buell as a heroic figure who was deeply and selflessly committed to the welfare of the Hmong people. For a more critical perspective on Buell's relationship with the CIA, see McCoy 1972. Several of the older Hmong men interviewed for this study knew Buell personally and recalled him with affection.

Chapter 2: Rumors, Ropes, and Redemptions

Epigraph. Lemoine 1972, 124.

1. Information in this chapter on Hmong-language writing systems is drawn from a few critical sources. Material on Miao writing systems in China comes almost

exclusively from Enwall's (1994) definitive two-volume history, which is a vital and overlooked resource on early Miao literacy. Information on Hmong-language literacy in Laos and Thailand is taken largely from the invaluable work of Nicholas Tapp (1989, 1982) and Jacques Lemoine (1972). And material on Hmong literacy in a general sense, in Laos and the United States, draws deeply from the scholarship of William A. Smalley and his collaborators (Smalley 1996, 1994, 1986, 1985, 1976a, 1976b, 1964; Smalley and Wimuttikosol 1998; Smalley, Vang, and Yang 1990; Vang, Yang, and Smalley 1990). As should be clear from the list of citations, my debt to Professor Smalley cannot be overstated and is to be found everywhere in this chapter and throughout this book.

2. See appendix C, number 1, Early Miao/Hmong Writing Systems.

3. See appendix C, number 2, Missionary Scripts for the Miao and Hmong.

4. There is an eighth, minor tone, which is a variant of one of the seven (Ranard 2004, 43).

5. See appendix C, number 3, National Writing Systems for the Miao/Hmong.

6. See appendix C, number 4, Hmong Spiritual Writing Systems.

7. The definitive account of the *Pauj Hauj* alphabet, its origins, history, and technical accomplishments are available in Smalley, Vang, and Yang 1990. A believer's perspective is found in Vang, Yang, and Smalley 1990.

8. See Smalley, Vang, and Yang 1990; and Ratliff 1996 for linguistic descriptions of Shong Lue Yang's achievements.

9. Information on the Sayaboury Alphabet comes from Smalley and Wimuttikosol 1998 and from a personal interview with William A. Smalley (June 28, 1997).

Chapter 3: Never to Hold a Pencil

Epigraphs. Spengler 1928, 150; Havelock 1988, 128.

1. Branfman (1972, 254) estimated that by 1969 U.S. bombing in Laos had displaced between 200,000 to 300,000 people in northern Laos.

2. The anthropologist Niko Besnier (1995) has argued that studies of the processes of globalization throughout history cast doubt on the empirical reality of preliteracy even in centuries past (4). The interaction of peoples and goods, in other words, undermines the idea of cultures "totally untouched by any knowledge of writing or print."

3. Nicholas Tapp (personal communication, August 9, 1999) has pointed out that while the Chinese had a writing system for their language, the majority of Chinese people did not read and write. This suggests that the absence of writing in Miao culture during the same period would not have been unusual relative to other peoples, though the Hmong still would have been distinguished by having no writing system of their own.

4. This statement applies to government schooling. Small numbers of Hmong Christians did attend bible schools in the 1950s and 1960s operated by the Chris-

tian Missionary Alliance and by the Catholic Church. Most students in these schools would have learned to read and write in the Hmong "missionary alphabet," the RPA.

5. The statements about education in Laos apply to regions controlled by the RLG. In areas controlled by the communist Pathet Lao in the 1960s, the situation was apparently quite different. In 1964, the Pathet Lao reported 36,200 children enrolled in "liberated" elementary schools, with another 250 students in secondary schools (Halpern and Kunstadter 1967). The Pathet Lao also claimed to have opened four teacher-training schools and two adult education schools, as well as having published 380,000 textbooks. These achievements are impressive considering that much of the teaching in Pathet Lao schools in the 1960s and 1970s took place in caves and jungles where students and teachers took shelter from U.S. bombings (Weinberg 1997, 180). In general, the Pathet Lao demonstrated a clearer understanding of the Hmong desire for literacy and education than did officials in the RLG. For example, while the RLG prohibited the use of a writing system in the Hmong language, the Pathet Lao developed and promoted their own writing system for the Hmong language. The Pathet Lao focus on education has generally been regarded as an important factor in their success in appealing to minority populations during the war (see Halpern and Kunstadter 1967, 244–245).

Chapter 4: Other Gods and Countries

Epigraphs. Balibar 1991, 94; Soltow and Stevens 1981, 22.

1. The role of messianic literacies should properly be included in this accounting. However, few of my informants had experience with these literacies, and so they are not discussed in this chapter.

2. The spelling of the village name is a transliteration. The woman who related this memory did not provide a Hmong spelling for this village.

3. Phoumi 1960.

4. See, among many, Ayers, Hunt, and Quinn 1998; Delpit 1995; Giroux 1983, 1991; Giroux and McLaren 1989; Rose 1989; Shor 1992.

5. The ingenuity shown by Hmong students in creating writing materials recalls that of African-American slaves in the United States. Janet Duitsman Cornelius (1991) has described how slaves overcame the shortage of writing materials in ways similar to Hmong students in the highlands of Laos. To compensate for the lack of pens and paper, for example, "one ingenious slave cut out blocks from pine bark and smoothed them for tablets, cut sticks from white oak or hickory for pens, and soaked knots from oak trees overnight to make ink. Others simply practiced by writing with their fingers on the ground or in the sand" (72).

6. It is important to remember that conditions for the majority of ethnic Laotian children were only marginally better. The Lao elite reserved for itself a type of education that was unavailable to the majority of the country, as discussed in chapter 3.

7. The spelling of this word is a Hmong transliteration of the Laotian word for "king."

8. These are Hmong words for village officials.

9. For a fascinating retrospective, see www.lib.ksu.edu/depts/spec/rarebooks/military.

10. I refer to "men" deliberately; no one interviewed on this subject spoke of women scribes.

11. The fact that the army was not actually teaching Hmong to read and write may explain why Hmong literacy scholars have largely overlooked the role of L'Armée Clandestine in promoting literacy development. While the contributions of missionaries, national governments, and messianic prophets to Hmong literacy have been recognized, military contributions, in comparison, have received scant attention. Perhaps the fact that the army had no systematic educational program, unlike the village schools and Christian missions, has caused scholars to discount the role of the military in promoting literacy. We must also acknowledge the relatively small numbers of Hmong who served as military scribes. Although the exact number is not known, the count is probably not very high. Interviews with Hmong men in one Wisconsin city who served as military scribes indicated that for every *koo phan* (kong pan), or battalion of approximately five hundred men, there were at least five people who had responsibilities involving reading and writing. Thus if we count ten scribes for each thousand troops, we arrive at approximately four hundred military scribes working with the Secret Army at the height of its military operations. This number, however, is speculative.

12. Recalling the different classes of scribes described previously, this particular activity describes the work of the *tus sau ntawv.*

13. The Steven Spielberg film about World War II, *Saving Private Ryan* (1998), has a scene depicting something similar. In the film, U.S. secretaries are shown typing letters from the U.S. military command that will be sent to families informing them of the deaths of family members.

14. This particular literacy activity describes the work of the *nai sai.*

15. Many Hmong have since used their reading and writing abilities on behalf of family, relatives, friends, and communities—meaning that they acted as scribes in more and less formal settings. For a good account, see Weinstein-Shr 1993.

16. Paoze Thao (personal communication, July 16, 1999) has stated that some Hmong who became scribes went through English courses in Vientiane, Laos, before entering the military. Other Hmong may have learned English through their contacts with Protestant missionaries from the United States. Thus the military was not the sole point of origin for English-language literacy, but was one of several sites where English literacy might be introduced. Thao suggested that communicative imperatives of CIA operatives and Hmong soldiers provided a "crash course" in the specific forms of English "required for successful military operations."

17. The testimony suggests that this man was probably what Paoze Thao identifies as a *tug xib paub maim,* a position in which Hmong soldiers provided information to CIA and Hmong pilots attacking enemy positions. The duties of Hmong

soldiers working with CIA pilots are elaborated in Robbins 1995, who provides a picaresque account of CIA personnel in Laos while typecasting the Hmong as loyal seconds to their CIA employers.

18. The term *Cob Fab* (Lord of the Sky) has two meanings, one specific and one general. The specific meaning relates the term to the followers of Shong Lue Yang, the creator of the *Phaj Hauj* writing system, as discussed in chapter 2. Hmong guerrilla soldiers who resisted communism after 1975 and adopted the writing system were called *Cob Fab*. In the general sense, the term refers to anyone who fought in the Hmong resistance after 1975, regardless of whether they knew the *Phaj Hauj* or subscribed to its religious teachings. Here I use *Cob Fab* in its general sense.

19. The testimony indicates that Lee was a *nai sai*.

20. Written translation by Peter Yang and LoPao Vang.

21. The rapid spread of Christianity among the Hmong recalled the earlier and even more fervent conversions of the Miao in China, described by the missionary Samuel Pollard in the early twentieth century (1919, quoted in Tapp 1989, 93): "Some days they came in tens and twenties! Some days in sixties and seventies! Then came a hundred! Then two hundred! Three hundred! Four hundred! At last, on one special occasion, a thousand of these mountain men came in one day! When they came the snow was on the ground, and terrible had been the snow on the hills they crossed over. What a great crowd it was!"

22. These functions of literacy speak to the broad aims of the missionary movement and not the motivations of individual missioners, which were diverse.

23. Written translation by Peter Yang and LoPao Vang.

24. According to Xiong, there was often at least one family in each village that owned a radio, and neighbors would gather at the home of the radio owner to listen to broadcasts from Long Cheng and elsewhere. In a sense, the owner of the radio performed a function similar to that of the literacy broker—conveying information by means of a technology not available to all. In this case, however, the technology was electronic rather than graphical.

25. See Adler 1995.

Chapter 5: Writing Hmong Americans

Epigraphs. Kronenwetter 1985, 329; Burke 1945, 105.

1. Statistics are available from the Southeast Asia Resource Action Center (SEARAC) at www.searac.org. (Accessed May 10, 2006.)

2. Hmong community leaders believe the actual number of Hmong in the United States in 2004 was closer to 250,000 to 300,000 (Duffy 2004).

3. The involvement of local churches in Hmong resettlement was not unique to Wausau. Religious organizations have long been central to refugee resettlement in the United States, assisting with the resettlement of displaced Europeans after World War II and with Cuban refugees in the 1960s and 1970s. Of the nine organizations selected by the U.S. government to assist Vietnamese and other Southeast Asian

refugees after 1975, four were associated with religious denominations, including the U.S. Catholic Conference, Church World Services, Lutheran Immigration and Refugee Service, and the Hebrew Immigration Aid Society (Robinson 1998).

4. Of the estimated 4,500 Hmong in Wausau by 1996, approximately 1,500 were Christians (information provided by the Hmong Methodist Church).

5. Early reports on Hmong educational achievement were generally promising, despite early difficulties. In his report on Hmong students in Wisconsin public schools, researcher Ray Hutchison (1997) noted that the earliest studies of Hmong students in the United States gave little reason for optimism. Downing et al. (1984), for example, estimated that 90 percent of Hmong girls in the Minneapolis-St. Paul area dropped out of high school. Yet Hutchison also noted substantial improvement in Hmong educational prospects in subsequent years. Rumbaut and Ima's (1988) study of Hmong students showed that they achieved above-average grades and high standardized results on a mathematics achievement test, while another study by Rumbaut (1995) found that Hmong students in California were less likely to drop out of high school than other recent immigrants. Similar findings were reported in a longitudinal study of Hmong high school students in St. Paul, Minnesota, which found that the high school GPA of Hmong students was nearly a full point higher than that of non-Hmong students—3.24 vs. 2.48 (McNall, Dunnigan, and Mortimer 1994). Hutchison's study of Hmong education in Wisconsin similarly found that the retention rate for Hmong students surpassed that of other groups, including white students, that the graduation rate for Asian high school students (95 percent) was higher than that reported for white and other non-Asian high school students, that Hmong children and adolescents at all levels studied more than other students, and that Hmong students had a better understanding of teacher expectations and were less likely to miss classes. All of these speak to the educational progress of the Hmong since arriving in the United States, which Hutchison attributes to the strong family bonds of Hmong families, the shared responsibilities among family members, and the high educational expectations that parents have for children (1997, 32). The picture that emerges, then, is one of increasing achievement. This suggests that Hmong students and their families resisted the category of "subordinate culture" to assert themselves as successful and upwardly mobile students.

6. We shall return to the relationship of literacy and gender in chapter 6.

Chapter 6: Hmong Americans Rewriting

Epigraph. M. Bakhtin, *The Dialogic Imagination,* 348.

1. While there have been many forms of literacy practiced by Hmong writers in the last decade—essays, letters, poetry, novels, political tracts, and commercial screenplays—this chapter limits itself to the forms of literacy practices that were most often brought up in the interviews and thus seemed most representative of self-directed writings practiced in one Hmong community at a particular moment in history.

2. In cases where I am discussing writers and their work, the actual name of the writer is used with permission.

3. For all these ease of word processors, their risks are understood. As least three Hmong writers told me they had erased or otherwise lost their entire autobiographies. One writer said he had lost as much as fifty pages!

4. During the course of the research for this project, I lived, as noted earlier, in the city where the letters were published and worked for the local Hmong Association as a consultant on English-language education. In that capacity, I lobbied the local newspaper to publish bilingual columns by Hmong writers and edited one of the Hmong-authored editorials discussed in this chapter. The newspaper agreed to publish occasional English-language editorials by Hmong writers. The essay I edited was "Heard a Hmong rumor? Check it out!" *The Wausau Daily Herald,* June 2, 1992.

5. There is a strong sense of class tensions in these letters. Many of the anti-immigrant letters were written by self-identified members of the working poor, and their letters reflect the apprehensions of people at the economic margins. It is worth keeping in mind that most of these letters were written in the late 1980s and early 1990s, which was the aftermath of the Reagan years and the economic recession that followed. Perhaps the sentiments expressed toward the Hmong speak as much to the anxieties of twentieth-century capitalism as to the resentment of immigrants.

6. The texts considered in this section were written by eighteen different individuals who published twenty-five letters and editorials between December 1989 and March 1994. Thirteen of these writers were male, five female. Of this group, I knew fourteen personally and interviewed ten of those. Those writers I knew personally varied in terms of age, occupation, and educational and language backgrounds. The oldest writer estimated his age to be in the mid-forties, and the youngest was in his early twenties. Seven worked for local nonprofit agencies, such as the Hmong Association and Lutheran Social Services, two were self-employed businessmen, two were teachers, one was a college student, one was a factory worker, and one was unemployed. In terms of U.S. education, six writers had graduated from college in the United States and the rest had taken various combinations of high school classes, adult education courses, and ESL instruction. One man had earned what he described as the equivalent of a PhD in Laos in French Literature. All of the individuals I knew could read and write English at varying levels of proficiency. Additionally, all could speak, read, and write Hmong, again at varying proficiency levels. Several also reported being fluent in Laotian.

7. Numerous advocacy groups have created guidelines for writing letters. Many of these are now online, including those by the American Civil Liberties Union (http://archive.aclu.org/action/editor.html), Amnesty International (www.amnesty.org/actnow/letter_guide.html), and the Sierra Club (www.sierraclub.org/takeaction/toolkit/letters.asp).

————. 1986. *The logic of writing and the organization of society.* Cambridge: Cambridge University Press.

Goody, J., and I. Watt. 1968. The consequences of literacy. In *Literacy in traditional societies,* ed. J. Goody. Cambridge: Cambridge University Press.

Graff, H. J. 1979. *The literacy myth: Literacy and social structure in the nineteenth century city.* New York: Academic Press.

————. 1987. *The legacies of literacy: Continuities and contradictions in western culture and society.* Bloomington: Indiana University Press.

————. 1995. *The labyrinths of literacy: Reflections on literacy past and present.* Pittsburgh: University of Pittsburgh Press.

Green, K., and S. Reder. 1986. Factors in individual acquisition of English: A longitudinal study of Hmong adults. In *The Hmong in transition,* ed. G. Hendricks, B. Downing, and A. Deinard. New York and Minneapolis: Center for Migration Studies and the Southeast Asian Refugee Project of the University of Minnesota, 299–399.

Grognet, A. G. 1997. Integrating employment skills in adult ESL instruction. *ERIC Q&A.* Washington, DC: National Center for ESL Literacy Education.

Gunn, G. 1990. *Rebellion in Laos: Peasants and politics in a colonial backwater.* Boulder, CO: Westview Press.

Halpern, J., and P. Kunstadter. 1967. Introduction. In *Southeast Asian tribes, minorities, and nations,* ed. P. Kunstadter. Princeton, NJ: Princeton University Press, 233–259.

Hamilton-Merritt, J. 1993. *Tragic mountains: The Hmong, the Americans, and the secret war for Laos, 1942–1992.* Bloomington: Indiana University Press.

Harris, R. 1986. *The origin of writing.* London: Duckworth.

Harrison, J. F. C. 1971. *The early Victorians, 1832–1851.* New York: Praeger.

Havelock, E. A. 1963. *Preface to Plato.* London: Cambridge University Press.

————. 1982. *The literate revolution in Greece and its cultural consequences.* Princeton, NJ: Princeton University Press.

————. 1988. The coming of literate communication to western culture. In *Perspectives on literacy,* ed. E. Kintgen, B. Kroll, and M. Rose. Carbondale: Southern Illinois University Press, 127–134. (Originally published in *Journal of Communication* 30 [1] [1980]: 90–98.)

Hayes, J. 1996. A new framework for understanding cognition and affect in writing. In *The science of writing,* ed. C. M. Levy and S. Ransdell. Mahwah, NJ: Lawrence Earlbaum Associates, 1–27.

Heath, S. B. 1983. *Ways with words: Language, life, and work in communities and classrooms.* Cambridge: Cambridge University Press.

————. 1988. Protean shapes in literacy events: Ever-shifting oral and literate traditions. In *Perspectives on literacy,* ed. E. Kintgen, B. Kroll, and M. Rose. Carbondale: Southern Illinois University Press, 127–134. (Originally published in *Spoken and written language: Exploring orality and literacy,* ed. D. Tannen. Norwood, NJ: Ablex Books, 1982.)

Heimbach, E. E. 1969. *White Hmong-English dictionary.* Ithaca, NY: Southeast Asia Program, Cornell University.

Hein, J. 1995. *From Vietnam, Laos, and Cambodia: A refugee experience in the United States.* New York: Twayne Publishers.

Higham, J. 1973. *Strangers in the land: Patterns of American nativism 1860–1925.* New York: Atheneum.

Hudspeth, W. 1937. *Stone gateway and the flowery Miao.* London: Cargate.

Hutchison, R. D. 1997. *The educational performance of Hmong students in Wisconsin.* Thiensville: Wisconsin Policy Research Institute.

Hvitfeldt, C. 1986. Traditional culture, perceptual style, and learning: The classroom behavior of Hmong adults. *Adult Education Quarterly* 36 (2): 65–67.

———. 1992. Oral orientations in ESL academic writing. *College ESL* 21:28–39.

Ivanic, R. 1998. *Writing and identity: The discoursal construction of identity in academic writing.* Amsterdam: John Benjamins Publishing Company.

Jensen, R. 2003. *Writing dissent: Taking radical ideas from the margins to the mainstream.* New York: Peter Lang.

Jiang, X. 1989. Miaowen tanjiu [Thorough inquiry into Miao writing]. *Xinan minzu xueyuan xuebao* [Journal of the Southwest Institute of Nationalities] 1:112–116.

Jiang Y. 1945. Xinan bianqu tezhong wenzi [Particular kinds of writing in the southwestern border areas]. *Bianzheng gonglun* [Frontier affair] 4 (1): 277–287.

Johnson, C. 1992. *Myths, legends and folk tales from the Hmong of Laos.* 2nd ed. St. Paul, MN: Linguistics Department, Macalester College.

Kaestle, C. 1991. Studying the history of literacy. In *Literacy in the United States,* ed. C. Kaestle et al. New Haven, CT: Yale University Press, 3–32.

Kelly, G. P. 1977. *From Vietnam to America: A chronicle of the Vietnamese immigration to the United States.* Boulder, CO: Westview Press.

Koltyk, J. 1995. New pioneers in the heartland: Hmong life in Wisconsin. Ph.D. dissertation, University of Wisconsin.

Kozol, J. 1991. *Savage inequalities: Children in America's schools.* New York: Harper Perennial.

Kronenwetter, M. 1985. *Wisconsin heartland: The story of Wausau and Marathon County.* Midland, MI: Pendell Publishing Co.

Kulick, D., and C. Stroud. 1993. Conceptions and uses of literacy in a Papua New Guinean village. In *Cross-cultural approaches to literacy,* ed. B. Street. Cambridge: Cambridge University Press, 30–61.

Lee, G. Y. 1982. Minority policies and the Hmong. In *Contemporary Laos: Studies in the politics and society of the Lao People's Democratic Republic,* ed. M. Stuart-Fox. New York: St. Martin's Press, 199–219.

———. 1990. Refugees from Laos: Historical backgrounds and causes. www.stolaf.edu/people/cdr/hmong/hmong-au/refugee.htm. (Accessed May 19, 1999.)

———. 1996. Cultural identity in post-modern society: Reflections on what is a Hmong? *Hmong Studies Journal* 1 (1).

Lemoine, J. 1972. Les ecritures du Hmong [The writing of the Hmong], trans. K. M. Cole. *Bulletin des amis du Royaume Lao,* 7–8, 123–165.

Levi-Strauss, C. 1964. *Tristes tropiques,* trans. J. Russell. New York: Atheneum.

Levy-Bruhl, L. 1923. *Primitive mentality,* trans. L. A. Clare. Boston: Beacon Press.

Lewallen, J. 1971. *Ecology of devastation: Indochina.* Baltimore, MD: Penguin Books.

Lockridge, K. 1974. *Literacy in colonial New England: An enquiry into the social context of literacy in the early modern West.* New York: Norton.

Long, L. 1993. *Ban Vinai, the refugee camp.* New York: Columbia University Press

Lowe, L. 1996. *Immigrant acts: On Asian American cultural politics.* Durham, NC: Duke University Press.

Lu, C. 1683. *Lu Yunshi zazhu* [Miscellaneous writings by Lu Yunshi].

Luke, A., B. Comber, and J. O'Brien. 1996. Critical literacies and cultural studies. In *The literacy lexicon,* ed. G. Bull and M. Anstey. Melbourne: Prentice-Hall, 31–46.

Marshall, C., and G. Rossman. 1995. *Designing qualitative research.* Thousand Oaks, CA: Sage Publications.

Marshall, H. W. 1991. *A mutually adaptive learning paradigm for Hmong students.* Paper presented at the International Teachers of English to Speakers of Other Languages, New York.

Mattison, W., T. Scarseth, and L. Lo. 1994. *Hmong lives: From Laos to La Crosse.* La Crosse, WI: The Pump House.

McCoy, A. W. 1970. French colonialism in Laos, 1893–1945. In *Laos: War and revolution,* ed. N. S. Adams and A. W. McCoy. New York: Harper and Row, 67–99.

———. 1972. *The politics of heroin in Southeast Asia.* New York: Harper and Row.

McGee, M. C. 1995. The ideograph: A link between rhetoric and ideology. In *Readings in rhetorical criticism,* ed. C. Burgchardt. State College, PA: Strata, 442–457.

McNall, M., T. Dunnigan, and J. T. Mortimer. 1994. The educational achievement of the St. Paul Hmong. *Anthropology and Education Quarterly* 25 (1): 44–65.

Moss, B., ed. 1994. *Literacy across communities.* Cresskill, NJ: Hampton Press.

Mottin, J. 1980. *History of the Hmong.* Bangkok: Odeon Store Ltd. Part.

Munslow, A. 1997. *Deconstructing history.* London: Routledge.

Ng, F. 1993. Towards a second generation Hmong history. *Amerasia Journal* 19 (3): 51–69.

Nixon, T., and F. Keenan. 1997. Citizenship preparation for adult ESL learners. *ERIC Digest.* Washington, DC: National Center for ESL Literacy Education.

O'Connor, M. 1996. The alphabet as a technology. In *The world's writing systems,* ed. P. Daniels and W. Bright. New York: Oxford University Press, 787–794.

Ogbu, J. 1983. Literacy and schooling in subordinate cultures: The case of Black Americans. In *Literacy in historical perspective,* ed. D. Resnick. Washington, DC: Library of Congress.

Okihiro, G. 1994. *Margins and mainstreams: Asians in American history and culture.* Seattle: University of Washington Press.

Olson, D. R. 1977. From utterance to text: The bias of language in speech and writing. *Harvard Educational Review* 47 (3): 257–281.

Ong, W. J. 1982. *Orality and literacy: The technologizing of the word.* London: Routledge.

———. 1994. Literacy and orality in our times. In *Landmark essays on rhetorical invention in writing,* ed. R. E. Young and Y. Liu. Davis, CA: Hermagoras Press, 135–146. (Originally published in *ADE Bulletin* 58 (1978): 1–7.)

Parker, J. E. 1995. *Codename mule: Fighting the secret war in Laos for the CIA.* Annapolis, MD: Naval Institute Press.

Peterson, S. 1990. Translating experience and the reading of a story cloth. *Journal of American Folklore* 101:6–22.

Phommasouvanh, B. 1973. The preparation of teachers and its role in the Laosization of public secondary schools in Laos. PhD dissertation, Southern Illinois University.

Phoumi, M. 1960. National anthem (adopted 1947). In *National anthems of the world,* ed. M. Shaw and H. Coleman. London: Pitman Publishing Company, 179–180.

Porter, D. G. 1970. After Geneva: Subverting Laotian neutrality. In *Laos: War and revolution,* ed. N. S. Adams and A. W. McCoy. New York: Harper and Row, 179–212.

Quincy, K. 1988. *Hmong: History of a people.* Cheney: Eastern Washington University Press.

Ranard, D. A., ed. 2004. *The Hmong: An introduction to their history and culture.* Washington, DC: Center for Applied Linguistics.

Ranard, D. A., and M. Pfleger, eds. 1995. *From the classroom to the community: A fifteen-year experiment in refugee education.* Washington, DC: Center for Applied Linguistics and Delta Systems Co., Inc.

Ratliff, M. 1996. The Pahawh Hmong Script. In *The world's writing systems,* ed. P. Daniels and W. Bright. New York and Oxford: Oxford University Press, 619–624.

Reder, S. 1985a. *The Hmong resettlement study.* Prepared by Northwest Regional Educational Laboratory, Portland, OR. Washington, DC: Office of Refugee Resettlement.

———. 1985b. A Hmong community's acquisition of English. In *The Hmong in the West: Observations and reports, papers of the 1981 Hmong Research Conference,* University of Minnesota, ed. B. Downing and D. Olney. 2nd printing. Minneapolis: Center for Urban Regional Affairs, University of Minnesota, 268–303.

Reder, S., and K. Wikelund. 1993. Literacy development and ethnicity: An Alaskan example. In *Cross-cultural approaches to literacy,* ed. B. Street. Cambridge: Cambridge University Press, 176–197.

Reimers, D. M. 1998. *Unwelcome strangers: American identity and the turn against immigration.* New York: Columbia University Press.

Reinharz, S. 1992. *Feminist methods in social research.* New York: Oxford University Press.

Resnick, D. P., and L. B. Resnick. 1977. The nature of literacy: A historical explanation. *Harvard Educational Review* 47: 370–385.

Robbins, C. 1987. *The ravens: The men who flew in America's secret war in Laos.* New York: Crown Publishing.

Robinson, W. C. 1998. *Terms of refuge: The Indochinese exodus and the international response.* London: Zed Books.

Rosaldo, R. 1993. *Culture and truth: The remaking of social analysis.* Boston: Beacon Press.

Rose, M. 1985. The language of exclusion: Writing instruction at the university. *College English* 47 (4): 341–359.

———. 1989. *Lives on the boundary: A moving account of the struggles and achievements of America's educationally underprepared.* New York: Penguin Books.

Royster, J. J. 2000. *Traces of a stream: Literacy and social change among African American women.* Pittsburgh: University of Pittsburgh Press.

Rumbaut, R. G. 1995. Vietnamese, Laotian, and Cambodian Americans. In *Asian Americans: Contemporary trends and issues,* ed. P. G. Min. Thousand Oaks, CA: Sage Publications, 232–270.

Rumbaut, R. G., and K. Ima. 1988. *The adaptation of Southeast Asian refugee youth: A comparative study.* San Diego: Southeast Asian Youth Study, Department of Sociology, San Diego State University.

Schanche, D. 1970. *Mister Pop.* New York: David McKay Company, Inc.

Schein, L. 2004. Hmong/Miao transnationality: Identity beyond culture. In *Hmong/Miao in Asia,* ed. N. Tapp et al. Bangkok: Silkworm Books, 273–290.

Scribner, S., and M. Cole. 1981. *The psychology of literacy.* Cambridge, MA: Harvard University Press.

Seufert, P. 1999. Refugees as English language learners: Issues and concerns. *ERIC Q&A.* Washington, DC: National Center for ESL Literacy Education.

Shor, I. 1992. *Empowering education: Critical teaching for social change.* Chicago: University of Chicago Press.

Shuter, R. 1985. The Hmong of Laos: Orality, communication, and acculturation. In *Intercultural communication: A reader.* 4th ed., ed. L. Samovar. Belmont, CA: Wadsworth Publishing, 102–109.

Smalley, W. A., ed. 1964. *Orthography studies: Articles on new writing systems.* London: United Bible Studies.

———, 1976a. Writing systems in Thailand's marginal languages: History and policy. In *Phonemes and orthography: Language planning in ten minority languages of Thailand,* ed. W. A. Smalley. Canberra: The Australian National University, 1–24.

———, ed. 1976b. *Phonemes and orthography: Language planning in ten minority languages of Thailand.* Canberra: The Australian National University.

————. 1985. Adaptive language strategies of the Hmong: From Asian mountains to American ghettos. *Language Sciences* 7 (2): 241–269.

————. 1986. Stages of Hmong cultural adaptation. In *The Hmong in transition,* ed. G. Hendricks, B. Downing, and A. Deinard. New York and Minneapolis: Center for Migration Studies and the Southeast Asian Refugee Project of the University of Minnesota, 7–22.

————. 1994. Codification by means of foreign systems. In *Writing and its use,* ed. H. Gunther and O. Ludwig. Berlin and New York: Walter de Gruyter, 697–708.

————. 1996. *Hmong culture and written language.* Paper presented at the Hmong Stout Student Organization Conference, Menomonie, WI, March 30.

Smalley, W. A., C. K. Vang, and G. Y. Yang. 1990. *Mother of writing: The origin and development of a Hmong messianic script.* Chicago: University of Chicago Press.

Smalley, W. A, and N. Wimuttikosol. 1998. Another Hmong messianic script and its texts. *Written Language and Literacy* 1 (1): 103–128.

Soltow L., and E. Stevens. 1981. *The rise of literacy and the common school in the United States.* Chicago: University of Chicago Press.

Spengler, O. 1928. *The decline of the west, volume II,* trans. C. F. Atkinson. 4th ed. New York: Alfred A. Knopf.

Stevenson, C. A. 1972. The end of nowhere: American policy toward Laos since 1954. Boston: Beacon Press.

Sticht, T. G. 1995. *The military experience and workplace literacy: A review and synthesis for policy and practice.* Philadelphia: National Center on Adult Literacy.

Stob, P. 2005. Kenneth Buke, John Dewey, and the pursuit of the public. *Philosophy and Rhetoric* 38 (3): 226–247.

Stone, L. 1968. Literacy and education in England: 1640–1900. *Past & Present* 42:69–139.

Stotsky, S. 1990. Connecting writing and reading to civic education. *Educational Leadership* 47 (1990): 72–73.

Strand, P., and W. Jones. 1985. *Indochinese refugees in America: Problem of Adaptation and Assimilation.* Durham, NC: Duke University Press.

Strauss, A. 1987. *Qualitative analysis for social scientists.* Cambridge: Cambridge University Press.

Street, B. 1984. *Literacy in theory and practice.* Cambridge: Cambridge University Press.

————, ed. 1993. *Cross-cultural approaches to literacy.* Cambridge: Cambridge University Press.

————. 1995. *Social literacies: Critical approaches to literacy in development, ethnography and education.* London: Longman.

————, ed. 2001. *Literacy and development: Ethnographic perspectives.* London: Routledge.

————. 2003. Foreword. In *Literacy and literacies: Texts, power, and identity,* ed. J. Collins and R. Blot. Cambridge: Cambridge University Press, xi–xv.

Stuart-Fox, M. 1986. *Laos: Politics, economics, and society.* London: Frances Pinter.

Takaki, R. 1989. *Strangers from a different shore: A history of Asian Americans.* New York: Penguin Books.

———. 1993. *A different mirror: A history of multicultural America.* Boston: Little Brown.

Tapp, N. 1982. The relevance of telephone directories to a lineage-based society: A consideration of some messianic myths among the Hmong. *Journal of the Siam Society* 70:114–127.

———. 1989. *Sovereignty and rebellion: The White Hmong of northern Thailand.* Oxford: Oxford University Press.

———. 2004. The state of Hmong studies (An essay on bibliography). In *Hmong/ Miao in Asia,* ed. N. Tapp et al. Bangkok: Silkworm Books, 3–37.

Tapp, N., et al. 2004. *Hmong/Miao in Asia.* Bangkok: Silkworm Books.

Terrien de Lacouperie, A. 1886. *The languages of China before the Chinese.* Transactions of the philological society. (Reprinted in Osnabruck by Otto Zeller, 1969).

Thao, P. 1999. *Mong education at the crossroads.* Lanham, MD: University Press of America.

Thompson, P. 1978. *The voice of the past: Oral history.* Oxford: Oxford University Press.

Timm, J. T. 1997. *The relationship between culture and cognitive styles: Implications for teaching in a diverse society.* Paper presented at the Midwest Educational Researchers Association Conference, Chicago.

Tollefson, J. 1989. *Alien Winds: The reeducation of America's Indochinese refugees.* New York: Praeger.

Topping, D. 1992. Literacy and cultural erosion in the Pacific islands. In *Cross-cultural literacy; Global perspectives on reading and writing,* ed. F. Dubin and N. Kuhlman. Englewood Cliffs, NJ: Prentice Hall, 19–31.

Trueba, H., L. Jacobs, and E. Kirton. 1990. *Cultural conflict and adaptation: The case of Hmong children in American society.* New York: The Falmer Press.

Vang, C. K., G. N. Yang, and W. Smalley. 1990. *The life of Shong Lue Yang: Hmong Mother of Writing.* Minneapolis, MN: Southeast Asian Refugee Studies Occasional Papers, Center for Urban and Regional Affairs.

Vial, P. 1890. *De la langue et de l'écriture indigenes au Yun-nan.* Paris: Ernest Leroux.

Volosinov, V. N. 1973. *Marxism and the philosophy of language,* trans. L. Matejka and I. R. Titunik. Cambridge, MA: Harvard University Press.

Walker-Moffat, W. 1995. *The other side of the Asian American success story.* San Francisco: Jossey-Bass.

Warner, R. 1995. *Back fire: The CIA's secret war in Laos and its link to the war in Vietnam.* New York: Simon and Schuster.

Weinberg, M. 1997. *Asian-American education: Historical background and current realities.* Mahwah, NJ: Lawrence Earlbaum Associates.

Weins, H.J. 1954. *China's march toward the tropics; a discussion of the southward penetration of China's culture, peoples, and political control in relation to the non-Han-Chinese peoples of south China and in the perspective of historical and cultural geography.* Hamden, CT: Shoe String Press.

Weinstein-Shr, G. 1993. Literacy and social process: A community in transition. In *Cross-cultural approaches to literacy,* ed. B. Street. Cambridge: Cambridge University Press, 272–293.

Wells, S. 1996. What do we want from public writing? *College Composition and Communication* 47 (3): 325–341.

Wen, Y. 1938. Lun Pollard script. *Xinan bianjiang* [Southwest frontier region] 1:43–53.

Wess, R. 1996. *Kenneth Burke: Rhetoric, subjectivity, postmodernism.* Cambridge: Cambridge University Press.

Wolf, E. R. 1982. *Europe and the people without history.* Berkeley: University of California Press.

Yagelski, R. P. 2000. *Literacy matters: Writing and reading the social self.* New York: Teachers College Press.

Yang D. 1985. Why did the Hmong leave Laos? In *The Hmong in the West: Observations and reports,* papers of the 1981 Hmong Research Conference, University of Minnesota, ed. B. Downing and D. Olney. 2nd printing. Minneapolis: Center for Urban Regional Affairs, University of Minnesota, 3–18.

———. 1993. *Hmong at the turning point.* Minneapolis: Worldbridge Associates, Ltd.

Young, M. 2004. *Minor re/visions: Asian American literacy narratives as a rhetoric of citizenship.* Carbondale: Southern Illinois University Press.

Index

HOPE Quarterly, 169
HOPE Women's Committee, 167–170
Hudspeth, William H., 38, 47–48
Hutchison, Ray, 223n.5
Hvitfeldt, Christina, 60, 63–65

identification, 15; patterns of, 16
ideology, defined, 17
immigrants: in American schools, 138, 144, 146; Asian, 5; Asian American, 141; Chinese, 5, 141; Filipino, 5, 141; German, 2; Japanese, 5, 141; literacy acquisition of, 18, 172, 191, 198–199, 223n.5; Northern European, 217n.2; Polish, 2; receiving public assistance, 150; rhetoric directed against, 141, 153, 170–173, 175–179, 182, 184–186, 224n.5; Scandinavian, 2
Immigration and Naturalization Service, 128
International Voluntary Services, 33, 74, 218n.7

Jensen, Robert, 179

Koltyk, Joanne, 217n.8
Kronenwetter, Michael, 124
kvw txhiaj, 117

Lansdale, Edward G., 31
Lao People's Democratic Republic, 29, 33
Laotian village schools: language policies of, 87–88; material conditions of, 83–85; rhetoric of, 79–91; teaching methods in, 85–97; writing assignments in, 88–90
L'Armée Clandestine, 1, 29, 31–32, 80, 94, 101–105, 107, 126, 197, 221n.11
Lee, Gary Yia, 25, 29, 35
Lemoine, Jacques, 37, 41, 45, 218n.1 (chap. 2)
Levi-Strauss, Claude, 5, 40
life history interview, 10–11

literacy, defined, 7
Lobliayao, Faydang, 28, 218n.6
Long Cheng military base, 32, 59, 91, 93, 97, 100, 107, 118, 222n.24
Lowe, Lisa, 6
Lutheran Immigration and Refugee Service, 222n.3
Lyfoung, Touby, 28–29, 31, 33, 157

Manchu Dynasty, 21, 26, 68
Marathon County Human Rights Committee, 173
Marshall, Helaine, 63–64
Mattison, Wendy, Laotou Lo, and Thomas Scarseth, 162
McCoy, Alfred J., 26–29, 35, 70
McGee, Michael Calvin, 183
Meo Maquis, 28
Methodist: church, 132, 134–135, 223n.4; Hmong, 132
Miao, 24–26, 38–48, 51, 56, 66–68, 110, 218n.1 (chap. 2), 219nn.2–3, 5 (chap. 2), 219n.3 (chap. 3), 222n.21
"model minority" narrative, 5–6
Mottin, Jean, 67
Munslow, Alun, 22

National Origins Act of 1924, 5
NATO Phonetic Alphabet, 100
Ndjuka Script, 54
Neo Lao Hak Sat (Lao Patriotic Front), 29–30
New Literacy Studies, 7–10, 191
Ng, Franklin, 146
Nixon, Richard, 33

Ogbu, John, 141
Okihiro, Gary K., 6
Olson, David, 60
Ong, Walter, 21, 38, 41, 60, 62, 65
opium, 26–28, 35, 54, 68, 218n.6
oral/orality. *See* Hmong preliteracy, presumed

Pa Chai Vue, 28, 31, 52–53, 110, 190, 196
Pathet Lao, 28, 30–31, 33, 51, 59, 185, 220n.5 (chap. 3)

Peterson, Sally, 22
Phaj Hauj, 53–56, 120, 219n.7, 222n.18
Phommasouvanh, Bounlieng, 70
Plain of Jars, 30, 33, 94
Pollard, Samuel, 46–48, 110, 222n.21
Pollard Script, 46–50
Porter, Gareth, 31, 35
preliterate/preliteracy. *See* Hmong preliteracy, presumed
Presbyterian missionaries, 108

qeej, 145–146
Quiet American, The, 31

Ranard, Donald, and Margo Pfleger, 122
Ratliff, Martha, 54
Reder, Stephen, 31, 35
re-education camps, 34
Refugee Act of 1980, 127
Reimers, David, 171, 173
Reinharz, Shulamit, 11
Resnick, Daniel P., and Lauren B. Resnick, 70
rhetoric/rhetorics, 15–18, 152; of Christian sponsorship in the United States, 126, 128–137; current-traditional, 143–144; defined, 15; of "Fair City," 154, 170–189; of Lao Schooling, 79–91; of military literacy, 80, 93–106; of missionary Christianity in Laos, 80, 107–116; of new gender relations, 154, 162–170; of preliteracy, 61, 64–66, 77–78; of public schooling in United States, 126, 137–146; of testimony, 153, 154–162; of workplace writing, 126, 147–150
rhetorical conception of literacy, 14–18
Robbins, Christopher, 221n.17
Romanized Popular Alphabet (RPA), 12, 29, 48–52, 56, 101, 109, 111–112, 116, 118–120, 132–134, 136–137, 155, 158, 219n.4 (chap. 3)

Rose, Mike, 7–8, 86–87
Royal Laotian Government (RLG), 25, 30, 33, 50, 79, 81, 155; educational policies of, 69–73, 83, 102, 155, 220n.5 (chap. 3)
Royster, Jacqueline Jones, 14
Rumbaut, Ruben, and Kenji Ima, 223n.5

Savina Romanized Alphabet, 50
Saving Private Ryan, 221n.13
Sayaboury Alphabet, 55–56, 219n.9
Schanche, Don, 218n.7
Schein, Louisa, 24
Secret Army. *See* L'Armée Clandestine
Sesame Street, 190, 195
Shong Lue Yang, 53–55, 219n.8, 222n.18
Shor, Ira, 8
Shuter, Robert, 61, 63–65
Sierra Club, 224n.7
60 Minutes, 2
Smalley, William A., 12, 37, 41, 48–50, 52, 54–55, 63, 109, 119, 218n.1 (chap. 2), 219n.9
Smalley, William A., Chia Koua Vang, and Gnia Yee Yang, 38, 55, 219nn.7–8
Smalley, William A., and Nina Wimuttisokol, 56, 219n.9
Soltow, Lee, and Edward Stevens, 79, 87, 197
Southeast Asian Resource Action Center, 127, 222n.1
Spengler, Oswald, 58
Spielberg, Steven, 221n.13
Stob, Paul, 16
Stone, Lawrence, 86
Stotsky, Sandra, 178
Strauss, Anselm L., 13
Street, Brian, 9, 86, 112–113

Tacitus, 93
Takaki, Ronald, 6, 60
Tapp, Nicholas, 21, 24, 39–41, 47, 53, 110, 115, 218n.1 (chap. 2), 219n.3 (chap. 3)
terministic screen, 39, 66, 199